MASTERING
KUNG FU

Featuring
Shaolin Wing Chun

Garrett Gee
Benny Meng
Richard Loewenhagen

Human Kinetics

Library of Congress Cataloging-in-Publication Data

Gee, Garrett, 1956-
  Mastering kung fu : featuring Shaolin wing chun / Garrett Gee, Benny
Meng, Richard Loewenhagen.
    p. cm.
Includes index.
  ISBN 0-7360-4568-6 (softcover)
  1. Kung fu. I. Meng, Benny, 1961- II. Loewenhagen, Richard, 1950-
III. Title.
  GV1114.7.G44 2004
  796.815'9--dc21

                              2003012257

ISBN: 0-7360-4568-6

Acquisitions Editor: Ed McNeely; **Production Editor:** Melinda Graham; **Assistant Editor:** Scott Hawkins; **Copyeditor:** Patsy Fortney; **Proofreader:** Pam Johnson; **Indexer:** Susan D. Hernandez; **Permission Manager:** Toni Harte; **Graphic Designer:** Robert Reuther; **Photo Manager:** Dan Wendt; **Cover Designer:** Kristin Darling; **Photographer (cover):** Mike Mathews; **Photographer (interior):** Allen Kong, Mike Mathews; **Illustrator:** Savi Kruoch; **Printer:** Versa Press

Human Kinetics books are available at special discounts for bulk purchase. Special editions or book excerpts can also be created to specification. For details, contact the Special Sales Manager at Human Kinetics.

Printed in the United States of America
10 9 8 7 6 5 4 3 2 1

Human Kinetics
Web site: www.HumanKinetics.com

United States: Human Kinetics
P.O. Box 5076
Champaign, IL 61825-5076
800-747-4457
e-mail: humank@hkusa.com

Canada: Human Kinetics
475 Devonshire Road Unit 100
Windsor, ON N8Y 2L5
800-465-7301 (in Canada only)
e-mail: orders@hkcanada.com

Europe: Human Kinetics
107 Bradford Road
Stanningley
Leeds LS28 6AT, United Kingdom
+44 (0) 113 255 5665
e-mail: hk@hkeurope.com

Australia: Human Kinetics
57A Price Avenue
Lower Mitcham, South Australia 5062
08 8277 1555
e-mail: liaw@hkaustralia.com

New Zealand: Human Kinetics
Division of Sports Distributors NZ Ltd.
P.O. Box 300 226 Albany
North Shore City
Auckland
0064 9 448 1207
e-mail: blairc@hknewz.com

CONTENTS

FOREWORD

This book illustrates the true roots of Wing Chun Kung Fu—the Southern Shaolin Temple (Siu Lam) and the monks and warriors who worked tirelessly in the Weng Chun Tong. The popular Wing Chun styles and arts practiced in today's general public properly trace their roots to the Red Boat Opera era. The complete systems of Chi Sim and Hung Fa Yi Wing Chun can only be described as "Shaolin Wing Chun." They represent the truth of Chan (Zen) philosophy, its health development in the form of Hei Gung (*Qi Gong*), and its evolution into martial science for the sole purpose of self-preservation and defense of the innocent. The very reasons for their creation (resistance to conquest and persecution by foreign invaders) mandated secrecy of their practice and employment for the past three centuries. Today they are free to be revealed.

This book represents the first detailed Hung Fa Yi material ever presented to the world at large. It will help preserve Shaolin truth in the 21st century. In this sense alone it represents a priceless gift to both the martial arts and military science communities.

It is a great honor to write this brief foreword for our "brother" Shaolin Wing Chun system. We proudly share the same roots; the same Chan philosophy; the same concepts of space, time, and energy; and the same passion for truth over illusion. I heartily congratulate Grand Master Garrett Gee and the Ving Tsun Museum team under Master Benny Meng for this milestone in Wing Chun history.

Andreas Hoffman
Grand Master
Chi Sim Weng Chun

ACKNOWLEDGMENTS

The authors would like to thank Jeremy Roadruck for his time and effort in collecting the Chinese terms used throughout this work from the Ving Tsun Museum. The nuance, beauty, and clarity of the original Chinese is an essential component of Wing Chun. Translations are useful but cannot capture the true depth of the original Chinese. Chinese terms are offered in this book in an effort to aid all people interested in Wing Chun to take their learning to a deeper level by being able to investigate the original language. The brief review of terms used in this book should be thought of as a springboard to further investigation and research.

For more Wing Chun terms and Chinese characters, visit the Ving Tsun Museum's terminology webpage at http://home.vtmuseum.org/terminology/index.php. Maintained by Mr. Roadruck, this free on-line resource presents Wing Chun terminology in Cantonese, using the Yale system, and Mandarin, using the Pinyin system. Always looking to expand the VTM's database of Wing Chun terms and phrases, Mr. Roadruck can be reached at meng.gamay@vtmuseum.org.

This scientific text is dedicated to our Kung Fu ancestors, the unsung Shaolin Warriors who poured 12 centuries of creativity and sweat into its creation. Their paradigm shift is a priceless treasure that will continue to inspire martial scientists throughout the eons.

Many thanks must also be given to the Ving Tsun Museum Founding Committee members who have labored for over 10 years to bring this information to light. In addition to the authors, Benny Meng and Richard Loewenhagen, committee members Chango Noaks, Michael Mathews, Jeremy Roadruck, and Dan Wells have all played crucial roles in this decade long journey. Their countless sacrifices and years of diligence will be forever remembered.

Lastly, and most importantly, Hung Fa Yi Wing Chun's future rests with today's disciples who have dedicated their lives to the preservation of Hung Fa Yi Wing Chun science via practice and teaching in the 'Hou Chuen San Sau' manner. Twenty first century Hung Fa Yi history will be determined by them.

Ninth Generation Hung Fa Yi Disciples
Benny Meng
John Murphy
Matthew Kwan
Allen Kong
Alex Oropeza
William Elliopulos
Tom Msgurk
Ricky Chu

Tenth Generation Hung Fa Yi Disciples
Richard Loewenhagen
Mike Mathews
Jeremy Roadruck
Wayne Schulz
Andy Kalish

Eleventh Generation Hung Fa Yi Disciples
Jason K. Walz
Savannaroth Kruoch

PREFACE

Humans exist as temporary positionings of mass and energy in space and time. Those who truly know, understand, and act on the space given them have an identity. If that identity is true and solid, their moment in time becomes a truth in itself that goes beyond their own temporal limitation. Truth is what endures the test of time. It carries an independent significance no matter the context of space, time, or energy. Reality is merely the momentary state of things; it is existence conditioned by circumstance.

The creators of Hung Fa Yi Wing Chun were aware of their reality with such a focus that their discoveries and experience are with us today, 350 years later. Their focus of space, time, and energy has indeed passed on scientific truth that goes beyond reality. For them, Shaolin Wing Chun was their identity, their way of life, their true existence. Their science evolved from the same passion experienced by any artist or musician.

The extremes, heightened experiences, and moments in time of the human condition come into focus during war and battle. Where else are true heroism and cowardice so hard to miss? Where else are life and death so intimate? The history of warfare is a chronicle of the best and worst of the human condition. The Shaolin creators faithfully captured the truths of the human condition. The art and science that resulted from that capturing provided a glimpse of truth to future practitioners.

The authors of this work know their moment in time. Grand Master Gee (Sifu) has recognized that each space and moment comes with its focus and responsibility. His task is to ensure that the truth of Hung Fa Yi Wing Chun and its creators is not lost to future generations. From a Shaolin Wing Chun perspective, this book represents a bold and unprecedented step in that direction.

After examining countless written works and legends, the Ving Tsun Museum researchers have found the ultimate historical artifacts of Shaolin Wing Chun to be the Chi Sim and Hung Fa Yi Wing Chun systems themselves. They must be experienced firsthand to appreciate the depth of their truth and science. No written treatise or hypothetical exposition can replace that actual experience—that reality! As so aptly expressed in Chan (Zen), you cannot *read* truth; you must *experience* it. This book focuses on Hung Fa Yi Wing Chun. The Ving Tsun Museum and Grand Master Andreas Hoffman are planning a future work highlighting Chi Sim Weng Chun.

I am most fortunate to have had an incredibly strong support base in my disciples and grand students. Likewise, the totally selfless support of my wife, Sunmi, makes the impossible forever feasible.

Benny Meng
Curator
Ving Tsun Museum

INTRODUCTION

This book is for accomplished teachers, martial arts practitioners, military instructors, and law enforcement professionals confronted with the need to attain an undistorted combat self-identity. It is designed to help them see beyond the limitations of training based solely on a "biggest, strongest, fastest" mentality. At the same time the book shows how to approach martial training as a complete science rather than as a personal expression.

Many people involved in martial arts today teach merely because they choose to do so, but they lack qualifications. In many instances there are no histories, philosophies, scientific consistencies, governing bodies, or formal education programs. Individuals create a style based on personal artistic expression, which in turn is based on their perspective, experience, and physical abilities—all subjective criteria rooted in personal interpretations. Students of such teachers try to imitate them, but their attempts are imperfect. As a result, the style changes with each new generation. Without scientific and philosophical continuity, performance criteria are lacking, and the creator's original concepts are soon lost forever. The style thus becomes diluted. True martial combat leaves room for only one perspective. The reality of combat can only be fully understood within a rational philosophical framework rooted in true science.

Throughout history, efforts to develop the most efficient means for humans to fight have driven the creation of military (or martial) science. A martial science focused on hand-to-hand combat must optimize use of the three dimensions of space in relation to the structures and kinetic functions of the human body. In hand-to-hand combat the martial science practitioner is not concerned with the art or style of an opponent. Instead, the practitioner identifies spatial reference planes and uses their height, range, and width to create three-dimensional zones in space for attack and defense. The inclusion of time and energy as factors in the use of the special volume of these zones completes the scientific basis for combat. In the Weng Chun Tong of the Southern Shaolin Temple 350 years ago, this cutting-edge scientific approach to combat caused a paradigm shift in combat and the evolution from martial art to martial science. The Shaolin Wing Chun that evolved into Hung Fa Yi Wing Chun is a combat martial science based on specific military science criteria. Seven specific military science criteria guided its creation and development:

1. It makes use of all available natural weapons. Their structure and motion comply with the harmony (physical laws) of their genetic construction.

2. It employs optimum efficiency in combat. It is most direct and employs the minimum required amount of motion, energy, and time.

3. It is logical to learn and efficiently retained.

4. It is lethal in deployment, yet it provides a full range of nonlethal options, thereby supporting choice consistent with morality.

5. It is survivable against a numerically or physically superior enemy.

6. It provides reactional combat speed rather than eye-brain–dominated speed.

7. The results of the system are consistently predictable and repeatable.

The southern Shaolin monks and the Ming military strategists discovered that time, space, and energy constitute the ultimate reality in combat and set about mapping the interrelationships between them and human physiology. Many martial artists focus on personal expression and style rather than on the science of human anatomical and physiological structures, motions, and energies. This book addresses each of these issues from historical, philosophical, and technical perspectives.

The history of Shaolin from the sixth century to the destruction of the Southern Shaolin Temple (Siu Lam) is examined in the first two chapters. This represents the first time myth has been dispelled from the Shaolin story. Ten years of research by the Ving Tsun Museum staff and contributors yielded verifiable facts and conclusions, many of which are revealed for the first time in this work. Chapter 2 identifies Chi Sim Weng Chun as the essence of all that is Shaolin art, and Hung Fa Yi as the militarized version of Wing Chun. It also illuminates Hung Fa Yi Wing Chun's history as it left the temple and expanded to the revolutionary fighters of the 18th and 19th centuries. Chapter 3 reflects Hung Fa Yi's Chan Buddhist philosophical and cultural bases, which strongly parallel Chu Hsi's emphasis on bounded learning. It provides an analysis of how Hung Fa Yi Wing Chun has been passed on to future generations. As such, it clearly reflects the means employed to ensure that Hung Fa Yi's martial science remained intact. This scientific foundation itself is thoroughly examined in chapter 4. The hand-to-hand technologies developed from the interrelationships of time, space, and energy form the basis of Hung Fa Yi Wing Chun and constitute the basis of the Wing Chun Formula and the original idea of Siu Nim Tau training. Both are examined thoroughly in chapters 5 and 6, respectively. Strategy and tactics, as well as Wing Chun's famous bridge arm and sticking hand (kiu sau and chi sau) training methodologies are examined in chapter 7. Chapters 8 and 9 briefly introduce advanced striking point technology, energy development and employment, and weapons. Each of these last three subjects could fill several texts in and of themselves. This particular work is oriented to giving the advanced reader a general picture of the knowledge and training required for further development.

Overall, this book is designed to encourage martial artists, military warriors, and law enforcement personnel worldwide to renew their focus on total martial training, which should include the historical, philosophical, ethical, mental, and physical development designed to explore true self-awareness in the real universe that surrounds them. Science must be at the core of their efforts.

Most systems taught today could not meet even basic combat training needs because they are more artistic expressions than scientific achievements of maximum efficiencies in a life-and-death reality. While taking 10 hits in a point sparring tournament and delivering 15 might win a trophy and give a practitioner a sense of accomplishment, that same performance would most certainly spell disaster in combat. The real danger in this type of training is that it leads to the *illusion of competence*. The first controlled hit in real combat with no rules and no restricted target areas would most likely be the last. Likewise, any injury shy of death is often more detrimental to friendly forces because it compels them to expend far greater resources to care for the wounded, resources that are desperately needed to continue the battle. This is the primary reason true martial training focuses on the containment of an opponent's forces through time and space control prior to releasing one's own weapons with guaranteed accuracy and lethality. A true fighter never gambles on the "lucky strike."

Along the way to developing true martial skill, the serious martial practitioner develops as a person as well as a fighter. Martial study must lead to self-awakening in the process of removing all illusion from one's reality. Development of martial self-awareness and one's true martial identity must become training imperatives. The reader will find chapters 4, 5, and 6 to be real eye-openers in this regard. Once understood, the material in them leaves no room for martial self-illusion. That same material will impart to a true practitioner a hunger for personal self-awareness that cannot be ignored. This hunger becomes the basis of recognizing one's own identity, thus enabling one to honestly interact in that reality. In order to fight (or succeed in any of life's struggles) in one's own reality rather than the reality of one's opponent, one must cease the acquisition of knowledge for its own sake and pursue knowledge for the express purpose of defining "self." The uniqueness of Chan Buddhism and the bounded learning philosophies of Chu Hsi (highlighted in chapter 3 and practiced in the Hung Fa Yi science discussed in the remainder of this book) will greatly aid in this pursuit. Practitioners must understand and embrace these philosophies as the creators of Shaolin Wing Chun understood and embraced them—as part of a complete science expressed in rational applications.

In total, the technical chapters of this book describe the science of Hung Fa Yi Wing Chun Kung Fu. This science arose from a 30-year military development project employing the talent of over a hundred experienced hand-to-hand combat masters (many inheriting over 1,100 years of Shaolin wisdom), scientific scholars, and military scientists and tacticians in a concerted effort to map out the most efficient use of the human body in combat. All body parts (hands, elbows, hips, knees, and feet) are continuously aligned to battle in space and time in accordance with strategies and tactics designed to maximize efficiency. No other hand-to-hand combat system has ever achieved this level of spatial and temporal marriage. It constitutes the one-on-one equivalent of today's high-tech fighting machines and control centers. Every weapon is deployed with precision measurement of range and advanced warning of threat.

Upon completion of this treatise on the history and application of martial science, the reader should be left with a greater awareness of the depth of hand-to-hand combat knowledge available in the traditional systems that trained practitioners to face opponents eyeball to eyeball. Hung Fa Yi clearly establishes the military imperatives for guided strikes and precise range measurements. It is every bit as high tech and cutting edge as today's long-range, digitally controlled fighting platforms. As we progress into an era of terrorism and counterterrorism and an ever increasing need to fight face to face with the enemy (in tight quarters while minimizing collateral damage), these skills are once again becoming essential. In short, this book represents a serious reality check!

Richard Loewenhagen
Lieutenant Colonel
United States Air Force (retired)

Northern and Southern Shaolin Kung Fu Development

CHAPTER

1

Apreponderance of evidence exists to conclude that the hand-to-hand combat skills thought of today as martial arts were practiced widely in China since well before the time of Christ. Chinese fighting systems were developed in parallel with philosophical traditions such as Taoism and Buddhism. During times of peace in China, martial arts development (and preservation) continued because of its unique relationship with Chinese philosophy and its focus on self-improvement. Such was not the case for Western fighting systems, which were tied to current science rather than philosophy. Combat science in the West was viewed primarily as a tool for military purposes—a tool that could be quickly replaced with another. Consequently, as science and the culture that supported it changed, fighting systems became obsolete and were quickly replaced with systems based on current science. Eventually, true hand-to-hand combat went "out of fashion," and those skills were principally lost to Western combatants.

Regardless of what text one reads on Chinese martial arts development, the discussion nearly always begins with the Shaolin[1] Temple located in the foothills on the north side of Song Mountain in the province of Hunan. Shaolin martial arts cannot be studied or learned properly without also studying the philosophy behind them. That philosophy is accepted as Buddhist, but it is unlike the forms of Buddhism practiced elsewhere. The form of Buddhism that evolved at this famous temple is unique, yet it has influenced martial arts development and practice throughout Asia. In China it is referred to as Chan Buddhism. In Japan it is referred to as Zen Buddhism. For the sake of brevity in this text, the authors have chosen to use simply Chan (Zen) or Chan.

HISTORICAL BACKGROUND PRIOR TO CHAN (ZEN) CREATION IN 600 A.D.

As a landmass, China appears isolated by her geographic borders. Surrounded by mountains, deserts, and oceans, Chinese people have always followed their own path to social and cultural development. Their centrist perspective has forever viewed the world outside the empire as barbarous, with the empire itself (meaning the Chinese people and their human condition) constituting the center of the universe between heaven and earth. The Chinese words for *China* (*Zhonggua*) and *Chinese* (*Zhongguaren*) literally translate to "Middle Kingdom" and "Middle People." With their perspective of "self" at the center of the universe, the Chinese evolved a view of man as inherently moral. The firm belief that the human mind is capable of moral order and perfection remains central to Chinese thought. Among the many schools of Chinese thought, three proved most influential in the development of martial art and science: Taoism, Confucianism, and Chan Buddhism. Table 1.1 offers a comparison of the three philosophies.

Taoism's Influence: The Way of Nature

The oldest form of philosophy in China is Taoism. Taoists do not accumulate knowledge by studying individual parts or functions. Rather, they examine the whole of a process or system. Individual parts bear significance only in terms of their contribu-

---

[1] Shao Lin (or Shaolin) is the Mandarin Pinyin romanization for the characters 少林. Siu Lam (pronounced **síu làhm**; see Glossary for pronunciation guide) is the Cantonese Yale romanization. Shaolin is the most often seen romanization and will be used throughout this text.

Table 1.1	Comparison of Taoism, Confucianism, and Early Buddhism		
Philosophy	**Beliefs**	**Source**	**Types**
Taoism	Avoidance of extremes, simplicity, harmony, meditation, knowledge gained by examining whole system	Developed in the mountains of China Laotzu Chuangtzu	Wen (literary) Wu (military)
Confucianism	Active leadership and social study as opposed to Taoist emphasis on nature; hierarchy of relationships: ruler/subject, father/son, husband/wife, elder brother/ younger brother, elder friend/ younger friend	Confucius	Confucius Mencius
Buddhism	Aim is self-awareness through asceticism, nonviolence, and renunciation of worldly things; Buddhism easier for common man to grasp than Confucianism (popular with educated, elite bureaucrats and rulers)	Buddha India to China via silk trade routes	Many branches that generally break down into - Philosophical - Religious

tion to the whole. The Taoist practice of martial arts was expected to restore energy balance and maintain the harmony among body, mind, and spirit. Taoist martial arts existed centuries before Buddhist-supported martial systems. The Buddhist systems developed along the same three lines as those of the Taoist systems centuries earlier: philosophical, military, and health.

Confucianism's Influence: The Way of Man

Confucianism was the second major philosophical and religious structure to influence Chinese culture and, for our purposes, Chan (Zen). Confucians believed that looking inside oneself would never result in enlightenment. In contrast, they sought enlightenment through rigorous use of the mind and body via examination of the knowledge and experiences of the sages. In other words, self-development could come only through work and effort conducted within the bounds of social wholeness. Chan's emphasis on good manners and proper respect for others is a direct result of Confucian influence.

Buddhism's Influence: The Way of Emptiness

The third major philosophical root of Chinese culture and the uniqueness of Chan (Zen) was Buddhism itself. Buddhists seek self-awareness through asceticism, nonviolence, and renunciation of worldly things. Freeing oneself from worldly trappings presumably makes the likelihood of reflecting true reality in terms of "self" possible. Reality can then be expressed only "mind to mind" based on shared experience.

The Resultant Chan (Zen) Buddhism: 527 A.D.

Chan Buddhism differs from traditional Buddhism in that it removes much of the emphasis on complex esoteric concepts and elaborate writings (called "Tantric"). It does not advocate withdrawing from worldly affairs, as does the Hinayana sect of Buddhism (often referred to as the "Little Raft" in the Buddhist context of using a raft to get to the other shore). The Hinayana sect is more suited to high priests and monks in a cloistered environment than to common people. In contrast, Chan Buddhism advocates remaining involved in everyday transactions, a practice gained from roots in the Mahayana sect, with its belief that man lives in the here and now and should act and think accordingly. The Mahayana sect is referred to as the "Great Raft" in Buddhist context. It is more suited to meeting the needs of the masses. In accordance with this perspective, Chan Buddhism places an even greater value on experience than does original Tantric Buddhism. It focuses on three key criteria: instant awakening, practicality, and completeness. Chan Buddhism had its roots in the Shaolin Temple, but today dominates more than 70 percent of the Buddhist temples throughout China. Yet, of all of these Buddhist temples, only the Shaolin Temple (northern and southern) was renowned for its martial arts. This begs the question, Why?

The official position of today's Shaolin Temple (and the official position of the government of China) is that both philosophy and circumstance contributed to the development of martial arts at the Shaolin Temple. Their brand of Chan Buddhism tolerates almost all forms of worldly behavior except killing, looting, robbing, and sex. The temple opened its doors to monks shunned by other Buddhist temples (such as those who drank wine or ate meat). This unusual level of tolerance probably provided the basis for the existence and development of Shaolin martial arts and the ultimate appearance of "fighting monks" and "cudgeling monks." Moreover, because Chinese history is a story of one dynastic or feudal struggle after another, retired or fleeing military generals, malcontents, and refugees from the law were always seeking acceptance and safe haven in the Shaolin Temple. They came to the temple because of its idyllic geographical location and professed philosophy of tolerance and brought with them martial skill and real world experience. When they came together at the temple, the trading of skills and theories was bound to occupy their attention. Gradually, Shaolin Kung Fu began to mature.

Before continuing, it is important to highlight Shaolin longevity in contrast to other temples and training disciplines. Chan Buddhists are very practical. They have a strong work ethic. They believe that if one doesn't work, one doesn't eat! Over time, this led the Shaolin Temple to build true self-sufficiency. They had their own means of education, food production, cultural development, socialization, and even defense. Kung fu became a by-product of their Chan philosophy and their environment of self-sufficiency.

Founders of Chan Buddhism

Many legends suggest that the 28th patriarch of original Buddhism and the first patriarch of Chan Buddhism, the Indian monk *Damo* (also known as the patriarch Aryan Bodhidharma, *Bodhi* meaning "awakening" and *dharma* meaning "teaching"), developed and taught his Chan Buddhism at the Shaolin Temple of Song Shang. According to legend, he was a Buddhist Indian prince tutored in both Taoism and yoga. Likewise, he was purportedly raised in the Mahayana Buddhist sect discussed earlier. The legend further asserts that, armed with this philosophical background, he chose to forswear a life of royalty for the freedom of practicing and espousing his own blend of Buddhism with Taoist seasoning and yogist meditation aids. In contrast, modern scholars have expressed serious doubts that Damo ever existed. The more accepted belief in academic circles is that Bodhidharma is a collective name for a series of masters who contributed to the development and spread of Chan Buddhism. For the purposes of this book, all references to Bodhidharma refer to the collective efforts of Chan Buddhism's creators and missionaries who took its principles and concepts to the Northern Shaolin Temple.

Bodhidharma traveled to China and ultimately arrived at the Shaolin Temple in the third year of the reign of Emperor Xiaoming (527 A.D.), approximately 30 years after its construction for the Indian Buddhist monk Ba Tuo. The emperor's gardeners planted bountiful numbers of new trees on the temple grounds. This gave rise to its name Shaolin, meaning "young forest."

The imperial mission given to the first abbot of the Shaolin Temple was to establish a model Chinese temple of Buddhism. While records do not exist of any martial feats or activity related directly to Ba Tuo, current temple records reflect that Ba Tuo's two disciples, Hui Guang and Seng Chou, possessed significant martial skills, even in adolescence. They are credited as being the first two Shaolin monks to practice martial arts.

Figure 1.1 Typical depiction of the bearded, blue-eyed master from the West.

Legends and today's Shaolin monastery claim that Bodhidharma sat facing a wall for nine years in meditative practice. His perseverance and the exercises he created during this feat (the famous 18 exercises of Arhat, also known as the 18 Buddha Hand exercises) purportedly produced a profound stimulus to the development of martial arts at the Shaolin Temple. In reality, these exercises are modified yogic health postures brought to the temple by Chan Buddhist practitioners. Nevertheless, because they do require physical acumen and devoted practice to master, they may have encouraged disciples who came to the temple to improve their physical condition. Bodhidharma strongly believed that Buddhism was to be experienced, not just with intellectual understanding. This attitude was the key to the development of future martial arts development within the Shaolin Temple. According to legend, Bodhidharma is credited with introducing to the temple two additional sets of exercises to add to the already existing Taoist internal *Qi* exercises: the muscle and tendon changing exercise (Yi Jin Jing) and the blood washing exercise (Xi Xue Jing). Modern scholars have stated that the first published book of this exercise was created as late as the early 1600s by a Taoist priest named Zi Ning. These exercises were similar to Taoist meditative practices, and they intertwined and assimilated into different branches of Chan Buddhist development. Although the preparations, details, and techniques are not universal in all branches, the principles and results are.

Qi (Life Force) Development in Kung Fu

Both Buddhist and Taoist internal practices were refined and developed into scientific disciplines based on Chinese cosmology. The 18 Buddha Hand, muscle/tendon changing, and blood washing exercises all emphasized breath control and cultivation of the life force called *Qi*. They developed health and internal strength in parallel with the development of Shaolin martial skills by combining additional internal breathing and meditation exercises with the existing internal and external training of martial systems. The breath, the *Qi*, in the form of heat current, when refined through the body's energy channels, created glowing health and produced a long life and deadly force when used with the external skills of Chinese boxing.

Qi is believed to surpass muscle power in its ability to heal, harm, or protect the body. Shaolin kung fu carried beyond the external bounds of physical training and into the mental realm of the power of intent. This power is developed through the performance of qi exercises universally referred to as *Qi Gong*. Qi Gong is usually defined as exercise and training of the internal organs to develop uncanny feats of fitness and health.

External *Qi Gong* practice is generally referred to as wei gong training. Northern Shaolin Kung Fu relied primarily on techniques requiring extensive physical attributes through training for speed, strength, endurance, and quick reflexes. Both external and internal training were employed in the northern Shaolin program. An underlying internal principle was followed called "essence, energy, spirit," implying that one's external work should harmonize with the internal, ultimately resulting in superhuman ability. One of Bodhidharma's concerns in meditation is the cultivation of *Qi*. The main center of one's *Qi* is the lower abdomen. Many statues of Buddha present him with a large belly—it symbolizes the abundance of *Qi*.

The division between internal and external is largely exaggerated. Shaolin internal and external kung fu were inseparable, as are body, mind, and spirit. Both internal and external kung fu were required by Chan (Zen) Buddhism's demands for "completeness." The truth of this demand becomes obvious to every practitioner at some point in life. The practicing of *Quan-Fa* (Mandarin) or Kuen Faat (Cantonese) (both meaning boxing or striking methods) without studying a breathing system will certainly end in failure as one ages. The generic term for skill and effort is kung fu.

SHAOLIN DEVELOPMENT FOLLOWING BODHIDHARMA

The century following Bodhidharma's leadership presented the temple with political challenges. First, the Sui Dynasty (581-618 A.D.) granted a significant tract of land (1,648 acres) to the temple in 618 A.D. The royal court's growing interest in the monastery radically increased the monastery's economic base, as well as its administrative needs. Ultimately, wealth in property and personnel brought with it the need for security and defense. Shortly thereafter, problems that arose between Qin Prince Li Shi Min and a General Wang Shi Cong ended in even greater landholdings for the monastery. According to temple records, the prince called on the monks to assist in apprehending the rogue general and pacifying the land. The monks responded to the prince's request with Shaolin warriors. Again, per current temple records, this represents the first time Shaolin Buddhist disciples collectively took part in battle. Prince Li went on to become the first Tang Dynasty emperor. He awarded the Shaolin Temple an additional 40 hectares of land (approximately 930 acres). Within a few short years, the Shaolin Temple and its buildings encompassed over 3,000 acres of land. The temple's defense needs continued to rise, as did their need for a general labor force. The ultimate answer was a permanent warrior class of monks referred to in today's monastery records as "monk soldiers," which significantly increased the temple population.

Approximately 60 years after the formation of the Northern Temple, a Southern Temple was built to commemorate the deaths of northern warrior monks who had traveled south at Emperor Li Shi Min's request to repress massive pirate incursions in the southern provinces. Evidence amassed by the Fujian Province Archeologists Association, the Fujian Museum, and the Putian Southern Shaolin Temple Investigatory Association establishes that Emperor Li Shi Min approved the site and construction of the southern temple at Putian in the province of Fujian. These same research organizations affirm that many of the northern warrior monks who had fought in the pirate wars remained at the Southern Temple to teach and further the development of Chan martial systems.

Current monastery records cite numerous relationships among the Shaolin monks and political authorities and military generals throughout the Tang, Song, and Ming Dynasties. Monastery records reflect that Tang Dynasty generals were often sent to the Shaolin Temple to exchange martial routines. Generals Cheng Yao Jin, Luo Cheng, Gao Huai De, and Yang family members are credited with teaching the monks their famous crescent axe, plum blossom spear, and black tiger hammer.

Two specific books purportedly survived the fire set in the Northern Shaolin Temple in 1928 by Chinese warlords: *Records of the Shaolin Monastery* and *Records About Shaolin Boxing*. Both books tell of the Supreme Monk Fu Ju inviting eighteen masters of eighteen different schools of martial arts to visit the monastery. The purpose of the visit was to obtain a demonstration of their skills and an agreement to teach the monks for three years for the purpose of absorbing each master's best knowledge and combining the knowledge into manuals on Shaolin boxing.

Some historical theorists have called these accounts myth and legend, whereas others consider them a part of both dynastic and Shaolin history. At a minimum, they provide ample precedent for the obvious political and military connections and activities described further in this work. By the temple's own admission, kung fu masters and military generals frequently came to the monastery and shared their skills with the existing monks.

Dispelling Myths

During the 20th century, myths about the origins of Shaolin Kung Fu abounded. The myths were exacerbated by records lost in wars and the political prosecutions of countless kung fu masters (Taoist as well as Shaolin). Many of the true masters fled China to safe havens in the West. Seven pivotal myths must be addressed here.

Myth 1
Damo (Bodhidharma) invented Shaolin Kung Fu.

Fact
Damo did not invent Shaolin Kung Fu. The Eighteen postures of Arhat represent health exercises based on yoga. Collective masters and missionaries were referred to as Bodhidharma. Their true contributions to the temple were Chan Buddhism and renewed impetus for health development.

Fact
Many of the monks present in the temple at the time of *Damo's* arrival already possessed martial skills from previous military and private backgrounds and, by the temple's own admission, were freely trading kung fu knowledge with one another.

Fact
The tolerant environment and self-sufficient attitude of the Shaolin Temple set it apart from other Buddhist temples. The method of Hou Chuen San Sau (mind understanding through bodily experience) was the key component to stimulate the growth of martial skills within the Shaolin Temple. Their environment and attitude permitted ready absorption of military and martial knowledge from the best of Chinese culture and leadership. Ample evidence exists to suggest that the monks received as much kung fu as they gave in the first few centuries of the temple's existence. 150 years after *Damo's* death, the Shaolin warrior monks had already earned a reputation as formidable fighters.

Myth 2
All Chinese Kung Fu comes from Shaolin.

Fact
Chinese history goes back several thousand years. The Shaolin Temple began its existence 1,500 years ago. Prior to that time, military and personal defense and combat training and skill were still needed. During the Chou Dynasty (1122-221 B.C.) the Chinese were already using sophisticated combat techniques in battle according to *Records of the Historians*. The same social and cultural seeds that later fueled Shaolin development existed in the earlier centuries as well. In truth, the earliest forms of Chinese kung fu were influenced by Taoists and came in many varieties across three separate, broad categories: combat, health, and spirituality. China's militaries from warlord fiefdoms to dynastic empires all employed some form of Taoist-influenced kung fu skills, and those militaries engaged in their own development efforts as well. Taoist monasteries and the Chinese military continued to create and refine their own

systems throughout the centuries of Shaolin influence. Even within Shaolin, there are two major systems of martial art and science development: Northern and Southern. In short, while the Shaolin Temples did have a significant impact on Chinese Kung Fu development, they did not have a monopoly. The real value of Shaolin Kung Fu lies in its marriage of health, moral, philosophical, and spiritual development with combat skill development. The results of this marriage were true martial disciplines leading to complete artistic genres and sciences.

Myth 3
Animal postures were used for combat.

Fact

Animal postures were used to enhance internal and external health development. They were also employed to develop specific physical attributes that, when employed within the bounds of natural human motion, could enhance fighting abilities. For example, leopard postures were intended to develop the attribute of speed. Tiger postures were used to develop power. When engaged in actual combat, practitioners of each look and act quite human. Just as leopards and tigers could not survive attempting to engage in fighting on two legs like humans, humans could not efficiently engage in combat attempting to behave like four-legged animals. This particular myth stems primarily from film industry and marketing romanticization of martial styles.

It is interesting to note that the Taoist systems of martial arts included animal postures for a twofold purpose. The first was for deriving the benefits of acrobatic training as indicated earlier. The second was to stay in tune or harmony with nature. Observation and mimicry of animals aided in this pursuit.

Myth 4
Buddhist monks did not engage in Chinese politics.

Fact

Anecdotes, legends, poetry, and dynastic as well as temple records abound of Shaolin warriors assisting in political and military events. The monks assisted in border patrols, quelling local uprisings, and even the defeat of pirate incursions. Shaolin landholdings and wealth grew considerably as a result of dynastic appreciation for their support.

Fact

The monks of the Shaolin Temple did not cloister themselves from the surrounding world. That world was very much a part of their reality. They were good citizens and very much a part of their community's culture, art, scholarship, politics, and defense.

Myth 5
Chan Buddhism and martial arts represent a contradiction in terms.

Fact

Supporters of this position clearly do not understand the most basic nature of Chan Buddhism. One of the major precepts of Chan Buddhism is comprehension of the differences between reality and illusion for the express purpose of removing illusion. The true root of all pain and suffering stems from illusion. There simply is no better way to contrast reality and illusion than in combat. Combat deals with life and death, the ultimate reality for all of us. Along the way, it tests courage and resolve, as well as both inner and outer strength. It leaves no room for false self-images. The very first symbol of Hung Fa Yi's logo is the Buddhist swastika. It is a symbol of the paradox of life and death: One must accept death to appreciate life. True knowledge interrelates all that is essential to human survival. Self-defense is included. A person who studies only Buddhist religion or philosophy and never martial arts can never make this connection. In contrast, a person who never studies Chan Buddhism and only studies martial arts cannot make this connection either. The connection is quite obvious to those who study both.

The principal implication of this myth is that warriorship is incompatible with the study or practice of Chan Buddhism (or any other moral philosophy). Nothing could be further from truth. The study of martial arts leads to a better understanding of violence. For a Buddhist monk, the highest level of knowledge and proficiency results in the ability to refuse an offering of violence or disharmony by merely returning it to the person who broke the harmony in the first place. Those who train professionally to defend society must be educated in this level of morality. How does society defend itself legitimately if its warriors do not train for it, both physically and philosophically? Maintenance of harmony in the face of aggression requires both proper training to resist aggression and the will to use that training in the interests of harmony. Self-preservation is natural, while denial of self-preservation by adopting a policy or position of total nonaggression is suicidal (unnatural). Chan philosophy requires compliance with the natural order, with reality.

Contemporary martial arts historian Harry Cook, in an excellent treatise entitled "The Shaolin Temple," noted that the first rule of the Bramajala Sutra (Chinese Fan Wang Jing) forbids killing, but it also commands Buddhists to save all living things from death and suffering. The 16th precept commands Buddhists to give up their own flesh, if necessary, to feed starving tigers, wolves, lions, and hungry ghosts! Likewise, Buddhists were expected to protect the trinity of Buddha (teacher), dharma (teaching), and sangha (community). Protecting temples, libraries, and the innocent against bandits and invaders necessitated the use of force. In view of these seemingly conflicting commands, it is easy to see why the staff became the core weapon of Shaolin monks. They aided mountain hiking and were convenient as carrying tools. At the same time, their lethality was determined solely by the ferocity of the attack repelled.

Myth 6
The Northern Shaolin Temple was burned by the Qing.

Fact
The original Shaolin Temple at Song Shan was never burned or razed by the Qing Dynasty. The Southern Temple (Siu Lam) in Fujian, which received the warrior monks of the north during the initial years of Qing incursion, was burned to the ground in the mid-17th century because of its involvement in revolutionary planning and insurgent activities. Chinese scientists and archeologists located the site of the Southern Temple in the mid-1990s and recently completed reconstruction on the same historic grounds.

Fact
The Northern Shaolin Temple was burned in 1927. The Qing government was overthrown in 1911 through efforts supported in part by Secret Societies. Chaing Kai-Shek became the Nationalist leader and initiated a campaign to remove the threat of regional warlords to unify China under a central government. In 1927, Chaing sent General Feng Yu-Xiang to Honan Province to fight the local warlord Fan Chung-Xiu.

During their skirmishes, the Shaolin Temple was burned and many buildings and priceless books of martial arts and Shaolin history were destroyed.

Myth 7
Today's Shaolin monks in China represent traditional Shaolin skills development and combat training.

Fact
The latest craze of acrobatic stunts to impress onlookers stems from the film industry's romanticization of combat training and the advancement of wushu performances for athletic competitions. They serve to entertain. If there is any truth to this myth, it only begins to take shape and form in the past 10 years when the communist government decided to restore training at the temple in support of a groundswell of popularity over kung fu movies and implications of their Shaolin roots. In truth, the most knowledgeable Shaolin teachers fled communist oppression to the Western world over 40 years ago. The real knowledge of traditional Shaolin as practiced and developed over the past 15 centuries is now spread (and fragmented) across the globe. A few truly dedicated teachers have humbly traveled extensively to study from numerous teachers and lineages in an attempt to piece the fragments back into a whole science.

These myths continue to confuse legitimate research into Chinese Kung Fu history. Their impact has been greatly magnified with the advent of the Internet. It is time to put them to rest and get on with legitimate research using traditional methods reviewed and challenged by competent research authorities. Once these myths are dispelled, a proper distillation of the true treasures of Shaolin Kung Fu is possible.

TRUE TREASURES OF SHAOLIN KUNG FU

After 1,500 years of Shaolin Temple work, effort, and experience, it is possible to discern the true essence of Shaolin Kung Fu—that which makes it uniquely Shaolin. Three treasures constitute the essence of Shaolin: Chan philosophy, internal and external health development, and true martial skill based on the reality of combat and the removal of self-illusion.

The first treasure, Chan, obviously began with its creators and missionaries, collectively referred to as Bodhidharma. It truly is the heart of all Shaolin Kung Fu development. The Chan emphasis on instant awakening rooted the monks' focus in the here and now. It is impossible to consider combat training without the ability to focus 100 percent of physical and mental resources on the moment at hand. Equally important is the Chan mandate for practicality. From a combat perspective, in the absence of practicality only illusion remains. Finally, Chan insistence on "completeness" provides the ultimate impetus for total knowledge of combat space and time and total tactical ability to control that space and time. Interestingly, each of these Chan requirements is circular; each evolves from the others, and each gives rise to the others. None can exist without the others. How very Taoist—of course, the Chinese did create Taoism. It's little wonder that Chan Buddhism with its Taoist undertones appealed to the Chinese people and evolved in the Shaolin temple, where monks engaged in the continuous exercise of instant awakening.

The second treasure of Shaolin, internal and external health development, had its roots in the then two-thousand-year-old Chinese Taoist investigations of Qi Gong study and practice. The addition of Chan (Zen) yogic exercises and breathing technolo-

Figure 1.2 "Song Shan Shao Lin Si" – Song Mountain Shaolin Temple

gies no doubt fueled their passions for health improvement even further. Even today that passion survives in the myriad of head standing, finger standing, and impressive "child exercises" demonstrated in road shows by the 21st-century "Shaolin Warriors" from the Northern Temple.

The final treasure, true martial skill, most likely had its roots in the Chinese military, as have real fighting skills in every society on every continent throughout the course of human history. The role of martial evolution outside the temple and its influence on the Shaolin Temple throughout its history cannot be downplayed. In truth, the Shaolin Temple constituted an incredibly unique laboratory for the development of combat skills. It was, for the most part, an apolitical institution focused on a single output product—true martial skill—that remained in existence with that purpose intact for almost 1,500 years.

Numerous sources suggest an interaction between the temple and the Chinese military throughout each dynastic rule, save for the Mongol (Yuan) and the Manchu (Qing.) The same type of interaction between laboratories and the military can be seen in virtually every society, even in the 21st century. Stanford, Harvard, Massachusetts Institute of Technology, Berkeley, and so forth, are all esteemed institutes of scholarship and human development, yet all service extensive defense grants and contracts for research and engineering. They are long-term institutions dedicated to the specific purpose of research and development of new concepts and solutions. They will always be cherished and courted by the military for their creative contributions to overall national defense. Yet their contribution is far less direct in terms of output product than was the contribution of the Shaolin Temple.

In addition to military contributions toward development of the third treasure of Shaolin, the philosophy of Chan with its strong orientation to self-sufficiency was also a prime contributor. Wing Chun (created centuries later) is nothing more than an extension of the Chan emphasis on attainment of reality. Wing Chun is nothing more or less than a complete expression of the pursuit of reality through the removal of illusion. From a martial sense, approximations of space, time, and energy control are illusions that can be challenged. Total knowledge of these constants on a clearly defined battlefield leads to a reality that cannot be challenged.

These three treasures represent the true essence of Shaolin Kung Fu. For more than 1,100 years they were probed and pressed in a daily onslaught by tireless monks until they became a raw gem—akin to a lump of coal subjected to the continuous onslaught of nature until it becomes a diamond. But as any gemologist can attest, a raw gem does not attain ultimate value until cut into a multifaceted true gem. Only then does it become priceless in its ultimate reality. By the time the Qing Dynasty conquered northern China and stifled Shaolin Kung Fu development at Song Shan, both temples' (north and south) kung fu had reached the raw gem stage. The newly forced military focus in the Southern Shaolin Temple in Fujian proved to be a blessing of sorts. It was in the Weng Chun Tong of the Southern Shaolin Temple that the monks and their Ming military counterparts turned the raw gem into the diamond of Wing Chun kung fu. All three came together in Shaolin Wing Chun.

The amazing history and the resultant treasures of the Shaolin temples (north and south) hold a special message for advocates of realistic martial study and self-development. True martial systems must provide the equivalent of Chan emphasis on instant awakening, practicality, and completeness. They must also provide for the training and promotion of internal and external health. Finally, they must produce martial skill that identifies and removes all illusion of self and capitalizes on the opponent's own illusions. Anything less, in the life-and-death framework of combat, must be considered "incomplete."

GENESIS OF WING CHUN FROM ITS HISTORICAL AND POLITICAL CONTEXTS STARTING WITH THE MING OR "BRIGHT" DYNASTY (1368-1644 A.D.)

Any serious study of Wing Chun Kung Fu origins must begin with the expulsion of the Yuan Chu (Mongol Dynasty formed in 1271) from China in 1368 by Chu Yun Cheung, the founder of the Chinese Ming Dynasty. The heroic leadership of Chu Yun Cheung became a rallying point centuries later in the formation of the secret societies surrounding the development and spread of Shaolin Weng/Wing Chun Kuen (everlasting/praise spring fist) and is the seed from which many of those societies' traditions and symbology took root.

Noted historian W.P. Morgan, in his superb book, *Triad Societies in Hong Kong* (Government Press, Hong Kong, 1960), posits that the decline and fall of the Mongol Yuan Dynasty parallels the legendary foundations of the secret societies. Following the demise of Kublai Khan, Mongolian leadership proved weak by comparison. As leadership weakened, the number and size of rebel organizations within both northern and southern China grew proportionately. No specific organization guided the many rebel groups, but they all shared a common goal—to rid China of foreign rule and return the throne to the Hon people. Among the many organizations and historical figures involved in rebel activities was a former Buddhist monk named Chu Yun Cheung. Chu left the monastery to join in revolutionary activity. His military and leadership skills proved to be far greater than those of the rebel leaders throughout China. These skills enabled him to influence many of the resistance groups in their efforts to oust the Mongolian emperor of China. When the dust settled from the revolution, Chu found himself in a position of strength. People revered him as a national hero. This status enabled him to claim the throne of China virtually unchallenged.

Historians past and present have noted the apparent influence of all the previously discussed factors on later secret society legends. Chu was a Buddhist monk, as were the founders of later secret societies, such as the Fut Paai Hung Mun and Hung Fa Wui. He was highly skilled in the arts of warfare, as were many of the secret society founders. Chu abandoned monastic life and robes to help his people drive a foreign dynasty out of China. Interestingly, this was the professed political intention of most of China's major secret societies, as borne out in their recruitment efforts, initiation ceremonies, codes of conduct, and military actions and campaigns over the next 450 years.

Chu Yun Cheung was born to a peasant family. Poverty and the death of his parents drove him to become a monk at the age of 17. By age 25 he had joined the insurgent Red Turbans (around 1352) and quickly rose to leadership, primarily because he was one of only a few members who could actually read and write fluently as well as fight. It was here that legends began that would influence poetry and astrological texts for centuries to come. When future poets and historians referenced Chu, they would write, "He walks on seven stars." This reference acknowledges that Chu had seven moles on the bottom of his feet. In Chinese astrological predictions, a mole on the bottom of a man's foot indicated a destiny of wielding great power. Literally speaking, if a man had a mole on the bottom of his foot, he would rule a thousand other men. Chu's military advisor, Bat Wan, was also an accomplished astrologer. He predicted that the seven moles on the bottom of Chu's feet meant that Chu was destined to rule an entire nation.

When Chu's forces took control of China, he founded the Ming Dynasty—a name that translates into "Bright Dynasty." The Ming Dynasty lasted from 1368 to 1644. History reflects that Chu Yun Cheung began his reign by ordaining himself with the regal title of *Hung Wu*[2], meaning "Magnificent Power." It must be noted that this *Hung* is also homophonous with another word for the color red. (紅) I-Hung in Cantonese, *Hong* in Mandarin). Additionally, it should be noted that one meaning for the word *Chu* (朱) is also the color red. The word *magnificent* (洪) is used in the famous Hung Mun society and many other political societies seeking acceptance and the semblance of legitimacy by referring to the greatness of the Ming Dynasty's founder and implying that their respective organizations were rooted in the magnificence of Chu Yun Cheung. The indirect reference to the color red points to that same implication of legitimacy. Many historians affirm that the name Hung was used repeatedly by subsequent secret society founders in deference to the heroic acts of the first emperor of the dynasty they sought to restore. Interestingly, just as Chu fought from a revolutionary society known as the Red Turbans, subsequent secret society members would adorn themselves in red sashes, streamers, or banners for an added touch of legitimacy. For over three hundred years, the fully trained masters and leaders of Hung Fa Yi Wing Chun have been referred to as "Red Bandannas." The reasons for such passionate loyalty to the Ming Dynasty and its founder are many.

The early Ming Dynasty marks the Chinese equivalent of Western history's Renaissance period rich in artistic, philosophical, religious, and cultural development. Chu's implemented measures produced a favorable effect on society. The booming economy brought forth a population explosion, from 55 million people at the begin-

---

[2] 洪 武 Hung Mo is Cantonese; *Hong Wu* is Mandarin. While *Hong Wu* is the more commonly see translation, this text makes use of the Cantonese.

ning of the Ming Dynasty to 150 million at the end. During this time, China was the most prosperous country on Earth.

This dynasty, more than any other, contributed heavily to the growth and development of the Shaolin monasteries. An understanding of this dynasty's relationship with the temples is essential to fully grasping the risks the Northern and Southern Shaolin Temple monks were willing to take three centuries later in attempting to help the Ming family and bureaucracy return to power despite the apparent corruption and weak leadership of its final emperors.

During the reign of Ming Dynasty Emperor Wan Li (1573-1620), China started to face increasingly dangerous pressure from the Manchu Tartars under the leadership of Narhachu. Narhachu sought control of the entire Tartar nation as well as China. His aspirations were not unopposed by his own people. Some Tartar tribes resisted him with successful appeals to the Chinese emperor for military assistance. His armies were destined to remain camped outside the Great Wall until after his death. Succession went to Narhachu's six-year-old son, but the true leaders of the armies were the father's military advisors. Continuing preparations for an invasion of China, they did not have long to wait.

The degeneracy of the Ming court in these latter years, the corruptness of officials, and the almost complete breakdown of central authority brought great economic hardships on the Chinese people. Droughts led to famine conditions in large geographic areas. The adoption of a closed-door foreign trade policy exacerbated problems further. Simultaneously, ever increasing demands from tax collectors and local political officials turned many members of an oppressed and hungry population against their ruler. Many people began to believe that the "mandate of heaven" had been withdrawn from the current ruler and that a new dynasty was needed.

The provinces of Shansi and Shensi became the tinderbox for a rebellion headed by Lei Ji Sing, who led a peasant army of nearly 200,000 troops. This gave the Manchu their opportunity to finally invade and conquer China in 1644 A.D. Lei's forces raided widely throughout northwestern China and even into the Yangtze River valley. This rebellion's successes were greatly facilitated by an indecisive emperor whose army was tied up at the Great Wall confronting the Manchu invasion potential. The rebellion ended with Lei's march on Beijing and the emperor's resultant suicide.

General Wu San Gui, the commander of the Chinese forces at the Great Wall, had entered into an agreement with the Manchu leaders to counterattack Lei. Both politically and militarily, Wu may have had no other choice. Had he withdrawn his forces from the Great Wall to aid the Ming emperor ousted by Lei, the Manchu would have invaded anyway, and his army could well have been trapped between Lei's rebels and the Tartars. His decision could also have been influenced by an aristocratic distaste for serving a rebel peasant leader on the Dragon Throne and the apparent anarchy beginning to overcome the Hon people. It is also interesting to note that Lei added insult to injury by executing Wu's family and concubine in Beijing.

Lei had dynastic succession within his grasp. His lack of bureaucratic expertise and apparent decision not to curry the support of the Chinese army following his capture of the throne led to his quick downfall. With the combined forces of the Manchu and Chinese armies, Lei's rebels were ousted from Beijing, and a Manchu prince was proclaimed the first emperor of the foreign Manchu (or Qing) Dynasty with the regal title of Shunzhi. The same man Lei shunned, General Wu San Gui, remained in the service of the new Qing emperor and accepted the role of hunting down Ming loyalists.

Remnants of the Ming royal family and numerous political and military support-ers held out for the next four decades after the fall of Beijing, but they remained on the run from the relentless pursuit of the new Qing armies. From the northern and central regions of the Chinese mainland they were driven southward toward the coast until the last members of the royal family were safe only within the borders of a few southern provinces. They referred to these provinces as the Southern Ming Dynasty. It is historically significant that the Ming Dynasty's staunchest and most loyal support ultimately came from these southern provinces. The last of the Ming royalty survived here for several years with the support of the local people. The Qing army's continual hounding of loyalists in these provinces left great bitterness in the hearts of the Hon people (Chinese). The ultimate pursuit of the remaining Ming royal family members in these provinces to Burma and their resulting death in historical obscurity curried deep hatred in South China for the Qing. Many historical researchers of secret society roots conjecture that this may be another reason the secret societies, dedicated to the Ming cause, became especially strong in the southern provinces.

A number of important historical figures planted the seeds for rebellion, first against corrupt Ming officials, and ultimately against the invading Qing. The most famous of these was Hung Ying, a very educated man and acknowledged expert in martial arts. He formed an organization dedicated to helping people engaged in the protection of fellow families and workers encountering persecution in certain trades or geographic areas. The activities of this organization were primarily political in nature and did not include the creation of a peasant army. The significance of this early political so-ciety is its name, which refers to the integrity and courage of the hero who founded the great Ming Dynasty and began China's greatest period of economic and cultural prosperity. To the common man and intellectuals alike, this reference lent credibility to secret societies. This lesson was not lost on the founders of Shaolin Wing Chun. The reader will see many references to it in the organizations that surrounded the development of the fielded system of Hung Fa Yi Wing Chun.

As indicated earlier, once the Manchu fully invaded China, the remnants of the Ming Dynasty escaped farther and farther south to repeatedly regroup. Hung Ying chose to support the Ming Dynasty rather than align himself and his secret society with the invading forces. The reason for this reversal of attitude toward the Ming is essential to understanding continued popular support of revolutionary activities over the next two centuries. It centers on the fact that the Manchu are a non-Chinese people called the Keih and have different habitat and heritage, language, and culture. They forced the Chinese to adopt the Manchu style of wearing a que (pigtail). This practice was particularly distasteful to the common people of China. Additionally, the Manchu (of Mongol descent) and the Hon[3] Chinese of the 17th century embraced distinctly different philosophies. To make matters even worse, the Manchu effectively instilled two separate governments in China with two separate sets of laws. One government applied to those of Manchurian descent; the second applied to all other Chinese peoples. This contributed to strong social distinctions between the two, with the conquering people sharing significantly higher status and privileges. Even people vehemently opposed to the corrupt excesses of the dying Ming Dynasty reversed their support following the implementation of the Qing Dynasty. The truth of this assertion is borne out by the nearly two hundred years of secret society activity in support of revolution during Qing rule.

---

[3] 漢 Hon is Cantonese; *Han* is Mandarin. While *Han* is the more commonly seen translation, this text makes use of the Cantonese.

QING ("PURE") DYNASTY: 1644-1911 A.D.

The Ming Dynasty finally collapsed under the weight of peasant rebellions, enabling Manchu forces, invited and aided by corrupt or disgruntled Ming Dynasty collaborators, to sweep into China to occupy Beijing and then carry out a systematic conquest of the rest of the country.

The essential point of the Manchu conquest of 1644 is that the Manchu at the time they came to power in China had already mastered the early Confucian philosophy and art of government and reconciled their own political institutions with it. Emphasis was on loyalty to parents and to the state, with its ruler viewed as a patriarchal family member. Little emphasis was placed on religious loyalty. This contrasted sharply with the new Buddhist bent of the Hon people and played a key role in the rising popularity of the secret societies.

As Hung Ying's efforts grew in support of the patriots rallying around the remnants of the Ming (Chu) family, revolutionaries and many prominent Ming loyalists joined him. Numerous oral traditions reference five elders (Ng Jou) in connection with loyalist activity. They are referenced here because later there were legends of five famous martial arts elders throughout Chinese martial arts lore, and it is important to note that these were distinct from the five political elders. Indeed, the five political elders may be a reference to five separate locations of loyalist activity. They should not be confused with the legends of particular martial arts players and teachers.

Hung Ying's organization continued to grow, becoming one of the earliest forms of the secret society called Hon Stay (Hon Lau), the first of its kind to appear during the Qing Dynasty. This organization was the genesis of the later Hung Mun secret society, which played a key role in the spread of Everlasting/Praise Spring Fist (Weng/Wing Chun Kuen) Kung Fu.

In 1647 the Qing Dynasty sent an invasion force south where Hung Ying had amassed about 20,000 troops. Resistance was fierce, but the outcome was inevitable. The better equipped Manchu army massacred Hung Ying's forces. Many escaped the battle including the five elders. In later records of this battle, most tales mention only the escape of the five political elders.

Another revolutionary leader and his equally famous son also played pivotal roles in furthering the formation and spread of secret societies during this period. Cheng Ji Lung was a maritime fleet owner of an enormous private navy. Between 1620 and 1683, he and his family battled the Qing Dynasty for control of the Xiamen (Amoy) area in Fujian. His son, Cheng Sing Gung, conducted anti-Qing resistance throughout the area. According to legends and oral traditions, the five political elders mentioned earlier cooperated extensively with Cheng Sing Gung and vice versa.

With his naval power, Cheng Sing Gung's fame grew. After many successful battles, he and his fleet were ambushed by the Qing Dynasty and lost. He was forced into retreat, taking his remaining troops to the island of Formosa (Taiwan). Cheng led 350 warships with 25,000 soldiers to conquer Formosa (under Dutch occupation since 1624) and reestablished his southern stronghold. Cheng not only established an anti-Qing base, but also expelled the Dutch, who were resented by the native Taiwanese. He also succeeded in developing the island politically and economically. According to legend, Cheng Sing Gung and close to four thousand of his closest followers and supporters took an oath committing themselves to continuing secret society activities. Their secret society later acted as the counterpart to the Hung Mun Society on China's mainland. Many other secret societies were also established during this same period. In all, they caused major problems for the Qing Dynasty in southern China. At one point, the Qing officials ordered an evacuation of the coastal areas of southern China in an effort to defeat Cheng Sing Gung by eliminating the population centers needed to fuel his merchant trade. This evacuation and its resultant battles and struggles in the late 17th century resulted in the loss of about 40 percent of the southern province of Fujian's overall population. The Manchu Qing recovered the island of Taiwan in 1683, thus putting an end to open, armed rebellion.

Expansion of the Secret Societies

After losing in open combat, these political organizations took on a much more secretive nature and went underground to form the first true secret organizations known today as the secret societies. In essence, China's secret societies started out as self-help and mutual aid brotherhoods. From there they evolved into political and military groups opposing the instabilities of the Ming/Qing transition. The values of patriotism, brotherhood, loyalty, righteousness, bravery in battle, and secrecy shared by "brothers-in-arms" throughout all human history became paramount in these societies. It is interesting to note that the 36 oaths common to many of the secret societies (including those still functioning today) can all be broken down into these categories. It should also be noted that from this point on, secret societies took on a new role as major institutions in Chinese history and culture. Although brotherhood societies focused attention on the plight of the common man throughout China's rich history, during this period they increased in number and ferocity and took on the role of permanent social institutions that would heavily influence and shape future Chinese social politics. It is easy to see why such a high emphasis was placed on maintaining the secrecy of their ultimate combat training and fighting system eventually fielded for guerilla warfare as Everlasting/Praise Spring Fist (Weng/Wing Chun Kuen).

As the Qing Dynasty gained more power and became more ruthless in its oppression of political opposition, the secret societies became more secretive. They adopted strict codes of conduct and ethics and employed blood oaths designed to defend them. The conduct they expected of themselves and their members was far stricter in terms of morality than that reflected by the established government ruling them. It was not until the latter half of the 19th century that a criminal element began to influence some of the secret societies.

It is important to note that the attitude of the Qing government was quite hostile toward the martial arts community. This hostility was probably deserved since the martial arts community had strong ties to resistance movements. For these reasons, government records reference members of the martial arts community as socially inferior and often call them criminals. In any revolution, the loser is branded a criminal and the winner is perceived as just and righteous. The same is true here. Many of these societies took on Robin Hood type roles by robbing from the rich and giving to the poor. In that sense, they were criminal from a Manchu perspective, but just as Robin Hood was revered as a hero in Western lore, so too were these secret societies in the minds and hearts of the common people. It is true that during the mid-19th century some societies turned to criminal activity in the opium trade. The British government took to calling these criminal societies "triads." The name *triads* itself references the three harmonies of heaven, man, and earth. Indeed, one of the greatest revolutionary societies of the previous two centuries was the Heaven, Man, and Earth Society.

Today's secret societies can be classified into three groups that evolved from a common background: political, criminal, and martial. Many secret societies of a political nature still thrive today, both within and outside of China's borders. The Hung Mun and Qing Bang remain quite active in Taiwan today. There the Hung Mun has over 100,000 active members. Taiwanese authorities openly affirm that there is no evidence these two organizations have any criminal involvement in Taiwan.

Those societies that have turned to criminal activity share similar names and ceremonial activities with noncriminal societies, but no longer possess the noble purpose of their political and martial counterparts. They do, however, remain quite secretive.

The martial arts societies still maintain their cultural and historical traditions, but they have no relation to today's political or criminal activities or associations. Many of these societies are no longer secretive.

The Essential Mix in the Melting Pot of the Southern Shaolin Temple

As they retreated southward from the onslaught of the Qing Dynasty invasion, the last remnants of the Ming Dynasty's imperial court traveled with a sizeable force of imperial troops, as well as many capable administrative officials and governing bureaucrats. Along the way they enlisted the assistance of numerous rebel leaders. At the final collapse of Ming rule, many of these civilian officials took refuge in Buddhist monasteries in the south. Temples particularly favorable to sheltering Ming refugees were located in Fujian, Gwongdong, and Gwongsai provinces. At the same time, most members of the armed forces either surrendered or turned to robbery for a living. A few of the best generals and combat-experienced warriors joined the new rebel base in the southern Young Forest Temple in Fujian Province to continue the fight against the Qing Dynasty. It served as a secret headquarters for their continued resistance activity.

The importance of their selection of a Shaolin Temple as a base of operations should not be understated. Many parallels can be drawn throughout recorded history of ruling families and governing bureaucracies who turned to religious and philosophical sentiment to fuel support for a government under attack. The Ming loyalists were no different. They most likely embraced the opportunity to pit the Chinese love of Buddhism as a faith and Taoism as a philosophy against the Manchu in an attempt to keep the struggle for power alive. From the Southern Shaolin Temple they could visibly shout the praises of the Ming Dynasty and emphasize its long history of support for the Buddhist religion and the teaching of Taoist philosophy. Indeed, many of the greatest Buddhist temples were built with Ming Dynasty patronage. Likewise, many of China's greatest Taoist writers and philosophers owed their popularity to Ming Dynasty bureaucratic support. At a minimum, they could continue to foment local interest in continued pursuit of Buddhist and Taoist teachings. Indeed, Buddhist and Taoist philosophies directly conflict with the Manchu insistence on universal acceptance of Confucianism. Fanning the flames of this philosophical conflict suited them in their efforts to keep the Qing from gaining dominance in the southern provinces of China and cementing control of the entire nation of Hon people. From a political standpoint, the Qing Dynasty needed wide acceptance of Confucianism because of its emphasis on paternal obedience to the current emperor as "Father of the People" in his role as head of state.

For these reasons, the Manchu government continuously suppressed martial arts practice in the temples and attacked suspected Ming family supporters on both religious and political grounds. These attacks were frequently evidenced in military attempts to uncover and eliminate the secret societies. Often, they played into the hands of the Ming strategists because they ultimately brought the victims closer together rather than driving them farther apart. This government suppression of martial arts practice and development was the primary reason for Wing Chun's initial secrecy and the resultant legends two centuries later as to its origins.

Key Political and Military Progenitors of Wing Chun Development

Among the revolutionaries, there were two significant people who influenced Everlasting/Praise Spring Fist development, one because of his political influence and the other because of his technical and military influence.

The first, Chiu Yun (also known as Chu Ming), was one of the last surviving members of the royal family. He assumed the role of Shaolin monk to hide from persecution and foment revolution. Because of his close association with the Buddhist teachings of the Northern Shaolin Temple, he established the Buddhist Sect Hung Mun to coordinate political activities in the Northern region. This was the first secret society related to the Shaolin Temple. Its importance lay in the fact that it was the first organization to form a bridge between Shaolin Buddhist supporters of the Ming Dynasty and Ming military and political revolutionaries.

As the Manchu gained control over Northern China, the remnants and supporters of the Ming retreated south, including Shaolin revolutionaries. Around 1646, the Southern Shaolin Temple revolutionaries developed the Red Flower Society (Hung Fa Wui) at the Red Flower Pavilion (Hung Fa Ting) for the purpose of coordinating their anti-Qing efforts. This highly secret organization closely aligned with the existing Fut Paai Hung Mun.

Figure 1.3 Official Entrance to the rebuilt Southern Shaolin Temple.

The name *Hung Fa* contains special meanings to the secret societies. The Chinese pronunciations of "Magnificent" (洪) and "Red" (紅) are virtually the same. The word "Hung" was used, again to enhance confusion of the enemy's spies. Additional cultural innuendoes for the words "Magnificent," "Red," and "Hung" must also be considered in any study of the secret societies. The name "Hung (Magnificent) Mun" was originally chosen for secret societies for two specific reasons. The first was to commemorate the efforts of Hung Ying, one of the earliest revolutionaries fighting the Manchu. The second came from the terms used to describe timeframe—Magnificent Martial Year Time period of the first Ming Emperor's reign. This emperor's name was Chu Yun Cheung. His family name "Chu" is another word for "Red." In the stories of the founding of the Ming Dynasty, he wore a red bandanna on his brow. From this historical link, the color red became the official color of the secret societies seeking to restore the Ming family to the throne of China. Two famous sayings among secret society members were, "A piece of a red banner in the hands" and "wrapped around the head is a hero," meaning that a man wearing a red bandanna is a hero. Finally, it is important to note that the final battle fought by Chu Yun Cheung in his quest to establish the Ming Dynasty was won under a brilliant red sunset. For these reasons, the secret societies chose red as their official color.

It is also important to understand the use of the word "Flower" in the naming of the secret sects surrounding the evolution of Everlasting/Praise Spring Fist (Weng/Wing Chun Kuen). The word "flower" reflects enlightenment in Chan (Zen) Buddhism. Additionally, the flower points back to the Shaolin roots.

By this point in time, the Shaolin warrior monks of the Southern Shaolin Temple were no longer living a peaceful, isolated existence. Their temple had become a gathering place for the Ming Royal (Chu) family members in hiding and the best military minds of the Ming Dynasty, all seeking refuge and a base of operations for military development and revolution. It should be noted that the Chu family (also spelled Chia, Ju, Choi, Tsoi, Gee, Zhu, and Jyu) possessed its own highly developed and tested Kung Fu called Chu Ga. In the interests of secrecy, the name Tong Long (Preying Mantis) was used to cover up the origins of the system. Today, this style is known as Chu Ga Tong Long. That knowledge, by association, was now also present in the Southern Shaolin Temple and played a contributing role in the development of the Wing Chun Kung Fu to come.

Accompanying these political refugees in the Southern Shaolin Temple were wealthy leaders, scholars, and businessmen of the previous Ming Dynasty, as well as a significant core of common Ming loyalists actively participating in the overthrow of the Qing Dynasty. In essence, the Southern Shaolin Temple had become a hotbed of revolutionary activity fueled by the best fighters of the Shaolin Temples and the greatest military minds and leaders of the previous Ming Dynasty. Together, they share the battle cry of "Fan Qing Fu Ming" (Oppose the Qing, restore the Ming). This decision became the genesis of future branches of secret societies and different branches of Southern Shaolin Kung Fu in the Fujian Province.

It was the Hung Fa Wui Secret Society in collaboration with the Southern Shaolin Monks that were instrumental in the creation of Hung Fa Yi Wing Chun Kuen.

The fighting effectiveness and revolutionary activities of the Southern Shaolin systems astounded the Qing Emperor at that time. In response, the Qing ordered the destruction of the Southern Shaolin Temple through the use of overwhelming odds. Surviving members scattered throughout the Southern Provinces. Supported by other secret societies, these revolutionaries

Figure 1.4 The only original building left standing from the original Southern Shaolin Temple, the Hung Fa Ting.

Figure 1.5　Bou Man Dim was the public name of the Hung Fa Ting.

continued to spread their activities and fighting style. Many of today's Southern kung fu systems trace their roots to the Weng Chun Tong, such as Chi Sim Weng Chun and Hung Fa Yi Wing Chun.

The second significant member involved was a military expert turned monk named Ng Dak Hei. His monk name was Maan Wan Lung. The Buddhist Sect Hung Mun called him Daat Jung. The different names were used to confuse potential spies and protect Ng Dak Hei and the temple itself. He was known to be actively involved in anti-Qing activities and is credited with bringing additional military knowledge of martial arts to the Hung Fa Wui and playing a role in the continuing development of new combat systems within the secret societies.

After the destruction of the Southern Shaolin Temple, Hung Fa Wui members continued to be active. During the reign of Emperor Kangxi (1661-1722), the main purpose of the Red Flower Society was twofold: to overthrow the rule of China by the Manchu and to function as a "Robin Hood" type group to fight against governmental corruption. It was most active during the 1673 revolt, called the War of the Three Feudatories. This revolt was due to three ex-Ming Generals that had decided to serve the Qing and then later revolted. For the next one hundred years, the Qing Dynasty under the leadership of Yongzheng (1723-1735) and Qianlong (1736-1795), China was expanded to its farthest reaches in terms of controlled territory.

Figure 1.6　Courtyard of the Southern Shaolin Temple.

Genesis of Shaolin Wing Chun and Hung Fa Yi History

Within the Southern Shaolin Temple a particular hall was designated for development of this new fighting system named Everlasting/Praise Spring Fist (Weng/Wing Chun Kuen); the hall was called Weng Chun Tong. Its name symbolized "a fresh start . . . current . . . in the moment . . . eternal spring . . . the continuous cycle of death and rebirth throughout life," all recurring metaphors in Buddhism. It also symbolized the rebirth of the Ming Dynasty and the hope that it would last forever. From the Pao Fa Lin Wing Chun lineage, the survivors of the Southern Shaolin Temple swore to resist the Qing and spread the revolution. To recognize one another, they used the phrase *Weng Yin Chi Ji; Mou Mong Hon Juk; Daai Dei Wui Chun* ("Always speak with determination; don't forget the Hon nation; again will return the spring"). Thus, Everlasting Spring (Weng Chun) was a name that maintained consistency with its Buddhist Shaolin roots, thereby rendering it even more effective as a code word bearing secret meaning only for those who had a need to know its true intent.

With the destruction of the Southern Shaolin Temple and its Everlasting/Praise Spring Hall (Weng Chun Tong), the character of *Weng* (永) meaning "always, perpetual, or Everlasting" was changed to *Wing* (詠) meaning "to sing out" or "praise." Chan Buddhism uses oral communication to pass on its teachings. This was a message to Wing Chun's disciples to pass the system on orally so that its details could not accidentally fall into enemy hands. The character *Chun* (春), meaning "spring, a time of new growth," stayed the same. Many loyalists saw the Hon nation as the "spring" of Chinese culture. By changing the characters, the Ming Dynasty loyalists were reminded to pass on the tradition and secrets orally while working to rebuild the Ming Dynasty government. The Chinese word *Yim* (嚴) means "to prohibit" or "secret." By adding *Yim* (嚴) to *Wing Chun* (詠春), the meaning was "to be discrete, secret, and pass on the revolutionary art orally." The initial intent was to return to the original name of Weng Chun following the successful rebirth of the Ming Dynasty. Such a success never happened, and the name remains Wing Chun today for all Hung Fa Yi practitioners.

Before the development of Weng Chun/Wing Chun, the monks' martial arts were created for the primary purpose of supporting their Buddhist beliefs of "nonkilling" and Taoist philosophical goal of attaining a nonmaterialistic and physiologically healthy lifestyle in harmony with nature. Consequently, heavy emphasis was placed on physiological training via the exercise of artistic postures. This new infusion of military and revolutionary minds of the Hung Fa Wui drove the need for changing the Southern Temple's martial arts focus. The development of a cutting-edge military fighting system that could be used to address all hand-to-hand combat threats in a relatively short time became imperative. At the same time, this new system had to be consistent with the philosophical venue of the Shaolin Temple and its Chan Buddhist faith.

This consistency made possible both a revolution and an evolution in Shaolin Kung Fu. For these Chan Buddhist warriors, the direct experience of reality was paramount. Their philosophy mandated a natural and simple existence, and they simply could not remove this philosophy from any prime activity, including martial training. The essence of Shaolin martial art training focused on understanding the nature of combat (to be in harmony with the universe) and learning how to avoid conflicts. Once an attacker possessed the mind to attack, he separated himself from the universe. From a Shaolin perspective, an attack represents an offering of violence. Rather than accept the offering, Shaolin warriors returned it to the sender. Initially, the offering would be returned in the form of a parry or block; if the attacker was both skilled and determined to cause harm, a more definite and conclusive solution was required. This could take the form of incapacitating joint locks, knockouts, or death. The more sophisticated and violent the assault, the more devastating became the return of the attack to the attacker. Shaolin followers did not see themselves as responsible for hurting an attacker; they were merely refusing delivery of intended harm. Consequently, in the Everlasting Spring (Weng/Wing Chun) training hall of the Southern Temple, only functional fighting and truly simple concepts were employed that maintained harmony with the Shaolin philosophy.

EVERLASTING/PRAISE SPRING FIST

This new emphasis on simplicity and directness provided a sharp contrast to the complex acrobatic styles taught and employed outside the hall and proved to be the key to Everlasting/Praise Spring Fist's (Weng/Wing Chun Kuen's) ultimate success as a combat system. To fully comprehend this point, students of history must understand that revolutionaries had to contend with separate regional armies who tended to adopt the fighting styles of their commanding generals, each of whom had his own training method. A new style was needed that could counter the styles of these different armies. Common soldiers had to be trained quickly to counter specific threats by using specific modules of the system rather than the complete system itself. Consequently, only a limited number of true masters of the entire system would be needed as teachers.

At this stage of development, the conceptual groundwork was being laid for the eventual development of the Everlasting/Praise Spring Fist combat system. To ensure that the accumulation of many centuries of philosophic and martial heritage was not lost during wartime, the Weng Chun Tong was designated for preserving the essence of their kung fu (the three treasures identified in chapter 1). The creation of this new system focused on optimizing human physiological expression in combat. At this early stage, traditional development structure still guided the endeavor. That development structure included five major components: form, intention, principles, methods, and art.

CHI SIM

The system of Everlasting Spring Fist (Weng Chun Kuen) developed and employed at this early stage (called Chi Sim by today's followers) is very closely related to the classical Shaolin postures in both appearance and training methodology. (*Chi Sim*, meaning "extreme compassion," is another metaphor from the Chan Buddhist teachings.) However, direct military influences are hinted at as well. In Chi Sim, weapons are trained first, and training for the hands and body progresses from the weapons experience. Chi Sim practitioners call the pole (Gwan) their teacher and the butterfly swords (Dou) their parents. This emphasis on training weapons up front is an obvious military necessity; this was not the first time this concept was introduced. Great combat knowledge and experience could already be drawn on. The times produced extensive weapons experience. Likewise, great knowledge of apparatus employment in training (i.e., the wooden man dummy) was also already available from northern Shaolin roots. It was a simple matter to translate this knowledge to support new development efforts focused on efficiency, simplicity, and directness. Therefore, the pole (or spear) became the instructor to those developing the hand and foot tools of the new system, and the wooden dummy was employed extensively in training the pole. Ultimately, the same would be true for Hung Fa Yi Wing Chun.

As a combat system, Chi Sim covered all ranges of combat including many kicking, fist and open-hand striking, elbow and shoulder, joint locking, and throwing techniques, all connected and directed through the use of the Centerline concept. Complete knowledge of all forms of attackers, including proficient grapplers, was present using Chi Sim's heaven, man, and earth orientation of body structures, space, and energetics. For instance, *Heaven* from a range perspective represented hand and foot strikes. *Man* represented the knee and elbow range, and *Earth* represented the shoulder and hip range. Figure 2.1 depicts these representations.

This heaven, man, and earth orientation is the original language which expresses time, space, and energy in Shaolin Chan and martial arts. Hung Fa Yi Wing Chun makes use of the same concept but primarily expresses it through language based on what is termed the "Wing Chun Formula." This formula forms the centerpiece of Hung Fa Yi training and employment, creating its unique structures and positions.

Chi Sim also incorporates the mastery of multifaceted hand-to-hand weapons such as the long and powerful Shaolin pole and the short, versatile double butterfly knives. Unlike popular Wing Chun of today, Chi Sim and its brother system, Hung Fa Yi, elegantly represent the three-pronged Shaolin approach to experiencing reality through philosophy, internal hei gung development, and combat preparation.

As indicated in chapter 1, of the many expressions of Wing Chun Kung Fu present in modern times, only Chi Sim and Hung Fa Yi trace their roots to the Southern Shaolin Temple. Hung Fa Yi Wing Chun represents the Shaolin expression of combat efficiency, owing heavily to the military influences of its fielding in the revolutionary societies engaged in two centuries of guerilla warfare against the Manchurians. Chi Sim Weng Chun rep-

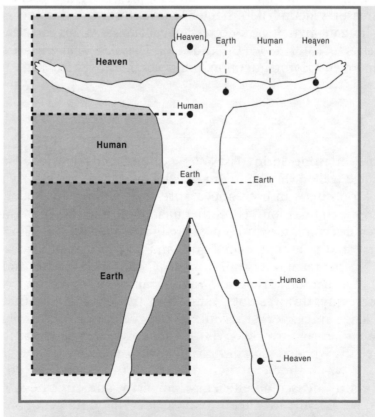

Figure 2.1 Heaven, man, earth. The foundations of three-dimensional fighting.

resents the culmination of Shaolin Chan learned through combat arts. All paths of Shaolin knowledge accumulated in the previous 12 centuries of Shaolin martial arts came together in Chi Sim Weng Chun. The Chi Sim Weng Chun system was the roots of many southern Chinese marital arts. When the warriors from the Northern Temple fled south to Fujian, they reaffirmed their centuries-long identity in the Weng Chun Tong.

Based on Ten Shaolin Wisdoms, Seven Shaolin Principles, Eighteen Shaolin Bridge Hands (Kiu Sau), heaven-man-earth structures and energetics, five hand forms, and two weapons forms, Chi Sim is well equipped to challenge the practitioner to a lifetime of continued development and self-improvement. From a Chi Sim perspective, kung fu is the special ability one receives suddenly after a long time of dedicated training. Wushu (combat skill) is only one aspect of kung fu in Chi Sim terms.

Before examining Chi Sim's approach to kung fu development, a quick review of who passed that approach from the Shaolin Temple to today's practitioners is appropriate. As always, the best measure of the true roots of a martial system is the system itself. In this case, the system as practiced today is richly Chan (Zen). There can be little doubt as to its roots once its methods and practice are fully understood.

Figure 2.2 Attacking the center while guarding heaven, human, and earth.

Chi Sim Lineage to the Present

The lineage chart on the next page depicts Chi Sim Weng Chun masters' oral and written legends of their heritage. Chi Sim actually represents a series of teachers from the Southern Shaolin Temple and their direct descendants. *Chi Sim* means "extreme compassion," a Buddhist concept, whereas *Sim Si* means "Chan teacher." During these years, there were both inner-circle secret society members and practitioners of Chi Sim, as well as public figures and representations of the system. The public figures were not taught all of the details of the system (particularly the identity with southern Shaolin) simply because of their public exposure. They were far too vulnerable to capture and torture to be given inner-circle access to details leading to possible identification of inner-circle members. A figure clearly documented in history was a well-known resistance participant named Hung Hei Gun. He is credited as the founder of today's Hung Ga (and ultimately other subsets such as Lau Ga, Choi Ga, and Lei Ga). That is why so many parallels exist between Chi Sim and today's Hung Ga.

It is held in the Chi Sim legends that these teachers referred to as Chi Sim eventually ended up at the Red Boat Opera Troupe (Hung Suen Hei Baan). This legend is virtually identical to Hung Fa Yi legend.

Chi Sim Training Overview

The foundations of the art of Chi Sim Weng Chun were based on Chan teachings at the Shaolin Temple that were handed down from the time of Bodhidharma. The essence of Chan teaches its followers to trust in their own experience and the understanding

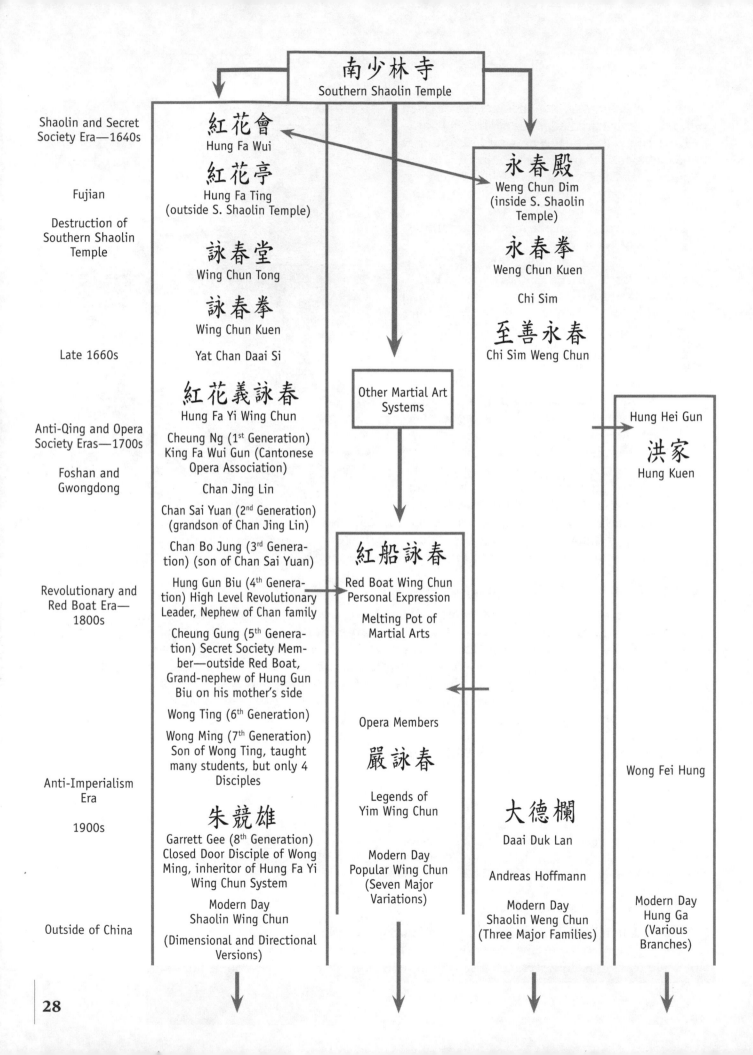

南少林寺
Southern Shaolin Temple

Shaolin and Secret Society Era—1640s

紅花會
Hung Fa Wui

紅花亭
Hung Fa Ting
(outside S. Shaolin Temple)

永春殿
Weng Chun Dim
(inside S. Shaolin Temple)

Fujian

Destruction of Southern Shaolin Temple

詠春堂
Wing Chun Tong

永春拳
Weng Chun Kuen

Chi Sim

詠春拳
Wing Chun Kuen

Yat Chan Daai Si

至善永春
Chi Sim Weng Chun

Late 1660s

Other Martial Art Systems

紅花義詠春
Hung Fa Yi Wing Chun

Hung Hei Gun

Anti-Qing and Opera Society Eras—1700s

Cheung Ng (1st Generation) King Fa Wui Gun (Cantonese Opera Association)

洪家
Hung Kuen

Foshan and Gwongdong

Chan Jing Lin

Chan Sai Yuan (2nd Generation) (grandson of Chan Jing Lin)

Chan Bo Jung (3rd Generation) (son of Chan Sai Yuan)

紅船詠春
Red Boat Wing Chun Personal Expression

Revolutionary and Red Boat Era—1800s

Hung Gun Biu (4th Generation) High Level Revolutionary Leader, Nephew of Chan family

Melting Pot of Martial Arts

Cheung Gung (5th Generation) Secret Society Member—outside Red Boat, Grand-nephew of Hung Gun Biu on his mother's side

Wong Ting (6th Generation)

Wong Ming (7th Generation) Son of Wong Ting, taught many students, but only 4 Disciples

Opera Members

嚴詠春

Anti-Imperialism Era

Wong Fei Hung

Legends of Yim Wing Chun

1900s

朱競雄
Garrett Gee (8th Generation) Closed Door Disciple of Wong Ming, inheritor of Hung Fa Yi Wing Chun System

大德欄
Daai Duk Lan

Modern Day Popular Wing Chun (Seven Major Variations)

Modern Day Shaolin Wing Chun

Andreas Hoffmann

Outside of China

(Dimensional and Directional Versions)

Modern Day Shaolin Weng Chun (Three Major Families)

Modern Day Hung Ga (Various Branches)

Figure 2.3   Grand Master Wai Yun receiving the tea from Sifu Andreas Hoffmann. Grand Masters Lau Chi Long and Cheung Kwong witness. Sifu Andreas Hoffmann was the last student of the Hong Kong Wing Chun "Mecca," Dai Duk Lan.

Figure 2.4   Grand Master Tang Yick (second from left) with three students circa 1960.

of nature rather than doctrine or history. Any fighting system based on Chan, such as Chi Sim Weng Chun and Hung Fa Yi Wing Chun, must have the following three key components:

1. It must be complete, taking all factors into account. For example, it must address all ranges of combat from kicking to striking, trapping, grappling, or employment of weapons.
2. It must be based on reality rather than theory.
3. It must be spontaneous, existing in the here and now rather than in the past or future.

Figure 2.5 Earth Kiu Sau from the Chi Sim system.

Figure 2.6 Grand Master Tang Yick circa 1950s.

In Chan, there is no ego or body, no past or future. By focusing on the moment, not being distracted by thoughts or emotions outside the immediate task at hand, and being in the here and now, practitioners are free to be aware of the total situation and react accordingly.

The chart in table 2.1 depicts the 10 Wisdoms of Shaolin, the seven principles of Shaolin Weng Chun, and the 18 Shaolin Kiu Sau (bridge hand) methods employed to fulfill the requirements of Chan Buddhist martial training.

The technical components of Weng Chun are likened to a five-petaled flower as described in table 2.2.

Chi Sim As Precursor to Several Southern Styles

Many southern styles claim a connection to the Southern Shaolin Temple, and most are technically, tactically, and philosophically similar. An examination of the sets of Chi Sim Weng Chun suggests that each set is the precursor to several southern styles. The Fa Kuen set, with its flowing motions, connected movements, and position of being the first set taught, may be the precursor to many of the family systems in southern China. The Sap Yat

Table 2.1 Chi Sim Weng Chun					
10 Wisdoms		**7 Principles (called 6½ points)**		**18 Kiu Sau**	
識	sïk (knowledge)	提	tàih (raise)	挑	tìu (pick up "with a stick")
膽	dáam (confidence and courage)	攔	làahn (to press or take space from an opponent, make space for oneself)	撥	buht (sweep aside, push open)
氣	hei (chi / energy)	點	dím (point–hard or soft)	打	dä (strike or hit)
勁	gihng (focused power)	揭	kit (deflect, short impulsive rotational force connected to opponent's centerline)	盆	pùhn (folding)
神	sàhn (spirit, attitude)	割	got (cut downward, sink)	抓	jáau (catch or grasp)
形	yìhng (form, shape)	環	wàahn (circle, absorb)	拉	làai (pull)
意	yi (understanding, meaning)	The above six principles encompass 50% of the focus of Chi Sim Weng Chun. The remaining 50% of focus and importance is contained in the seventh principle, thus the name ½ Point, reflecting ½ the total system emphasis and importance. In essence, the seventh principle is a constant in Chi Sim Weng Chun. It is called "Lau" meaning to flow continuously toward the holes in an opponent's offense and defense.		撕	sì (tear/rip, shear–two energies moving in opposite directions at once)
理	léih (principles)	漏	lauh (flowing continuously)	扯	ché (quick pull, jerk)
法	faat (reality, methods)			擒	kàhn (capture)
術	seuht (expression, showmanship, and skill)			拿	nàh (control)

(continued)

Table 2.1 Chi Sim Weng Chun (continued)		
10 Wisdoms	**7 Principles (called 6½ points)**	**18 Kiu Sau**
Note: The most important of these wisdoms is correct knowledge. In Buddhist philosophy, all suffering comes from not knowing and living in harmony with reality. This gives rise to suffering. Correct knowledge is the way out of suffering.		封 fùng (close off, prevent free movement)
		閉 bai (tighter control, allow no movement)
		逼 bïk (press)
		恰 häp (follow-up, aggressive flowing/continuing)
		吞 tàn (swallow)
		吐 tuo (spit)
		搏 bok (attack is your best defense)
		殺 saat (eliminate, beat down completely)

Note: For every principle there is a *Qi/Hei* (internal energy) and *Ging* (focused power) movement. In essence, the 10 Wisdoms and the 7 Principles are intertwined. Both must be properly expressed in each of the 18 Kiu Sau.

Kuen, with its emphasis on economy of movement and short bridge power, could have been the foundation for further refinement into what is known as today's Wing Chun with the three forms of Siu Nim Tau, Chum Kiu, and Biu Ji. The Saam Bai Fut and Jong Kuen, with emphases on whole body energy and all ranges of combat, could have been the precursor to modern Hung Ga.

In several oral legends of Hung Ga, a person by the name of Chi Sim is credited as being the creator of the style, and the founder of Hung Ga, named Hung Hei Gun, is said to have learned directly from Chi Sim. As noted earlier, the term *Chi Sim* refers to a series of master teachers whose names are not recorded. The existence of Chi Sim as an individual is open to historical debate. Regardless, legend supports the assertion that Hung Ga is a modern day version of Chi Sim, with its ultimate roots in the Weng Chun Tong of the Southern Shaolin Temple. A similar parallel exists with Hung Fa Yi Wing Chun and today's popular Wing Chun system.

Whatever the possible connections of the southern Shaolin to today's modern martial arts, strong evidence exists to support the hypothesis that Chi Sim Weng Chun was directly involved in the evolution of modern Wing Chun. The core of the Chi Sim system is the weapon sets of long pole and double knife along with the dummy sets. It should be noted that these three training sets had their origins in the Northern Shaolin Temple. Throughout the martial arts community, the unique hallmark of all Wing Chun lineages is the long pole, the double knives, and the dummy. The hypothesis

Table 2.2	Five Petals of Chi Sim Training	
Technical components	1. Saan Sik	Separate motions
	2. Kuen Tou	Fist sets consisting of seven core development sets depicted in table 2.3
Flow and reaction training	Exercises focused on three-line references on limbs to develop distance awareness and proper geometry for leverage. Ultimately, these support kiu sau development	Wrist/ankle (Tin Pun Kiu Sau or Heaven Kiu Sau)
		Elbow/knee (Yan Pun Kiu Sau or Man Kiu Sau)
		Shoulder/knee (Dei Pun Kiu Sau or Earth Kiu Sau)
	Capture and control exercises	Kan Na (Chin Na) exercises similar to modern day wing chun laap sau, except focus expands to all lines with continuous flow—even on the ground
Subdue further struggle	Emphasizes center of balance, control, and incapacitation	
Saan Sau (separate hand)	Emphasizes sparring with all the physical, mental, and emotional rigors of combat	
Principles, poems, Chan, history, and Hei Gung	Mental training to include science, philosophy, and culture	
	Internal and external health and energy training employing Ng Jong Hei Gung as a training core	

that Wing Chun was a series of loose movements that later added the dummy and weapons does not match the evidence presented by both Chi Sim Weng Chun and Hung Fa Yi Wing Chun. These systems were founded on the pole and knife, using the dummy as an integral part of the training. In ancient China, priority was placed on weapons training due to the reality of combat in those times. A warrior did not have years to learn empty hand sets before uniting body and mind through weapons training. Chi Sim and Hung Fa Yi philosophy and technical knowledge constitute credible evidence that they were most likely the foundation for all modern Wing Chun some considerable time before the advent of the Red Boat Opera Troupe.

Chan Teachings Attest to Chi Sim's Shaolin Heritage

Although many styles lay claim to a direct connection with the Shaolin temples, Chi Sim Weng Chun backs up its claims with a training system based on Chan teachings and training methods that support Chan philosophy. A complete system that trains

Table 2.3	Seven Core Training Sets of Kuen Tou	
Fa Kuen (flower fist)	Basic energy training emphasizing use of whole body spiraling energy	
	Introduces all hand- and footwork for both short- and long-distance combat	
Sap Yat Kuen (11 fists)	Develops economy of motion and the shock power known throughout the Wing Chun world as "inch power"	
	Based on movements and concepts of the long pole	
	11 empty hand concepts taught via the 18 kiu sau bridging arm two-man drills	
Saam Bai Fut (three bows to Buddha)	Inner sanctum training paralleling sup yat kuen above	
	Multiplies energy through waist turning and bending	
	Emphasizes heaven, man, earth concepts in all directions and dimensions	
Syeung Kung Jong Kuen (internal/ external structure fist)	Highest level of training	
	Combines all hand sets, weapon training, and wooden dummy sets	
	Develops harmonious power through muscle, intent, and energy focus	
Muk Yan Jong (wooden man post)	Three sets emphasizing heaven, man, and earth concepts	
	Each set has seven sections, each in turn describing the seven principles of Chi Sim and introducing two or three kiu sau concepts	Heaven set stresses upper gate and long-range tactics
		Earth set teaches lower gate and close-range tactics
		Man set teaches middle gate and midrange tactics
Gwan (long pole)	Emphasizes long-range concepts, strategies, and tactics	
	Teaches "live energy" and develops responsiveness to changing situation	
Fu Mou Seung Dou (swords)	Called "father mother double knives'" because the weapons are viewed as the ultimate teacher of the kung fu	
	Teaches absolute subduing of an adversary	

in all ranges of combat in addition to long and short weapons within a complete set of strategies and tactics, the Chi Sim Weng Chun system represents the culmination of all that is Shaolin martial art. This completeness is most obvious in Chi Sim's seven principles. All easily represent different, yet cohesive and mutually supportive, ways to destroy the opponent's centerline (when *centerline* refers to balance mentally, emotionally, and physically) while simultaneously retaining one's own balance. Perhaps with more communication and closer ties between martial art families, more people will come to know this lineage and appreciate the roots, depth, and breadth of this "flower" among Chinese martial arts. It can only be described as the epitome of all that is "art" from the Shaolin temples, both north and south.

The stage is now set for the paradigm shift to the use of time and space control for hand-to-hand combat as seen in Hung Fa Yi Wing Chun.

Figure 2.7 Grand Master Andreas Hoffmann outside the Chi Sim Headquarters in Bamburg, Germany.

PARADIGM SHIFT OF HUNG FA YI WING CHUN

Hung Fa Yi Wing Chun was developed along a true paradigm shift in hand-to-hand combat thinking. Before this point, systems of combat were based on individual performance and self-expression. Hung Fa Yi was created in an environment based strictly on human physiology and the physics and control of time, space, and energy. This version of Wing Chun may have been created by a different group within the same Weng Chun Tong or by the same group heavily influenced by military thinking from Ming Dynasty officers and the Hung Fa Ting's secret group; either way, members of the Chu royal family, the former leaders of the Ming Dynasty, heavily supported them. This is the first time in the development of Shaolin fighting systems that time and space themselves became the focal point of design consideration. The military implications of this decision are alluded to in the preface of this text. They are far too extensive for technical discussion in this chapter. Suffice it to say that the physical science expertise of the monks, resulting from their relentless pursuit of the laws of nature and universal harmony, paired with the tactical and logistical training necessities confronting the professional soldiers in their midst, yielded the ultimate fighting system in terms of efficiency and effectiveness.

Both Chi Sim and Hung Fa Yi lineages contain strong Chan Buddhist philosophy and traditions, which remain at their cores in the 21st century. However, in Hung Fa Yi the major components of the Wing Chun fighting system's modern day identity take on its key structures and form. This is where the paradigm shift in thinking occurred and the radically different forms of Siu Nim Tau, Chum Kiu, and Biu Ji were first seen. They are far more efficient in motion than previous expressions of forms. Time, space, and energy focus demanded absolute efficiency and economy of motion. Many of Wing Chun's techniques existed in previous Shaolin systems, but the new emphasis on ultimate efficiency drove the need for more refined expression, and new forms were required.

As will be shown in chapter 4 and beyond regarding the science of Hung Fa Yi Wing Chun, this new fighting system was consistent with nature itself. From a rational philosophical perspective, nothing can be added or subtracted from nature; it exists as a totality. The Hung Fa Yi Wing Chun system exists in that same state; nothing can be added or subtracted. The teaching methodology might evolve or change relative to the audience or an individual's understanding, just as the expression of nature might evolve, but that does nothing to the original nature of Hung Fa Yi Wing Chun. It remains the ultimate efficiency in mapping human physiological structure to battlefield strategies and tactics. Without altering the DNA of its practitioners, further efficiency is not possible. Other postures may come close, but there can be only one "most efficient" position in battlefield space and time for placement of weapons for any feasible strategy or tactic. This is the gift the Southern Shaolin Temple's brilliant warrior monks and the Ming Dynasty's finest military strategists left to the world in the form of Hung Fa Yi Wing Chun. Interestingly, following countless centuries of martial arts development, it remains the only system to undergo the paradigm shift of melding human structures and energies to the mission of controlling battlefield spatial and temporal realities.

DESTRUCTION OF THE SOUTHERN SHAOLIN TEMPLE

The Southern Temple was recognized as a hotbed of revolutionary political activity. During this same time, someone inside the temple betrayed both the Red Flower Society and the Southern Shaolin Temple. Their activities were made known to the Qing army, and the Qing decided to execute a full-scale surprise attack. While organizing in secrecy was difficult, the Qing army nevertheless successfully launched an expeditionary force of specially trained combat troops in a surprise attack against the southern Shaolin warrior monks. The Chinese government today has provided proof of these actions via excavation of massive ruins on the ground traditionally believed to be the site of the original Southern Shaolin Temple as well as burial sites of the last Ming royalty.

It is currently believed that only a handful of warrior monks survived the temple's destruction. Five of them, known later as the five elders of Shaolin (not the same persons as the five political elders referenced in chapter 1) allegedly came into contact with Chan Gan Nam. Nam, also known as Chan Wing Wah, was a military general and

Figure 2.8 Burning of the Southern Shaolin Temple.

former right-hand man of Cheng Sing Gung. Following the Qing Dynasty's ambush of Cheng's navy by a Qing Dynasty general, Chan Gan Nam went into hiding on the mainland at the White Crane Cave, earning the nickname White Crane Taoist. The Hung Mun referred to him as Sim Jung.

It should be noted that the five Shaolin elders may be a metaphor for five different secret societies founded by the monks. They may also simply be a historic metaphor for other variations of southern Shaolin martial systems. Those systems can overall be referred to as the Fujian system. Some of these systems are so technically related that they seem to be just variations of each other, and they all share similar legends about their origins. Their differences seem to grow with the passing of each new generation as they become more and more public. With their public identity, they became increasingly focused on individual personality and the passing on of that expression rather than on the principles, concepts, and structures that were aggressively adhered to when they were secret societies. The following systems, which share some serious similarities to Chi Sim or Hung Fa Yi Wing Chun, reference their roots to the Southern Shaolin Temple and can be considered part of the Fujian system: Chu Ga Tong Long (Southern Praying Mantis), Ng Jou Kuen (Five Ancestors Boxing), Fujian Bai He (White Crane), Bak Mei (White Eyebrow), and Lung Ying Kuen (Southern Dragon Boxing). They all share similar legends and employ many similar techniques.

Hung Fa Ting

According to legends, the Red Flower Pavilion was another name for the Gun Yam Tong, a gathering place of the Heaven and Earth Society on mainland China. Membership included descendants of the Ming royal family and former Ming bureaucrats and military and political leaders. Some revolutionaries referred to this place as the Secret Hidden Room, where politics and strategies were discussed and cemented. The Red Flower Pavilion became the new headquarters for the Hung Mun. It was at this time that the practice of blood-oath ceremonies began. Red Flower Righteousness Praise

Spring Fist disciples continued this practice throughout the 20th century. Along with the blood oaths arose a famous phrase, "Of one heart to return the Great Ming."

With the development of Shaolin Weng/Wing Chun, the Southern Shaolin Temple came to an untimely end. Politically, the Qing had not yet cemented their control of Southern China. Three former generals of the Ming Dynasty, who had loosely changed allegiance to the Qing when they successfully captured control of Northern China, supposedly governed the Southern provinces. These generals revolted against the Qing in the Rebellion of the Three Feudatories (1673-1681). Numerous Ming sympathetic secret societies like the Red Flower Society (started in the Southern Shaolin Temple in a gathering place called the Hung Fa Ting) continued to engage in revolutionary activity as well. The proof is in the Hung Fa Ting itself. The archaeologists who excavated the Southern Shaolin Temple in this past decade found the Hung Fa Ting still intact. There can be no question of its existence. In response to these revolutionary activities, the Qing Dynasty had no choice but to act quickly and dramatically.

By the mid-1680s, the Red Flower Pavilion group had many successes against the local Qing authorities. Ironically, it was at this time that the Qing Dynasty consolidated its overall national power and increased efforts in prosecuting revolutionaries. The Qing government created a cruel punishment for revolutionaries involved with secret societies or rebellious activities. In this punishment, called "nine relatives involved in crime," not only was the revolutionary killed, but also his family extending out nine levels of family relationships.

By now the Qing Dynasty had enough power to send a large army south with the intent of crushing all rebellious activity there and on the island of Taiwan. After a decisive battle, the Qing Dynasty had again put down a major rebellion, destroying or scattering secret society members. It was during this period that the Manchu effectively attained control of southern China. With this final shift in power, the Qing Dynasty had finally cemented its control of all of China in the fourth decade of its reign. From this point to about the middle of the 18th century the Qing experienced the zenith of its prosperity. China's sphere of influence covered a territory larger than that of any previous or succeeding government in Chinese history.

Up to this time, Ming supporters remained in constant and often open revolt. They were now forced underground. As other historians have noted, this shift from active, open rebellion within an environment that permitted freedom of movement to a somewhat more subtle resistance due to dispersion of resources and the need for secrecy, created an additional need for shared traditions, aims, and rituals among the revolutionaries. The adaptation and secret use of identifying gestures and signs, including passwords, helped ensure safety and provided some sense of belonging, as well as unity of purpose and action, to revolutionaries now disenfranchised from their government and many from their homes. It is little wonder that Wing Chun revolutionaries became experts in secret communications and disguise of their true identity. By the turn of the 18th century, the official Qing government began recording the activities of the secret societies. These records reflect the names of the Hung Mun (Magnificent League), Tin Dei Wui (Heaven and Earth Society), and Saam Hap Wui (Triad Society or Three Harmonies Society). In the southern part of China, these three are virtually interchangeable as they refer to a single secret organization with many faces and branches.

The remaining rebels scattered and established their own secret society bases throughout China. Many meeting halls, called Tong, were established including the Ching Lin Tong and Hon Seun Tong around the Fujian and Gwongdung areas. The remnants of the warrior monks kept their own Everlasting Spring Hall with roots going back to the Southern Shaolin Temple and secret societies. After decades of military development for guerilla-like warfare and battle-tested trials, this time period was an era of refinement and completion for Praise Spring Fist (Wing Chun Kuen).

The public period of Wing Chun did not begin until the Red Boat Opera activities around 1850 A.D., over a century and a half after Wing Chun's initial battlefield deployment in the secret societies. Only secret society members were exposed to Wing Chun up to this point in time. This is the period referenced by the modern day legend of a young woman named Yim Wing Chun, who purportedly created the system in conjunction with a Buddhist nun named Ng Mui. Historically, the other southern Shaolin systems employ variations of this same legend when referencing their own roots. Such legends were inevitable considering the secrecy with which this system and the others were guarded and trained. This multiple use of the same legend lends credence to the hypothesis that it was an organized cover story employed as tactical deception in the form of misinformation to keep the details and origins of the complete systems secret. Certainly, in Hung Fa Yi Wing Chun's case it was never openly documented to ensure that the art was not abused or did not fall into the wrong hands. However, covert documentation in the form of Shaolin poetry does exist in the hands of a select few, but it remains simply elegant poetry in the absence of the cipher words needed to interpret the true martial meaning behind the artistic expressions of poetic language. Some Red Boat performers were ultimately exposed to certain pieces of Wing Chun science and techniques via secret society leader Hung Gun Biu and his Siu Lin Tau drilling methods.

CHEUNG NG AND THE BEGINNING OF THE OPERA CHAPTER OF THE RED FLOWER SOCIETY ASSOCIATION

Of those who survived the Manchu massacre at the Southern Shaolin Temple (159 years prior to the Red Boat Opera), two known Shaolin Temple disciples were able to keep the Praise Spring Fist System alive. The senior, a monk, was the 22nd generation Shaolin Temple grand master, Yat Chan Daai Si. The other, his disciple, was named Cheung Ng.

Not much is known about the history of Yat Chan Daai Si besides the knowledge that he was originally a high-level monk from the Northern Shaolin Temple who later migrated to the Southern Shaolin Temple and was directly involved in the Praise Spring Hall development of Shaolin Wing Chun.

It was said that Cheung Ng had come from a family of generations of military men serving the Ming Dynasty in the province of Hubei. This family came to a merciless end at the hands of the Manchu. Cheung Ng was the only member who escaped death. In addition to his military education, Cheung Ng was also known to possess extensive knowledge of Chinese opera, specifically Beijing Opera. Such a mixture of military and performing arts knowledge is not unprecedented. Many historians have noted that stage drama's progression in the 10th through 14th centuries of Chinese history included military entertainments

Figure 2.9 Yat Chan Daai Si in front of the Hong Fa Ting.

as a part of performances. Martial demonstrations later became a major attraction in the famous Beijing Opera, where impressive acrobatic feats became an anticipated part of every performance.

This operatic knowledge ultimately allowed Cheung Ng to maintain an effective disguise later in life (around the 1720s) while operating in a highly threatening political environment. Seeking refuge and fleeing persecution after the death of his family, Cheung Ng fled to the south and encountered Yat Chan Daai Si, one of the creators of Shaolin Wing Chun. He became Yat Chan Daai Si's disciple and the eventual inheritor of Shaolin Wing Chun, which the secret societies later called Hung Fa Yi Wing Chun in honor of its creators. The name is significant in that it honors the Hung Fa Wui secret society that sprang up inside the Southern Shaolin Temple to hide the actual identities of Wing Chun's creators and their revolutionary activities with Ming Dynasty supporters.

After becoming a disciple of Yat Chan Daai Si and a member of the Hung Fa Wui, Cheung Ng once again sought refuge from Qing persecution. His flight took him to *Foshan*, a southern Chinese city that was long a center of commerce and martial arts training. Foshan was given its name during the Tang Dynasty under the reign of Emperor Zhenguan (627-649 A.D.). Legend has it that local people discovered colorful lights emanating from one of its hillsides and set about excavating it. The excavation revealed three ancient Buddhist statues. They subsequently named the place Foshan, meaning "Buddha Hill." Foshan is located in Gwongdung Province (also called Canton).

Cheung may have picked Foshan for his continued revolutionary activities specifically because of its strong mixture of commerce and martial arts cultures. Well known for its metallurgy, ceramics, and textile industries, it was a prime place to discreetly recruit troops and obtain the resources needed to keep a revolutionary effort alive. At a minimum, it was here that he is credited with keeping the Hung Fa Yi system alive and actually deploying it to the societies engaged in revolutionary activity. Under his direction and that of his successors, Hung Fa Yi Wing Chun grew to become one of the primary combat systems of the secret societies.

To keep his identity and southern Shaolin background hidden from Qing loyalists, Cheung Ng organized the opera chapter of the King Fa Wui Gun (Beautiful Jade Flower Association) to cover his revolutionary activities. The King Fa Wui Gun was akin to a chamber of commerce in Foshan. This opera chapter was a perfect front because opera activity enabled him to remain in public disguise while allowing freedom of movement throughout the southern provinces. The inside name of this opera chapter was Hung Fa Wui Gun (Red Flower Association). Only the members engaged in revolutionary activity used this name. It was this organization that 140 years later gave rise to the Red Boat Opera so often referred to in popular Wing Chun history.

For the next 180 years Hung Fa Yi Wing Chun had to be kept secret from the Qing army. It represented truly superior fighting science. Likewise, the Qing policy (referenced earlier in this chapter) of killing nine generations of relatives for every rebel found made it absolutely imperative that Hung Fa Yi practitioners maintain the secrecy of their science, its roots, and their own identities. The blood oaths adopted by other secret societies for maintaining this secrecy were also an integral part of the Hung Fa Yi.

Cheung Ng's opera fame grew quickly, and his influence spread throughout the southern provinces. Numerous historians believe he included anti-Qing phrases, allusions, and commentaries in his poetry, lyrics, and performances. He may also have been responsible for the production of plays that promoted dissatisfaction with the Qing bureaucracy.

In addition to operatic fame, Cheung Ng became widely known for his martial skill as well. Indeed, all have noted his famous nickname, Taan Sau Ng. Tan sau is one of the pillar hand techniques of Wing Chun Kung Fu. He was known to the opera as Taan Sau Ng because of his skillful ability to use one technique to subdue others in combat. His level of understanding allowed him to use one motion to represent over a thousand techniques. His demonstrations were possible only because he understood that a technique must be realized in both concept and application before learning the next 100 techniques. After understanding a concept, all techniques become one.

Some nonacademic forums in recent years have suggested that perhaps Cheung Ng's nickname is a homonym for another Chinese word meaning "cripple," and that perhaps he was given the nickname because he always had a beggar's hand out for food and money. Such conjecture may be quickly dismissed because it runs counter to the preponderance of evidence present even in the 21st century. Both historical pointers and scientific principles lend credence to Cheung Ng's exalted position in Chinese opera and his contributions to Wing Chun.

Historical pointers begin with numerous opera records referring to Cheung Ng as respected for both his military and operatic skills. No beggar could garner such respect from the highly sophisticated opera societies that required their members to possess and demonstrate academic, musical, and martial skills equally. Today's Cantonese opera groups still revere him as a Si Jou (the term for founding ancestors in martial arts cultures), and numerous opera history books refer to him as Cheung Si (Master Cheung). Indeed, Cheung Ng is recognized as the creator of the *Eighteen Plays of Cantonese Opera* made famous by the Red Opera (the opera chapter of the King Fa Wui Gun). Likewise, his contributions earned him a place in Chinese opera heaven, where he, along with the god of Chinese Opera, Wai Gong, is worshipped by Disciples of the Pear Garden at every performance.

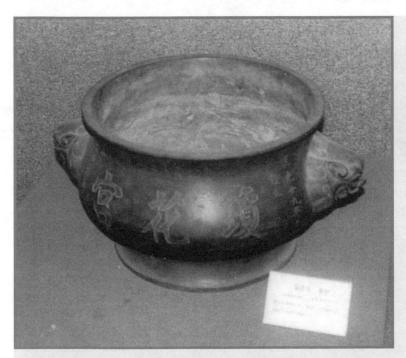

Figure 2.10 One of the few artifacts from the King Fa Wui Gun.

Figure 2.11 A cornerstone from the King Fa Wui Gun.

Figure 2.12   Hung Gun Biu training his followers.

The *Foshan* Museum in China also possesses historical evidence of Cheung Ng's life as both an opera performer and martial artist. Their historical analyses make no reference to Cheung Ng as either a cripple or a beggar. Corroborating research into Wing Chun family lore done by the Ving Tsun Museum supports the extensive historical evidence referring to Cheung Ng as both a martial arts and opera master. Indeed, Hung Fa Yi Wing Chun practitioners have a 300-year history and have always recognized Cheung Ng as the first generation grand master of Wing Chun Kuen. Museum records, opera records, and Hung Fa Yi traditions universally attest that Cheung Ng's Tan Sau technique was peerless throughout the martial arts world.

One of the first people to ferret this information about Cheung Ng out of opera records was modern day Wing Chun Grandmaster Ip Man's eldest son, Ip Chun. Many of the moves expressed as syllables or techniques in Hung Fa Yi Wing Chun are openly employed for stage movement and expression in Cheung Ng's operas. This places their origination at least 150 years before the time of the Red Boat Opera Company that today's popular Wing Chun practitioners reference as the root of Wing Chun. Artifact evidence alone clearly establishes that Wing Chun Kung Fu is far older than the Red Boat Opera Company.

Cheung Ng's clandestine revolutionary involvement eventually led him back into hiding to escape Qing persecution. He took up final refuge with a sworn brother, Chan Jing Lin, a member of a prominent Fujian business family, Chan Si Sai Ga. The Chan were well established and wealthy, possessing the resources necessary to keep Cheung hidden for the remainder of his life. Although the members of the Chan family were not recorded as direct secret society members, they may well have engaged in the financial backing of revolutionary activities. They did have close ties and connections to the Chu royal family of the Ming Dynasty.

Cheung Ng taught Hung Fa Yi Wing Chun Kung Fu to his sworn brother s grandson, Chan Sai Yuan, who in turn taught it to his own son, Chan Bo Jung. The younger Chan ultimately passed the system on to a high-level revolutionary leader (during the early 1800s) known in Hung Fa Yi lore only by the name of Hung Gun Biu (meaning Red Bandanna Biu). In the secret societies, the term *red bandanna* referred to a top leader of society activity. It is known in Hung Fa Yi traditions that Hung Gun Biu brought a public version of Hung Fa Yi to the Red Boat Opera, including Siu Nim Tau and Siu Lin Tau together with principles and drilling methods. Hung Gun Biu continued to lead Hung Fa Yi secret society members in revolutionary activity and kept the details of the system closely held among revolutionary members, but a public version was introduced to the opera players, most likely for recruitment purposes. Later on, this public display of Wing Chun was referred to as Hung Suen Wing Chun Kung Fu.

Secret society histories make reference to a leader named Chan Biu who lived during this same period of time. Considering the Chan family relationship to Hung Fa Yi Wing Chun and Hung Gun Biu, some have inferred that Hung Gun Biu and Chan Biu are the same person; however, this inference has not been historically verified.

Throughout this time, the King Fa Wui Gun opera chapter continued to flourish and became an underground headquarters for many revolutionaries who remained active up to the mid-19th century. Other opera societies did the same. Indeed, Goon Wai (anti-Qing undertones in story lines) was introduced into Cantonese opera after an unsuccessful anti-Qing coup led by Cantonese opera performers. Many other such uprisings followed.

RED BOAT OPERA ERA

Recent historical excavations of a Heaven and Earth headquarters complex in south central China, professionally dated to the early 17th century, contains four buildings shaped like a boat. Each building contains either 36 rooms or 108 rooms. The numbers 36 and 108 are important in Hung Fa Yi numerology. Secret society lore often refers to a red boat as a solar barque that carries brave souls to eternal bliss. The boat also symbolized that members of the secret societies were all together in the same effort, quite literally "in the same boat." This may be why there was such a close association between secret societies and the Red Boat Opera Company around 150 years later. It may also have had much to do with the Red Boat Opera support of revolutionary activities in the latter half of the 19th century.

Known for its discipline and rules of conduct, the Red Boat Opera was an organization of talented stage performers and martial artists who traveled up and down the rivers of southern China in three red junks. The junks were named Heaven, Man, and Earth, and each bore two staterooms with the names of Green Dragon and White Tiger. The influence of Shaolin Chan Buddhism and its kung fu was still obviously present 180 years after the destruction of the Southern Temple.

Figure 2.13 The Red Boat.

All lineages of today's popular Wing Chun trace their roots to this era. Their kung fu shows similarities to Shaolin Wing Chun, but many details and most principles and concepts are radically altered. Obvious reasons exist for these differences. Cantonese opera served as a mixing ground for many styles of kung fu, including northern Shaolin, southern Shaolin, non-Shaolin external and internal styles, military-derived styles, hand styles, leg styles, and acrobatic styles. This synthesis provided performers with a wide exposure that invited blending of patterns and techniques for theatrical display and performance. Wing Chun was affected by this synthesis, as were the other systems.

The Red Boat performers were known to be as equally supportive of anti-Qing activity as other opera troupes and performers in southern China. One such opera performer, Lei Min Mou, also a member of a notorious anti-Qing group, the Heaven and Earth Society in Foshan, led his and numerous other opera troupes into an uprising at the same time as the Great Peace Heaven Country (Tai Ping Tin Gwok) Christian uprisings of 1850-1861. The combined efforts of these groups made this the largest attempt at Chinese revolution in the 19th century. King Fa Wui Gun opera members (Hung Fa Wui Gun), dressed in full operatic costume, joined in with their martial skills. During this revolt, many members of the King Fa Wui Gun, along with members of other secret societies, wore red bandannas on their heads as a sign of bravery and an allusion to the legitimacy of the conduct of the first Ming Dynasty emperor in his earlier struggles against the Mongols. By this time, the Qing was too well established throughout southern China to be overthrown by rebels, and the uprisings ultimately failed. In retaliation, the Qing finally burned down the King Fa Wui Gun and disbanded the Red Boat Opera. Many opera members were killed. The remainder scattered throughout southern China, and their kung fu scattered with them.

By the mid-19th century, the fervor for the return of the Ming family to the throne of China had dissipated. The Qing dynasty was firmly established, and public dissent was focused more on political corruption and fighting Western imperial expansion. With the dissipation of the opera companies and the flight of the opera refugees throughout southern China, the doors were opened for the dissemination of Wing Chun. Nevertheless, after two centuries of secret society culture, discussion of the true roots of Wing Chun was virtually impossible. Likewise, with the spread of Red Boat Opera refugees throughout southern China, the skills of Wing Chun as a fighting style also spread. Because of the revolutionary nature of the system, even without total system knowledge practitioners often had an edge over practitioners of other styles. Only a handful of individuals were actually trained in the system's totality. The eighth generation successor, Grand Master Garrett Gee, is responsible for bringing this style out to the public after more than 300 years of secrecy.

Figure 2.14 Two Opera performers training on the Jong.

Figure 2.15 Wong Ting, Wong Ming, and Garrett Gee.

PUBLIC AWARENESS ERA

This next phase of Wing Chun evolution is best referred to as "modification and public awareness." Over the next hundred years Wing Chun went through its third major change in form, footwork, and structure. Environmental and cultural factors such as exposure to life on boats in the southern coastal regions of China may have heavily influenced stances and training methodology. At a minimum, the Wing Chun system began a transition from military battlefield employment to civilian use and support. As a direct result of this transition, Wing Chun outside the Hung Fa Yi tradition began to discard its Chan (Zen) orientation and revert to a focus based on individual expressions and personal street experience rather than life and death battlefield experience. At the same time, students were no longer required to endure hours of initiation ceremonies and blood oaths to fight to the death for a specific cause. Nevertheless, Wing Chun's fighting effectiveness proved adequate to meet the challenges of other systems making similar transitions to the modern world.

The majority of today's most popular lineages stem from Wing Chun roots in this era of personal expression. Three of those lineages stem from one man alone: Gu Lao, Chan Yiu Min, and Ip Man all originated from Dr. Leung Jan. He learned his Wing Chun outside of the secret society culture, through direct interaction with former Red Boat Opera players Wong Wah Bo and Leung Yi Dai. Dai Fa Min Kam, also an opera member, spread his art to Fung Siu Ching. The Chi Sim Weng Chun family carries on this lineage today. Other modern lineages include Pao Fa Lien, Yuen Kay San, Pan Nam, Cho family, Cheung Bo, Mai Gei Wong, Yip Kin, Yuen Chai Wan, and numerous subsystems practiced throughout Southeast Asia. After hundreds of years, most Weng/Wing Chun oral histories point back to the Shaolin Temple as the origins of Weng/Wing Chun.

All of these lineages appropriately trace their roots to the Red Boat Opera, as indeed the scattered opera performers began teaching bits and pieces of their knowledge. Most reflect the name of the teacher, rather than the traditions, philosophies, and history on which the original system was based. These systems appeared most likely

Figure 2.16 Chan Wah Shun (left) training with Leung Jan (right).

because their teachers achieved significant skills with the portions of Wing Chun that they learned. The personalities and knowledge levels of these respective opera performers directly affected the depth of knowledge passed on in these individual expressions of kung fu—expressions that ultimately became systems of their own, regardless of name. Consequently, most practitioners of modern Wing Chun have no knowledge of their predecessor's Shaolin roots, and most forms bear little resemblance to the original Wing Chun, despite adherence to the name. Without the original principles on which the science of Wing Chun was built, these modern systems will continue to change with the prevailing personalities of the dominant teachers arising in any given decade.

Today's popular legends of Wing Chun's origins also took root during this era. The now famous story of a young woman trained by a Buddhist nun creating and disseminating the art through the Red Boat Opera became quite popular. Ex-revolutionaries distancing themselves from the secret societies and government persecution most likely promoted this legend. Many popular Chinese fictional books and magazines were written and published at the turn of the century. Many fables about martial arts orientation resulted from the stories in these works, including the legend of Yim Wing Chun. It is important for all students of history to note that these were purely fictional works, not historical treatises. Nevertheless, they still fueled legends.

The next evolutionary phase of Wing Chun is best referred to as the commercialization phase. This phase represents Wing Chun's rapid expansion in a modern world. This stage was fueled by the mid-20th-century flight of Wing Chun teachers from mainland China as a result of political instability during China's civil war. Its popularity quickly spread across the globe, due primarily to the renowned public fighting success of Ip Man's Gong Sau (talking hands) fighters and the movie-making success of his fighting student, Bruce Lee. A strong parallel exists between this modern era martial arts icon and the southern Shaolin monks of three centuries prior. All believed that experience had to form the basis of true knowledge. No fighter in the modern era trained harder than Bruce in search of that experience. Like the monks, he too was looking for ultimate efficiency in hand-to-hand combat. Consequently, he tried to look beyond the known systems of his time (Hung Fa Yi was only practiced secretly at that time and was therefore unknown to him). The systems available to him simply could not give him that ultimate level of combat efficiency. He knew there had to be one most efficient position in space and time for any given strategy or tactic, and he never stopped looking for it. Nevertheless, he retained great respect for his roots in modern day versions of Wing Chun Kung Fu and stated so on many occasions.

Today the Ving Tsun Athletic Association in Hong Kong serves as a nexus for the Ip Man lineage. Along with rapid growth came the politicization of the system in the form of arguments over who inherited the real Wing Chun and the resultant rights to control its commercialization via franchises, certifying associations, publications, videos, Internet entities, and so on.

The current evolutionary phase of Wing Chun is just getting under way, and it may well signify the demise of Wing Chun's popularity. This era is most appropriately referred to as the cyber era. It is rapidly becoming characterized by Internet Web sites, chat rooms, and mailing lists populated by self-proclaimed experts with little or no true kung fu credentials. Credentials attained through years of training and testing are apparently unnecessary when expostulating positions and theories behind a keyboard and cathode ray tube. After all, in an Internet exchange, there is no one immediately present to physically confront or challenge these expostulations. Wing Chun's time-honored tradition of letting the "fists do the talking" is rapidly giving way to letting the "fingers do the talking." In the past, it was considered honorable to select appropriate fighters from individual families and test their kung fu within an environment strictly controlled by etiquette. Following the challenge match, the players and their supporters proceeded to teahouses to share experiences in a respectful fashion that allowed all to save face and actually benefit from the experience.

The nature of kung fu demands that it be learned through direct, personal interaction. That involves effort, time, and personal commitment. Along the way, a student of the martial arts must develop knowledge of good kung fu customs and courtesies and practice them at all times. While today's modern technologies of the Internet, e-mail, and video assist in the teaching process, these modalities cannot supplant direct experience with a teacher.

In discussions of kung fu outside of one's immediate family, courtesies and respects for credentialed masters, regardless of personal opinion about character, should be expressed. Insulting others through virtual environments is simply unacceptable from a martial arts perspective. If such an insult were offered in person, the threat could well involve facing the reality of the other's fists. Every action in life has a consequence. The same can be said for historians and researchers of Wing Chun. Many promoting themselves as such on the Internet have no formal research credentials and no formal historical credentials. Personal agendas are frequently promoted via verbal and written challenges to legitimate research—challenges based on conjecture and, in many cases, pure fabrication. In lieu of these credentials, they have taken to cyber garbage collection and named each conjecture gathered as a contributing piece of historical evidence. The danger in this era is that these skilled webmasters and cyber travelers will influence the direction Wing Chun development takes in the 21st century. Without Hau Chuen San Sau (face-to-face instruction and real experience), both the science and the culture of Wing Chun martial training may be forever lost.

Figure 2.17 The late Grand Master Ip Man with his student, the late superstar Bruce Lee.

In contrast, as the remaining chapters of this book will show, the rich science of Wing Chun Kung Fu has not yet been lost to commercialization. Practitioners can still find all the pieces of the art and its history spread across all four stages of its historical evolution. Collectively, they represent a science with its roots in the Southern Shaolin Temple and its application reflecting all that is Shaolin.

VTM Mission Statement

In recognition of Ving Tsun as a living art form, the Ving Tsun Museum's express mission is the preservation and advancement of the Ving Tsun art into and beyond the 21st century by:

- Documenting and researching its history.
- Archiving its treasures and artifacts.
- Updating its training methods with proven scientific teaching aids, tools, and certifications.
- Expanding its practitioners' comprehension and use of the system through examination and distribution of knowledge.
- Recognizing its greatest contributors, both past and present.
- Providing a home for all Ving Tsun families to gather and share their rich heritage, regardless of lineage, in an atmosphere free of prejudice, personal gains, or political considerations.

Figure 2.18 Ving Tsun Museum Curator with seven direct students of Grand Master Ip Man at the opening of the Ving Tsun Museum, in Dayton, Ohio, 1998. (left to right) Benny Meng, Chu Shong Ting, Moy Yat, Mak Po, Moy Bing Wah, Hawkins Cheung, Ip Chun, Ip Ching. First time in history of the Ip Man Wing Chun family that seven direct students gathered together for a common martial arts goal, the recognition of the VTM project.

Philosophy and Etiquette of Hung Fa Yi Wing Chun

The philosophy of learning and training in a Shaolin monastery cannot be separated from the unique Shaolin practice of Chan (Zen) Buddhism. Whereas Buddhism itself is of Indian origin, the unique brand practiced by Shaolin monks bears the mark of strong Chinese historical and cultural influences as well. Although it is not the purpose of this text to address the nature and extent of general Buddhism as a philosophy or religion, it is important to understand the uniqueness of Shaolin Chan (Zen) Buddhism because it emphasizes the need to learn the truth of reality via "experience"—also a requirement, interestingly enough, of Confucianism, a philosophy stemming from Chinese roots. Chan (Zen) Buddhist philosophy focuses on spontaneity, completeness, and practicality, all of which are learned by experiencing reality in the here and now.

By resolving to live each day as if it is the last, the Chan Buddhist warrior discovers how to experience life fully, without indecision or regret. This means developing the ability to focus the mind completely on one thought or activity, or "bounding" the mind's learning process and thereby forgetting oneself. Most people have had the experience of concentrating so deeply on an activity that all awareness of self is eliminated. At these moments time flies, and one is able to continue engaging in meditational activity for extended periods of time without tiring. It amounts to a kind of peak experience. In Chan (Zen) this equates to being spontaneous and focused on the here and now. Moreover, when real skill is achieved in any action, one is primarily aware of what is happening at that moment, rather than of the self or the body. That which is crucial bounds the learning experience. Extraneous matters remain outside the bounds of that experiential learning session.

Through martial discipline, the warrior can achieve a readiness for death, the strength to advance in life, and the ability to fulfill the duties of focusing and prevailing in combat. Within the Shaolin hall, a warrior monk studies and practices potentially life-threatening movements. In a certain sense, the monk dies regularly by facing mortality and, ideally, discovers the true meaning, as well as the value, of existence. The process itself forces the practitioner to encounter true reality. In facing combat reality, one has to look at all the dimensions of combat from weapons to close-range hand-to-hand combat. The martial practitioner eventually arrives at a philosophy and way of living that transcends fear and ultimately the self. This brings about self-actualization and assists the practitioner in developing a martial way of life. To practice Hung Fa Yi Wing Chun, the practitioner must train the body, mind, and spirit with equal fervor and discipline. This reflects the Chan (Zen) characteristic of completeness.

CHINESE INFLUENCE OF CHU HSI (AND CONFUCIANISM) ON FORMAL EDUCATION AND LEARNING

Chu Hsi (1130-1200 A.D.), spelled Zhu Xi in Mandarin Pinyin, is widely recognized as one of the most influential men in Chinese history in terms of educational orthodoxy. For nearly eight centuries his emphasis on and prescription for "greater learning" (called Da Xue, also translated as "ultimate learning") formed the basis of China's formal education system and civil service examinations. Besides having been a prefect (governor) in three different provinces or principalities in southern China, Chu Hsi was also a prolific writer, a renowned teacher, and one of China's most respected philosophers. Indeed, his influence spread beyond China's borders to most Asian countries, including Japan and Korea. Virtually all prestigious academies of learning, public and private, adopted Chu Hsi's approach to education. For the student of Southern Shaolin Kung Fu, it should be noted that Chu Hsi was born in the province of Fujian and performed much of his public service, government leadership, and teaching there. This is the same province that gave rise to the Southern Shaolin Temple (Siu Lam), which in turn ultimately created Shaolin Wing Chun.

There are three important parallels among the Chu Hsi, Chan Buddhist, and ultimately the Hung Fa Yi Wing Chun approaches to self-development. All either directly or indirectly emphasize (1) bounded learning, (2) ultimate understanding of the true nature of things, and (3) the traditional passing on of true learning through disciples.

Bounded Learning

If one were to choose a martial attribute that is most akin to the heart of Chu Hsi's approach to learning, it would have to be focus. Chu Hsi's emphasis on greater learning is all about focusing on the educational process. Chu Hsi believed that learning for the sake of learning was pointless. Learning for the sake of self-improvement was all that mattered. He taught that self-improvement could only be attained by apprehending "principle" (Li). Chu maintained that all things in the universe possessed principle. Principle was both their reason for existence and the rule by which they existed and thrived. Many scholars have described Chu Hsi's principle as the "cosmic blueprint." Chu further maintained that this principle was the same in all things, but that it was manifested differently in each. Man shares this same principle, and it is the same in each man—inherently moral and constituted of benevolence, righteousness, propriety, and wisdom. All things are also endowed with "psychological stuff" that distinguishes them from others. This stuff can mask reality or give it meaning. According to Chu Hsi, man's ultimate challenge is to fulfill his innate moral potential by harnessing his psychological stuff rather than being harnessed by it. To accomplish this, principle must be consciously and actively given realization.

The same can be said for true martial potential. The warrior can allow it to be masked by psychological stuff, such as preconceptions of skill, style, strategy, tactics, or others' sporting successes. In contrast, he can eliminate preconceptions via focus on scientific concepts rooted within the same time, space, and energy boundaries adhered to in the "cosmic blueprint," or principle, described by Chu Hsi.

Chu believed that the only way to understand this principle was through focused study. To focus, one must define boundaries to the investigation and then learn all there is to learn within those bounds. The key is to define boundaries that truly reflect what is important and filter out what is not essential to learning. Chu called his focus or bounds "greater learning." In greater learning, the works of the ancient Confucian philosophers—the classicists—form the bounds of investigation. These classical philosophers were known to be highly moral men, so using their teachings as boundaries for focused learning was the most efficient approach to true education and self-development in Chu Hsi's eyes. In essence, Chu sought ultimate knowledge about the nature of things through focused investigation. A strong parallel can be drawn between Chu Hsi's emphasis on bounded learning and the methodology employed in training Hung Fa Yi Wing Chun.

Just as Chu Hsi believed that any serious investigation of the nature of man should be bounded by the efforts and investigations of the classical Confucian philosophers (all of whom were experts on human nature), Hung Fa Yi practitioners believe that any serious study of the nature of human physiology and strategy in combat should be bounded by the 12 centuries of knowledge accumulated by the great Shaolin warriors and Ming Dynasty military officers who created Shaolin Wing Chun, all of whom were experts on human physiology and hand-to-hand combat. A famous Chu Hsi phrase describes the essence of greater learning and Hung Fa Yi learning philosophy: Gaak Mat

Figure 3.1 Sign authored by Chu Hsi, during his visit to the oldest Confucian college in Korea, Seonggyun-gwan. This prestigious university, originally established as Gukja-gam during the late Goryeo Dynasty (918-1392 A.D.), was the center for the study of Confucian philosophy and the political and moral ideals of the Joseon Dynasty (1392-1910 A.D.)

Ji Ji meaning "Know the ultimate truth within a defined bound." Direct parallels can be drawn between this emphasis on ultimate truth and Hung Fa Yi's six gate concept.

The bounds of Hung Fa Yi learning and employment are efficiency, economy of motion and resources, and clarity. The physical bounds are described by the practitioner's own body parts via six gates of offense and defense. The Hung Fa Yi practitioner strives to learn all there is to know about what happens within these six gates and to be in control of that activity at all times. Learning all there is to know means becoming fully cognizant of the use of geometric structures and energetics to control the space/time/energy relationships of all objects within these bounded gates. The Hung Fa Yi practitioner seeks ultimate knowledge of the nature of all possible attacks and defenses within these bounds and the physiological tools required to control them. Anything outside these bounds is inherently inefficient. From a combat perspective, such inefficient activity will never engage a vital target and is therefore superfluous to learning.

Figure 3.2 depicts the six gates of Hung Fa Yi Wing Chun that define the bounds within which ultimate knowledge is sought. The range dimension of each gate is described sideways via elbow and striking point position in relation to the three reference points called Saam Ming Dim and individually named (1) Tan Jung (which correlates to the heaven gate), (2) Yang Jung (which correlates to the man gate), and (3) Dan Tin (which correlates to the earth gate). It should be emphasized that the range of these gates represents the inner gate or inner hand distance from the body. This range is called Mun Jong. The vertical dimension of the two upper and two middle gates is described by "elbow to striking point" length. The vertical dimension of the two lower gates is described by "striking point (lower bound) to toes" length. The width dimension of all gates is determined by one and a half shoulder widths in each direction from the centerline with the body positioned so that both hands reach equally throughout the width.

The six gates, and their corresponding number six (6) in the Hung Fa Yi Wing Chun Formula, represent a combat formation structure that is based solely on human anatomical form. Hung Fa Yi Wing Chun is a scientific approach to combat and is designed for life-and-death situations. The six gates are used to determine the areas of attack and defense, and to harmonize the human anatomy with the reality of the four dimensions of time and space. The use of time and space by the practitioner is predicated on the opponent's position and movements. In combat you take what is given. Hung Fa Yi Wing Chun practitioners respect life and can use the element of control in combat because they have many options.

Knowledge, translated militarily as intelligence, when properly employed through sound strategy and tactics, can be more powerful than conventional weapons. In conventional hand-to-hand combat, which is confined to single or dual dimensions, a fighter must learn to attack and seize vast amounts of space in all directions. After the seizure is accomplished, he must then expend considerable resources maintaining protective vigilance over the controlled area to prevent incursion and sneak attacks by his enemy. To physically control such a large space requires that the fighter employ a significant arsenal of techniques and attributes at every range of combat. The size of a potential battlefield could grow to two or three times larger than the fighter's personal space as defined by the Hung Fa Yi six gate concept.

However, scientific hand-to-hand combat uses all the dimensions of the temporal volume of space and requires the fighter to see and act on distortions in the space and time dimensions of the existing battlefield. Use of the improved intelligence provided by the Hung Fa Yi Wing Chun space and time concept radically reduces the size of the potential battlefield. The Hung Fa Yi Wing Chun fighter does not need

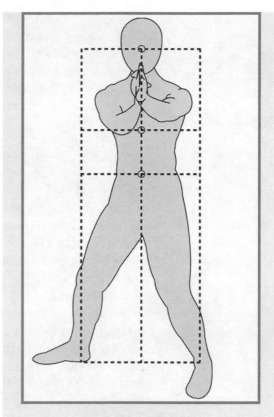

Figure 3.2 Six gates.

to seize and control large amounts of space simply to protect from attacks. He has no imperative to structure his fighting mobility for the dissipation of his forces over a large area simply to engage and repel perimeter incursions. Superior fighting intelligence, coupled with multidimensional strategy and tactics, enable the fighter to concentrate his forces on key areas of range. The Mun Jong range covers all three vertical dimensions within the six gates and enables the Hung Fa Yi fighter to keep the weapons delivery system, the limbs, mutually supported and reinforced for concentrated firepower. The surgical use of firepower is triggered with maximum efficiency against the enemy. The conventional fighter, on the other hand, is weakened through the dispersion of resources while maintaining an inordinately sized battlefield. That battlefield size is mandated by a conventional approach to hand-to-hand combat.

Use of the six gates gives Hung Fa Yi practitioners the ability to analyze an opponent's structural weakness and identify potential threats. Through this awareness and assessment of potential challenges, the practitioner can minimize an opponent's offense while maximizing the practitioner's own. Proper six gate alignment can force an opponent to self-destruct by either luring the opponent to attack an area that is seemingly open or forcing the opponent to attack from a bad position, creating telegraphic motions.

Ultimate Understanding of the True Nature of Things

This parallel to Chu Hsi's search for true reality could be described as Hung Fa Yi Wing Chun's bridge from philosophy to the science of time, space, and energy. As a science, Hung Fa Yi Wing Chun's logic flow is crucial to maintaining its integrity. The sequence of learning must follow this logic flow closely. From a historical point of view, Hung Fa Yi was created in the Southern Temple during the Qing/Ming Dynasty struggles. During times of war, paradigm shifts happen, and new developments in combat systems can occur quickly. Old habits and mind-sets are quickly overcome by necessity and survival instinct. Since 600 A.D., Shaolin had developed into a disciplined systematic approach of developing defense arts in a philosophical and academic environment uninterrupted for centuries. The nature of the universe and attendant philosophies was paramount. The other source of knowledge was the Ming military involvement and imperatives of the 17th century. These two sources of development came together at the Southern Shaolin Temple in the Weng Chun Tong to create the system of Wing Chun.

Within the Weng Chun Tong (and other Shaolin training halls preceding it) was a concept contained in the sutras called Tin Yan Dei, meaning "heaven, man, and earth," which described the Shaolin levels of reality. A direct connection exists between this concept and the three levels of reality practiced in Hung Fa Yi Wing Chun Chan (Zen) philosophy called saam mo kiu, meaning "three connecting bridges." In essence, they represent parallel universes of philosophical study and self-development. Both physical and spiritual connotations can be drawn from these connections. The physical connotations are drawn from the Heaven gate (the upper reference point of the Wing Chun Formula), the Man gate (the middle reference point of the Wing Chun Formula), and the Earth gate (the lower reference point of the Wing Chun Formula).

Three principal characteristics of Hung Fa Yi Wing Chun Chan are employed to attain a mind-set necessary to find reality (the true nature of things) identified by Saam Mo Kiu. First, Chan Buddhists look at the whole, not individual parts. Second, they deal with the here and now—they are spontaneous. Third, they try to attain complete practicality and directness. The previously referenced three levels of Chan (Zen) reality give rise to Hung Fa Yi Wing Chun's way of viewing combat in the framework of three connecting bridges.

Every hand, every stance, and every tactic in Hung Fa Yi Wing Chun is examined and trained in this same fashion. For example, the nature of Tan Sau is to disperse incoming energy within the upper gate. Simultaneous offense and defense are only possible when Tan's nature is employed in the upper gate at Mun Jong range. Any other range will negate simultaneous offense and defense or allow penetration of one's own defense, resulting in suffering a strike or the jamming of one's own weapons. In other words, at the wrong time and space, tan's true nature simply cannot be expressed.

The key to unlocking Hung Fa Yi Wing Chun as a combat system is the Wing Chun Formula (1, 2, 3, 5, 6, 5), and the key to understanding the formula is the concept of time and space. (This formula is detailed in chapter 5 of this text.) The key to properly approaching the concept of time and space is embracing the philosophy of Saam Mo Kiu.

A Wing Chun fighter in combat employs five elements or energies called Ng Jan Chiu Min Jeui Ying (to determine proper employment of tactics). From Baai Jong to Wui Ma the fighter must recognize Saam Mou Kiu to determine the proper mix of energies, structures, and tactics. (All five elements are detailed in chapter 7 of this text.) Saam mo kiu as used in Wing Chun refers to three specific time frames. A properly trained Wing Chun fighter employs Saam Mo Kiu to identify his opponent's knowledge of time and space, and from that to determine which strategies and tactics to employ to ensure the enemy's self-destruction. The Saam Mo Kiu is used in conjunction with the Wing Chun Formula and is supported by its principles and concepts. Together they enable the Wing Chun fighter to completely understand both his and his opponent's strengths and weaknesses within the space and time of the confrontation. Saam Mo Kiu as a Wing Chun concept posits that there are only three types of bridges between opponents, employing "time frame" as the guide to which bridge is in play. This allows the Wing Chun practitioner to determine the time frame used in combat and to understand the true nature of combat. Once the Wing Chun practitioner reaches a level of understanding nature itself, this concept is no longer concerned with just techniques. It extends to one's total interaction with the world.

The three connecting bridges of Saam Mo Kiu are as follows:

1. Fau Kiu—"floating bridge." Another frequently used expression of this same concept is Hoi Fau, meaning "illusion, cloudy, or unclear." Philosophically, the Fau Kiu stage is the stage of confusion and wandering—searching for direction and not knowing exactly what to focus on. At the Fau Kiu stage of reality, the level of one's existence is primarily the basic subsistence level of Maslow's famous hierarchy of needs. There is no time for higher-level development or life. In terms of combat, Fau Kiu represents "lucky strike" time. At this stage the practitioner is violating the Wing Chun time frame as he possesses no realized comprehension of space or time. In a physical confrontation it would be the same as standing right in front of the opponent and trading blows with him. Another example would be rotating the elbow out for a straight punch from the shoulder plane back to the opponent. This means the practitioner and his opponent can hit or kick each other as chance dictates. Fate will select the winner. Philosophically, this represents a stage at which both combatants are unclear of their path or reason for existence. They exist in an illusion. As martial artists, they are unaware of the basics of time and space and have failed to recognize any higher level of knowledge. In the Wing Chun system, this stage of reality also represents initial Siu Nim Tau training wherein one is looking for his true martial self-identity.

2. Saan Kiu—"separate bridge." This is also referred to as the awareness stage—understanding general direction, but possessing no knowledge of exact focus. This stage represents partial nature or understanding of the true time frame in combat, but practitioners still do not possess concrete ability to identify and deal with the intricacies of the interactions between time and space. They cannot express both together in harmony. At any moment, they may be able to express one or the other in their kung fu, but not both simultaneously. An example would be a long-range strike. The fighter knows about time or space, but the technique only succeeds because of speed. If his speed is not great enough, he does not succeed. At this level, the practitioner moves from establishing self-identity to establishing identity in relation to others in temporal and spatial reality. In the Wing Chun system, this represents the initial Chum Kiu stage of development; the practitioner is seeing how Siu Nim Tau techniques are put into motion. Philosophically, at this level practitioners are beyond the basic level of subsistence. They have the capacity and the time to engage in incomplete considerations of religion and philosophy.

3. Weng Kiu—"everlasting bridge." It is important to note that the character for *weng* is the same character employed in the name of the Weng Chun system. It represents the everlasting nature of the real science on which it is based. Weng Kiu is also referred to as the focus stage. Another phrase used on the journey to this stage is Hoi Gong, meaning "open light" or enlightenment. It is used in the Siu Nim Tau level of training to represent that the practitioner has been exposed to this idea (Nim) and is aware of Saam Mo Kiu, space and time, and the Wing Chun Formula and the relationships among them. Philosophically, the Weng Kiu stage reflects a practitioner's comprehension of the true reason for his own existence. He is approaching real enlightenment in terms of the universe surrounding him. His perceptions of his universe are in harmony with reality. In a physical confrontation, the practitioner's every motion is in harmony with space and time with no distortion of either. Practitioners who have the Weng Kiu time frame should be able to strike with all four limbs without needing to adjust their position. This is the highest level of combat skill. Harmony with reality replaces struggle. The opponent's own distortions are self-defeating, while the practitioner maintains harmony with the realities of space and time.

There will always be four dimensions in our physical universe—the three spatial dimensions of length, width, and height plus the temporal dimension (time). From a Hung Fa Yi perspective, at any given moment you may possess both spatial and temporal control, or one but not the other, or neither. Having proper space and time, coupled with proper use of energy, constitutes true action. In Wing Chun, this is the Biu Ji level of skill. At this level, practitioners know precisely what they are focused on; they have functional understanding of exactly where and how to strike.

HOU CHUEN SAN SAU: TEACHING ONE-ON-ONE

The third parallel of Shaolin Wing Chun to Chu Hsi's approach to learning lies in the practice of teaching one-on-one in the form of discipleship. The Chan (Zen) phrase *Hou Chuen Saan Sau* describes learning. *Hou Chuen* literally means "passing on orally." The intent is that a student needs direct, person-to-person interaction with the teacher. The instruction itself can take any form such as a story, a question and answer session, even a beating. *San Sau* literally means "receive with the body." The intent is that the student has to understand the lesson with his whole being, but the teacher doesn't have to be around for this to happen. The San Sau can take the form of meditation in stillness, meditation in motion, or physical training with a partner. The key is that San Sau is a personal discovery or realization on the student's own part, and it requires action. Oral instruction is needed to identify what the student is looking for, but the student must also physically experience the knowledge for it to become true. Students given only oral instruction in the form of concepts or ideas, or only experience without the concepts, will have illusions about reality. They will possess only blind dogma constituting partial knowledge divorced from reality. This represents the Saan Kiu level of skill and awareness expressed in Saam Mo Kiu philosophy.

With this emphasis on Hou Chuen San Sau, Hung Fa Yi teachers insisted that true learning be passed on personally from teacher to student in a close day-to-day, one-on-one fashion. Because Hung Fa Yi was created to train revolutionary armies to fight the Qing invasion of China, two tracks of training were employed. One was intended to create fighters to be employed against specific threats and specific strategies. It used body mechanics drills to develop martial skills in warriors without necessarily giving them detailed knowledge of geometry and space and time dynamics. It was called Siu Lim (drilling) Tau training. The second was detailed technical training that allowed the practitioner to attain the Weng Kiu level of awareness across the entire spectrum of hand-to-hand combat. This level of training was called Siu Nim (idea, knowledge) Tau training and was given only to a few disciples. Both of these levels of training are outlined in chapter 6.

Despite Chu Hsi's authorship, the vast majority of his teachings were oral in nature and later documented in the *Conversations of Master Chu* by his disciples. The same is true for Hung Fa Yi Wing Chun, which was passed on in its entirety only by word of mouth to disciples. Chu Hsi's insistence that his disciples literally memorize the works of the great classical philosophers, as well as his own teachings, bears close resemblance to Hung Fa Yi Wing Chun's teaching methodology. Hung Fa Yi disciples must literally memorize and experience the concepts, principles, structures, and strategies

Figure 3.3 An example of Hou Chuen: direct, personal interaction and instruction from the Grand Master. Direct experience is the method of San Sau.

passed on by the master. In the words of Grand Master Garrett Gee, "It is all about Wing Chun DNA. If I give you a horse, don't give me back a mule."

The essence of Chan Buddhist Hung Fa Yi philosophy and its parallels to Chu Hsi's greater learning are most apparent in the Hung Fa Yi creed and motto that follow.

Hung Fa Yi Creed

- True knowledge comes from comprehension and willing acceptance of the three levels of intelligence: wandering, awareness, and focus.
- To be a martial artist, one must know oneself by understanding time, space, and energy in terms of combat.
- To know one's opponent, one must recognize the true nature of all things in the universe outside of oneself.
- Only after knowing oneself and one's opponent can one find the harmony needed to truly survive in the real world.

Hung Fa Yi Motto

Harmonizing one's true identity through time, space, and energy.

ETIQUETTE OF HUNG FA YI

The etiquette of Hung Fa Yi is best described through examination of formal bowing, the Hung Fa Yi logo, and Chan teaching. Great emphasis is placed on respect for ancestry, truth, and self.

Formal Bowing

Formal bowing in Hung Fa Yi Wing Chun begins with the right hand, *Wu Sau* (guarding hand), positioned on top of the left hand, *Yat Kuen* (sun fist), and lined up on the middle reference point (Yang Jung) centerline position. The left hand represents the Ching Lung (green dragon—fist), while the right hand represents the Baak Fu (white tiger—palm). Both are traditional Shaolin symbols dating back to Northern Shaolin Temple origins, and both are reflective of the two systems that form the physiological root for Shaolin Wing Chun Kung Fu. Aligned in this position, the hands symbolize that the discipline comes from Shaolin (young forest) warrior monks. In the old Northern Shaolin Temple, the hands were reversed, with the right hand as the fist and the left hand as the palm, symbolizing the mind (left reflecting heaven) restraining aggression (right reflecting earth). As a result of the Southern Shaolin warrior monks' support of revolutionary activity, the nature of the universe was reversed in Shaolin symbology. In this Southern fashion, these hands also symbolized the sun and moon, both symbols of the Ming Chiu (Ming Dynasty—the Bright Dynasty). Finally, the Southern reversal of the hand positions reflected the paradox of facing death in order to live.

From this centerline starting position, the arms are extended to the high reference point (Tan Jung) and followed by a bow. The hands are then separated so that the knuckles of the fist and the fingertips of the palm point toward the temples of the practitioner. This gesture symbolizes the monks going out of the temple to the martial arts community. The hands in this position mimic the character used to depict the name of the Ming Dynasty, called "facing oneself." The ideogram "bright" consists of two parts—the Yat (sun—fist) and Yuet (moon—palm), the brightest objects in the sky. This is yet another reminder to the persons performing and viewing the motion to remember the Ming and the struggle to return the Ming to power.

From this extended position, the left hand changes to Taan Sau (dispersing hand), and the right hand changes to Dar (punch) at the high reference points with both elbows on their respective Yin lines. This gesture states that the practitioner is from the Weng Chun Tong (Everlasting Spring Hall) in the Southern Shaolin Temple.

The formal bow concludes by pulling both hands back to the temples open and then dropping the arms slowly to the sides.

Hung Fa Yi Wing Chun Logo

The Chinese characters in the Hung Fa Yi logo (see figure on next page) translate literally as Red (homophonous with the sound of the word for Magnificent) Flower Righteousness Praising Spring Fist. Their golden color alludes to the royalty of the Ming Dynasty line. The emblem represents a simple, yet philosophically complete statement of Hung Fa Yi reality and history. Each element of the logo has specific significance.

- The Buddhist symbol (backwards swastika) is originally derived from the Sanskrit term *svastika,* meaning "well-being." In Hung Fa Yi Wing Chun it comes from Shaolin Chan (Zen) roots and represents the Buddhist heart. It also

symbolizes the master key that opens the door to every science. The four arms express the succession of generations and the different stages of life (birth, life, death, and immortality) when it faces a clockwise direction. They also point to the four harmonies of nature when oriented clockwise. The symbol itself depicts the paradox of life: the fact that without death there is no life. This is the heart of Buddhist belief about life and death within nature: You have to understand death to know life. As realities change, there are always paradoxes. Understanding these paradoxes helps one to cope with one's immediate reality more effectively. The Chinese also linked this symbol with the

(continued)

number 10,000—a symbol representing eternity and infinity in classical Chinese literature. In the Hung Fa Yi logo, this symbol relates to its "everlasting" nature in both name and science.

- **The six-petaled flower** represents the six gates that bound Hung Fa Yi science and the human combat formation. It also recognizes the Buddhist roots of its creators by alluding to the six senses or sense bases of Buddhist philosophy (salayatana = eyes, ears, nose, tongue, body, and mind). The blossom itself is that of the plum flower, a uniquely tough and hardy plant. It blooms not only in the summer months when weather is favorable, but also in the wintertime when elements are harsh and cold. This courageous flower sets a fine example for all to follow.

- **Hung** (homophonous with the color red) represents the first emperor of the Ming Dynasty who overthrew the Mongols. The Hung Fa Ting, Hung Fa Wui, Hung Gun Biu, and Hung Mun societies all make reference to the color red, representing the first emperor's success as a hero throwing foreign invaders out of China.

- **Fa** (flower) represents Shaolin Chan (Zen) via the Buddha parable about a lecture on reality while holding out a flower. One student, Makashyapa, comprehended the essence of the flower's reality and only smiled without saying a word. The flower now represents "wordless transmission of the mind." This simply means that words can never express total reality.

- **Yi** (righteousness) represents the sacrifice and high personal standard of character needed to be a martial hero.

- **Wing** (praise) represents the character used to name the art after the destruction of the Southern temple. It alludes to passing on the art orally.

- **Chun** (spring) is a Chan (Zen) concept symbolizing rebirth—in this case, the rebirth of the Ming Dynasty.

- **Kuen** (fist) graphically represents the ultimate close-quarter combat nature of the system.

- **The yellow star** in the center represents Hung Fa Yi's origin from the Hon nation (the Yellow River Valley people). Hung Fa Yi was created to protect them. The star also symbolizes wisdom, Hung Fa Yi's five-line concept from the Wing Chun formula, and Hung Fa Yi's five phases of combat arrays.

- **The Baat Jaam Dou** expresses the struggle between the Ming and Qing dynasties. It presents the Hung Fa Yi warriors as martial heroes. It is a distinct trademark of Southern Shaolin kung fu.

- **Yin-Yang** (the Taai Gik—grand poles) represents harmony, the highest level of combat capability. This symbol is universally identified as one that represents the harmony of all things. It stems from Taoist roots and clearly reflects the military's Taoist martial influence on Southern Shaolin development.

Teaching the Chan Buddhism of Hung Fa Yi

In Chinese culture, a teacher with a high level of skill is called Sifu. This person is an expert in a particular field of study. For example, the head chef in a Chinese restaurant is called Sifu; a master electrician or master carpenter could also be considered a

Sifu. In the martial arts, an instructor is also called Sifu. A Sifu is one who, traveling along the same path, is farther ahead than the student and serves as a guide to the student's journey. *Sifu* also implies a relationship between student and teacher much like a master teaching a trade to an apprentice. The Sifu has a responsibility for both the technical skill and the social and ethical understanding of the student.

Another term is reserved for a different kind of teacher coming from the Chinese Buddhist culture. This teacher is called *Bun Jyun,* meaning "exclusive roots." *Bun* is the roots of something and has the sense of being tied to the ancestors. *Jyun* means "exclusive" and has the sense of being the only person with a right to something. When put together, *Bun Jyun* refers to the person possessing exclusive right to represent the ancestors and roots of the body of knowledge. The Bun Jyun decides how much of the system should be taught and to whom. The Bun Jyun is the lineage holder and the head of a generation. In Buddhism, reference is given to a generation patriarch, such as Hui Neng, sixth patriarch of the Sudden School of Chan Buddhism. He is the sixth patriarch as traced from *Damo,* also known as Bodhidharma, the man who brought Chan Buddhism to China. The patriarch of Hung Fa Yi is the Bun Jyun. In the Hung Fa Yi lineage, Yat Chan Daai Si, "Grand Teacher Speck of Dust," was the Bun Jyun of the system in his generation. After this time period, the lineage moved outside the Buddhist temples. As *Bun Jyun* originally referred only to a Buddhist monk, the term fell out of use in the generations following Cheung Ng.

A Bun Jyun serves a twofold purpose as safe-keeper of the system, the one responsible for the whole system: to maintain the purity of the knowledge and to serve as the guide for the students. By being under authority, students' actions and activities can be guided to a definite goal. Without the presence of authority, student actions quickly become unfocused and unclear. Actions, thoughts, activities, and experiences begin to lose their connection to the foundation of the body of knowledge. The student learning in such a situation must "reinvent the wheel" by developing personal ways to understand reality. This personal action might never be enough to reach the goal of full enlightenment. While individual experience is important, it is equally important to have a qualified teacher and receive quality instruction.

Sifu and Bun Jyun are two different types of teachers. Being a Sifu does not automatically make someone a Bun Jyun. However, to be a Bun Jyun one must also be a Sifu. The second prerequisite for being a Bun Jyun is being the leader in the Chan Buddhist tradition in an established lineage with a clear identity. Only systems with direct connections to the Shaolin Temples in the martial arts world, the Gong Wu (River Lake) led by a Buddhist monk, use the term *Bun Jyun.* Modern Wing Chun's Ip Man, while being a great martial artist and teacher, was not a Bun Jyun. He neither claimed to lead a lineage nor claimed to be a successor to his teacher while he was alive; it was only some of his students who made this proclamation after his passing. The term *Bun Jyun* was used in the Shaolin Temple for martial arts teachers because the art was both a Chan Buddhist teaching to reach enlightenment as well as a combat system.

In the Hung Fa Yi lineage, each generation has one head master or Bun Jyun. This is the reason the family tree is a straight line from the origins of the system. A master in the Hung Fa Yi lineage has the responsibility and the right to lead students to the realization of reality and their own true nature. In the past, only inside members were taught the details of the system and given this level of responsibility. The inside members acted as instructors and Sifu to the general students. General students were not always directly connected with the Bun Jyun nor taught the full details of the system. To understand the reason for this lack of information to the general student population, the discussion must turn to the history discussed earlier. While several people might be qualified to teach the whole system as Sifu, only one person bears the responsibility and authority to preserve the system of Hung Fa Yi as Bun Jyun. Thus, although several people knew the full details of the system, only one person was given the authority to declare how and in what manner the principles of the system were communicated to future generations.

HUNG FA YI RANKING

No study of a martial discipline actually deployed for combat purposes would be complete without a brief examination of ranking. Hung Fa Yi ranking identified both the function of a practitioner and the skills (physical, mental, and leadership) required to fulfill that function. Four primary ranks represented by four corresponding colors were used to accomplish this: blue, green, black, and red. Blue represented entry-level troops and junior fighters to be employed against general fighters, as opposed to specially trained opponents. Specifically, fighters at the Siu Nim Tau (and Siu Lin Tau) levels wore the color blue. The color itself symbolized the concept of Taam Lou (seeking the way). Practitioners at this level were still seeking the ultimate knowledge of martial reality. Just as blue represented entry into the system of Hung Fa Yi training, it also represented entry into the secret society as well. In this regard, blue lanterns (Laam Dang) were hung outside the training grounds as symbols to local residents of the training or meeting in progress. All concerned were well aware that nonmembers did not cross the light of the blue lanterns. To do so, of necessity, meant death.

Green symbolized Gong Wu (the martial arts world). It was the color of Chum Kiu–level practitioners possessing the strategy, tactics, and footwork necessary to combat much more advanced (and multiple) opponents. The phrase describing this level, *Luk Lam Ho Hom*, made two specific references. The first is a poetic reference (*Luk Lam* meaning "green forest") to the martial arts world. It implied that the wearer was a true martial practitioner, a skilled warrior. The second (*Ho Hon* meaning "righteous man") implied that the wearer had proven his integrity. He was trusted within the secret society to handle significant challenge.

Black symbolized waiting for the rising sun. The color black was used to represent the time immediately before the rising sun, a time of darkness. During the era of fighting the Qing, the rebels considered themselves to be in dark times, and their battle cry called for the reinstatement of the "Bright Dynasty" (Ming). From a strictly martial arts perspective, the practitioner was nearing his rise to becoming a true martial expert, which corresponds to the Biu Ji level in Hung Fa Yi training.

The final color used in ranking was red and signified completion of the system, to include both the Siu Nim Tau and Siu Lim Tau training tracks. Red was the color of a hero (Ying Hung). This was the color of the bandanna the first Ming emperor wore when he won the last battle that established his dynasty. He was revered throughout subsequent Ming history as a great hero. Hung Fa Yi warriors who wore red have always been respected as heroes worthy of great respect and unquestioned allegiance because of their significant contributions to Hung Fa Yi's mission.

STEPS TO BUILDING A HUNG FA YI IDENTITY

Serious study and reflection on the philosophy of Shaolin Wing Chun, coupled with a conscious embracement of Hung Fa Yi etiquette, is the only true path to developing a Hung Fa Yi identity devoid of illusions in combat skill. To this end, four key steps should be taken to economize the journey from "wandering" to "focus."

Know the History

Knowledge of history enables the practitioner to learn from the paths walked by others who came before on the same journey. Ultimately, the goal of historical study is to understand the background that led to a true paradigm shift in martial thinking and combat application. In military strategy and tactics, a paradigm shift is a change in the fundamental thinking of a group caused by technology or ideology. Examples from World War II include radar, the microwave, rockets, jet airplanes, nuclear weapons, stealth technology, and so on. Paradigms are challenged and changed most often in life-and-death struggles; this is also the time that the best and worst of humanity are displayed. In the history of Hung Fa Yi Wing Chun, the ancestors who experienced the paradigm shift that resulted in a complete combat system of fighting were 17th-century Southern Temple Shaolin Chan monks and Ming Dynasty military officers. The monks brought great wisdom and focus on seeing what is real and harmonizing with nature, and the Ming military experts brought extensive knowledge and experience in tactics, strategy, and the realities of life-and-death struggle.

Understand the Root Philosophy

The Saam Mo Kiu concept was a Southern Shaolin Temple tool to recognize reality. Knowing what is real is applicable to both life and combat situations. Knowing what is real is also used to recognize nature and learn to harmonize with it. The essence of Hung Fa Yi Wing Chun is the philosophy of Saam Mo Kiu. The paradigm shift of time, space, and energy reality in training and fighting has its roots in Saam Mo Kiu.

Experience the Paradigm Shift of the Time, Space, and Energy Concept

The time, space, and energy concept describes reality as four-dimensional space and time. By being consciously aware of it, the practitioner learns to appreciate what is real and what is illusion. When the philosophy of Saam Mo Kiu and the concept of time and space are combined, the practitioner can build an understanding of what is real. This is where the paradigm shifts from art to science. Once that paradigm shift occurs, the practitioner is able to approach kung fu from a scientific point of view. The practitioner can now understand how the shape of space is changed to add or subtract reaction time when dealing with a faster opponent, and how time is controlled to deny a stronger opponent the space required to use that strength. Likewise, the practitioner can now view space in terms of structure and position. Structural space is defined by proper bone alignment for optimal balance, mobility, and strength. Positional space deals with battle formations. It is the result of optimal alignment of the weapons (hands and feet) with the six gates.

Embrace the Wing Chun Formula

The Wing Chun Formula (detailed in chapter 5) is a tool used to harmonize the human body with time, space, and energy. Through this formula, the practitioner can quantitatively measure resources and energies to find optimum efficiency and find the level of performance that optimizes every human structure or position and energy contraction and release. Nothing can be added or subtracted to improve the output. Any distortions in the formula decrease the efficiency of the practitioner. This science can also be used to reproduce exact results in the next generation. With the Wing Chun Formula as a system-wide reference check, the system's integrity can be maintained from generation to generation. Quality replication is assured as long as the formula is applied correctly and honestly.

Core of Hung Fa Yi Science: Space, Time, and Energy

MARTIAL ACTIVITIES FROM FITNESS TO SCIENCE

If Chi Sim Weng Chun represents all that is "art" from the Shaolin temples, Hung Fa Yi represents all that is "military science" from the same. The military martial influence on Hung Fa Yi is unmistakable.

The need for maximum efficient use of time, space, and energy as the ultimate reality created a paradigm shift causing an evolution from personal interpretations to martial science. This scientific shift constituted the basis for Hung Fa Yi Wing Chun, which reflects the true meaning of Siu Nim Tau (little idea beginning) and has been maintained intact for centuries. The information is not open to subjective interpretations based on personal style and experience.

Martial arts training in the 21st century tends to follow four general types of programs: fitness and health, martial sports and recreation, martial entertainment, and self-defense and combat. Today many people mistakenly believe that all martial activities will lead to martial combat reality. Fitness, sports, recreation, and entertainment all have their place and contribute to basic development of physical attributes, but they do not give the practitioner military combat skill. All martial arts activities must be grounded in some form of fitness activity. To that extent, fitness and health programs serve a worthwhile purpose. However, the practitioner must guard against the illusion that fitness and health–oriented programs, in and of themselves, can teach self-defense, combat, or both.

Martial sports are the most popular martial activities today. They provide great physical and mental challenge to the participant. These sports include modern day Wushu, Muay Thai, kickboxing, Taekwondo, Judo, and others. Taekwondo and Judo have achieved Olympic sport status and have been promoted as tournament activities by many masters. By the year 2008, the Chinese Wushu competition forms will be featured in the Olympics as well. Most practitioners in these sports participate in light-contact to full-contact sparring and both empty-handed and weapon forms. Those that compete at the top levels must have focus and dedication, which will result in a disciplined and well-conditioned athlete. However, these sports limit their combatants by their rules and regulations. True practitioners training for the reality of combat remain fully aware that tournaments cannot be the ultimate goal of study and practice, nor can they be the ultimate measure of readiness to engage in combat. Tournaments produce champions; true martial arts produce survivors. Point scoring tournament contenders must, by necessity, pull power from techniques, thereby training improper use of energetics and power. All tournaments restrict lethality, in terms of both targets and weapons. Even allowing for safety concerns, this misuse of techniques, energetics, and strategies creates habits detrimental to a fighter in a real-life struggle.

Gichin Funakoshi, the father of karate, had the same predisposition toward tournaments. He threatened to dismiss, and did dismiss, any student, regardless of rank, who entered tournaments for the purpose of sport. Further evidence of this same attitude toward tournament activity was reflected in the creators of Eastern martial arts, the Shaolin monks. True monks never participated in tournaments or performed public demonstrations. They used their combat kung fu only in situations in which life was threatened—the ultimate reason for training martial skill.

Traditional martial arts have relied on duels or battle to truly develop skills. The stark reality is that, in combat, only the survivor's skill gets developed. In the true philosophy of martial arts, the traditionalist remains aware that tournaments and matches for prizes cause students to develop a need for external verification of their abilities, which gradually erodes their own internal verification of skill and ability.

WING CHUN: STYLE VERSUS SCIENCE

Among the many versions of Wing Chun taught and practiced today, one is most widely practiced and accepted. For purposes of comparison, we will refer to this most widely practiced version as Popular Wing Chun. Popular Wing Chun kung fu is an example of a classical martial arts style. In martial arts styles, the ultimate expression is determined by each individual based on mastery, personality, experience, and sometimes blind loyalties. Even in the Popular Wing Chun system there are many variations, and each new generation will modify the system according to its interpretation and perceived loyalties. The arts will always have variations due to their subjective approach to reality. In comparing martial styles to martial sciences, the styles have variations because of interpretations in expression. Martial sciences, however, are based on universally true concepts and principles that remain consistent through the ages and follow exact formulas. Any expression of that science by an imperfect being becomes "art."

Combat and self-defense reality cannot be based on health, sports, entertainment, or style! These must be based on a reality grounded in science. When it comes to the reality of combat, only one thing counts—efficiency. Combat survival is not about health, games, entertainment, or artistic expression. All of the elements of science must come together to make efficiency real rather than illusionary. *Martial science* is synonymous with *military science*. The Latin derivation for *martial* is *martialis*, the name of the Roman god of battle. Thus, *martial* refers to military activity. Science refers to knowledge or a system of knowledge covering general truths or the operation of general laws, especially as obtained and tested through scientific method. An exact science (such as physics, chemistry, or astronomy) is based on laws capable of accurate quantitative expression. In other words, the system can be measured and predicted accurately. A true military science must be exact. It must fully define optimum efficiency, economy of motion, and economy of energy/resources through quantitative measurement.

Hung Fa Yi is the only martial system to ultimately reach maximum levels of efficiency. Maximum efficiency is the attainment of a level at which nothing can be added or subtracted without violating the concepts of economy of motion and economy of energy or resources. Economy of motion can be defined as employing the least amount of movement (space) with the least amount of energy in the shortest period of time. Economy of energy or resources becomes employment of the least amount of resources (energy) within the minimum motion (space) in the least amount of time. Without science and the reality of time, space, and energy, one cannot attain optimum efficiency.

The concepts of time, space, and energy are relative to the universe in that they have always existed and will continue as long as that universe exists. To gain a realistic perspective of these concepts, we must also understand their relevance to each other. Time is the element used to measure the expeditious movement of objects via energy within a defined space. As such, it derives its meaning from space and energy. Space provides the area all objects occupy and in which they move. Energy is the force that is generated to move objects within that space. Time, space, and energy are harmoniously interrelated. Collectively they form the basis for scientific reality. Individually, they have specific functions.

In the final analysis, fitness, sports, entertainment, and the reality of combat science represent separate disciplines of study and practice—a fact that is often overlooked.

Consequently, it is not uncommon to witness martial artists engaging in physical activities without knowledge of martial skills, historical precedents, and true potential. Although they may appear at first glance to be practicing martial skills, they are actually engaging in sport or fitness programs. This gray area is not wrong as much as misleading. Only through attainment of clear knowledge and a maintenance of proper attitude for learning can the martial arts practitioner follow the path of true martial skill. The essence of Hung Fa Yi Wing Chun is consistent with the teaching of Shaolin—namely, understanding and harmonizing with reality.

HUNG FA YI MARTIAL SCIENCE

Hung Fa Yi Wing Chun evolved as a martial science for dealing with the realities of life's challenges physically, mentally, and spiritually. As such, it is formulated to maximize the three components of time, space, and energy in developing the anatomical, mental, and spiritual constructs of the human body, brain, and psyche. Basing martial arts training on anything less than the reality of three-dimensional space and the fourth dimension of time leaves one open to attack from many angles. In hand-to-hand combat the Hung Fa Yi Wing Chun practitioner does not consider the art or style of his opponent. Instead, he focuses on the dimensions of time and space with proper employment of energies. In essence, the practitioner seeks out and attacks his opponent's distortions of them. The reference planes are identified and the height, range, and width are used to create a three-dimensional volume in space of zones for attack and defense. Angulations and tactics for penetrating and controlling the opponent's spatial volume with proper energetics form the basis for control of the fourth dimension—time. In the physical world, nothing goes beyond time, space, and energy.

How then did this Hung Fa Yi science evolve from the Chan (Zen) battlefield experience of its creators? The harsh realities of their environment taught them the seven criteria for martial science referenced in the introduction of this book. Those criteria are detailed here as viewed from Hung Fa Yi experience.

Criterion One: Combat Reality Demands the Use of All Available Natural Weapons

In combat there is a proper time and place for everything such as finger strikes, punching, biting, and so forth. Humans, however, have no anatomical abilities that can compare to the fangs, claws, and other physical attributes of animals. Humans must use their primary weapon, intellect, to maximize the combat effectiveness of their weaker anatomical parts. Some of the body's combat tools are fingers, knuckles, elbows, knees, heels, and insteps. The body's bone structure, joints, and muscles support these combat tools. Many of these bones and joints were not designed to be used as weapons. To prevent injury, the practitioner must understand their proper anatomical structure and the alignments that give them the greatest amount of support and integrity.

These bones and joints must be used with natural body mechanics if they are to provide effective offense and defense. For example, to employ a straight punch with the hand, humans must first curl the fingers inward beginning with the little or "pinky" finger and following with a sequential closing of the remaining fingers and thumb to effectuate proper alignment and weapon density or hardness. The knuckles and the flat surface of the three fingers from the little finger toward the thumb serve as the striking surface or Saam Dim Kuen (three-point fist). The wrist must support this surface by being locked and straight. Thus, a straight line is formed from knuckles to elbow, both of which support and are supported by the natural structure of the human arm. The elbow itself must be sunken to a position that allows energy transfer to and from the hip and, ultimately, the root. This formation of the hand and arm produces the most impact to the opponent while yielding the least amount of recoil when combined with proper throwing energetics. This is the single best way to employ the human hand in close-range punching while maintaining the six gate structure. It is called Yat Ji Chung Cheui (sun character thrust hammer). To mistakenly punch with the first two knuckles of the fist causes the striking surface of the knuckles to be out of line with the arm and elbow. This misalignment is not consistent with the natural structure of the arm. A bent wrist or misalignment of the elbow is not natural and can therefore cause unnecessary damage to the weapon (fist—fingers, knuckles, or wrist).

In striking with Yat Ji Jeung (palm strike), humans use the same alignment as in throwing Yat Ji Chung Cheui, but replace the fist with an open hand that locks the wrist into a specific position and employs the palm heel for target penetration. To chop or Saat Geng Sau (kill neck hand), the practitioner uses the striking point at the intersection of the wrist and arm (the small bony part of the palm heel on the pinky finger side of the hand known as the pisiform bone). Likewise, when kicking, the heel is used as the primary striking point. The heel is designed for the impact of walking or running. When a practitioner kicks, he generates the same impact with the surface under the heel as he would walking or running. This is the most structurally sound (and natural) blow that can be thrown to an opponent. These constitute examples of efficient use of natural human weapons as opposed to making less efficient contact with misaligned joints and bones or just hitting with any parts of the body.

In addition to experiencing an understanding of natural anatomical weapons, Hung Fa Yi's creators needed to also fully comprehend the natural motions behind human movement. Proper motions for combat must be the same motions humans instinctively employ for any other movement purpose. For example, humans walk upright; therefore, in combat it is more natural to remain upright. The movement of feet should be as natural as possible and akin to walking. In walking, humans lift their feet, shift their weight, and place their feet in the direction they are going. They do not slide across the ground because it would not be appropriate in many terrains. In combat it is most efficient to use the same natural motion. Although flips and spins look impressive, they represent wasted motion that is both unnatural and impractical for combat. The proper use of natural weapons and natural anatomical motions will

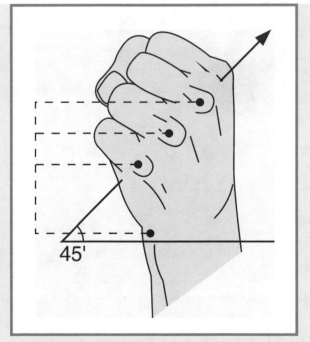

Figure 4.1 Saam Dim Kuen (3-knuckle punch).

lead to combat efficiency. Understanding proper combat structures and positions for the human body constitute Hung Fa Yi's self-space identity.

Criterion Two: Combat Reality Demands Efficiency

In combat the execution of offensive and defensive measures must be efficient without giving the opponent any warning or making the opponent prematurely aware of offensive or defensive intent. The fighter must avoid any overt or wasted movements while entering into or engaging in combat. One must maintain "positional efficiency" in stances for the efficient execution of techniques. The equipment worn by fighters is often heavy and cumbersome, further complicating combative measures and movements. Any technique that does not take this reality into consideration, such as high jumping or spinning, would not be efficient. Energy in hand-to-hand combat can be likened to ammunition. Each soldier carries a limited amount. The penalty for wasting it could be death. *Energy must be treated in the same way as ammunition; it must be employed with greatest attention paid to efficiency.*

Efficiency is gained by three-dimensional use of space, time, and energy. When considering combat space, three different spaces must be analyzed and controlled. The first is the combatant's own personal space. The second is the opponent's space. The third is the space of the arena in which they engage. The combatant must first control the arena and reduce it until the opponent is within proper range. He must then be aware of his own space and set up a position with his opponent that allows him to use his six gates of offense and defense. Before the conflict begins, he must identify the voids in his opponent's space and position himself to flow into those voids for interception or deflection of incoming weapons. Next, he harmonizes with his opponent and sinks or destroys his natural anatomical bridges (arms, legs, body, centerline, or facing). With his bridges destroyed, the opponent is vulnerable to attack and pursuit. In this manner, the combatant does not fight with his opponent. Rather, he harmonizes with space and time. By harmonizing with his opponent's space and time, he reaches maximum combat efficiency.

Figure 4.2 Most often, a flying kick is used for demonstration and entertainment purposes. In real combat, a technique such as this is unrealistic as it requires a large amount of energy and takes a lot of space, requiring too much time to execute.

Criterion Three: Combat Tactics and Techniques Must Be Logical to Learn and Efficiently Retained

The use of natural weapons in conjunction with efficient motion is logical in combat. It relates directly to the practical side of (Chan) Zen by dealing immediately with the here and now. The resultant fighting system is logically learned and efficiently retained. In preparing warriors for combat, the amount of time necessary for their training is absolutely critical to mission success. Consequently, great emphasis is placed on reducing the quantity of motions, tools, concepts, strategies, and tactics that warriors must learn and remember. The system itself must be based on principles and concepts rather than quantity of techniques. It is wholly pertinent that the conceptual information be formatted in a manner consistent with quick learning, ready retention, and easy application in real life situations. What can be naturally (quickly) learned and readily recalled can be instinctively applied under the stress of life-and-death conditions. Knowledge that is easily recalled is inherently most effective in the "reactionary time frame" in which there simply is no time for contemplation or thought. In short, training drills must make these scientific principles and concepts come alive in natural body motion. The techniques become merely tools for accomplishing this end. For example, the Hung Fa Yi centerline concept trains the fighter how to maintain his own center while destroying his opponent's center, regardless of the grappling, kicking, or striking techniques employed.

Unlike most martial arts and martial sports predicated on inefficient artistic motion requiring years to learn and countless hours of drilling to retain, Hung Fa Yi Wing Chun training leaves the practitioner with instinctive, natural motions and responses that remain efficient and effective for life. What makes this possible is Hung Fa Yi's ability to analyze all other systems' strategies, tactics, and techniques within the framework of the common denominators of time, space, energy, and human anatomical structures. One complete system designed from the ground up to address all ranges of combat is inherently easier to learn and employ than a series of techniques and concepts gained from cross-training systems with often diverging philosophies.

Criterion Four: The Combat System Must Be Lethal in Its Deployment

A true hand-to-hand combat system must be lethal. It must contain philosophical conditioning that enables professional conduct in the act of destroying enemies. Chan (Zen) philosophy provides the necessary framework for mentally preparing a warrior to face the realities of the life-and-death paradox. At the same time, a hand-to-hand combat system must provide the tools for lethality in the form of techniques for attacking the vital targets and pressure points of human anatomy while simultaneously destroying human structure. These tools are fully developed in Hung Fa Yi Wing Chun's Chum Kiu and Biu Ji training levels. Coupled with cohesive strategies and tactics, these tools and capabilities give the practitioner the weapons of true martial science. When the conflict begins, the response must be lethal and quickly deployed. Combat methods must be deadly not only in concept, but also in the reality of employment. In true combat there are no rounds or points given. Killing in combat, however, is the extreme condition: Any moral system must enable the practitioner to temper an attack to permit capture and control whenever possible.

Criterion Five: The Combat System Must Enable the Combatant to Survive in the Face of a Numerically Superior Enemy

In combat the unpredictable will often occur, and the enemy may outnumber or outflank a combatant. He must rely on sound, logical strategies and tactics when dealing with multiple opponents. He must be prepared to recover, regroup, escape, survive, and defend against or attack a superior force. He must also be able to improvise and have the technical knowledge to do so efficiently and effectively. A key to accomplishing all of these actions in hand-to-hand combat is the ability to remain mobile and physically upright. This means not going to the ground unless forced there. If multiple attackers move in, engaging any on the ground will allow the remainder to overrun one's position. Relinquishing his upright position and his mobility, he becomes easy prey for the remainder of the enemy's forces. Likewise, going to the ground makes one vulnerable to small or hidden weapons. In today's environment, small or hidden weapons are a real threat that simply cannot be ignored. Intentionally hugging an opponent or going to the ground represents an unacceptable risk in a true self-defense scenario.

Criterion Six: The Combat System Must Provide Reactional Combat Speed Rather Than Eye-Brain–Dominated Speed

In real combat, vision may be distorted or completely obliterated. The deployment of an attack must not depend solely on visual assessments. There is a proper time and space for the use of eye-brain control in combat, such as long range. Long range allows the use of the relatively slow eye-brain control process to set up strategies and tactics through position realignments. Inside that time and space, however, faster physiological control processes must be employed. The sense of touch is far faster and must be trained through arm bridge, leg bridge, and sticking hand processes to control all body reactions and responses in a fashion consistent with time, space, and energy domination. In Wing Chun, we call this "reactional combat skill." The eye-brain process begins with a relatively slow visual receptor that is buffered. A signal must then be sent to the brain, analyzed, and retransmitted to a hand, foot, etc. In contrast, reactional combat skills bypass the buffers of eye-brain. The bridge point between opponents becomes the control center for unified body motion. Reactional combat skills allow for maintenance of a sense of all combatants' positions and battlefield time in relation to self. In close combat one must train to maintain a true sense of touch and must react accordingly.

Criterion Seven: The Combat System Must Be Consistently Predictable and Repeatable

If results of strategies, tactics, techniques, and motions cannot be predicted with accuracy and repeated on the battlefield, the system is neither viable nor survivable.

Hung Fa Yi's Use of the Seven Martial Science Criteria

The Shaolin monks and the Ming military strategists discovered the use of time, space, and energy as the ultimate reality in accomplishing the previously listed criteria in combat. This created a paradigm shift in thinking that resulted in an evolution from martial art to martial science. It might be interesting to note that Western military strategists made many of the same paradigm shifts in battlefield thinking four decades later, as indicated in Carl Von Clausewicz's classic military work entitled *On War*. The basis for Hung Fa Yi Wing Chun is this same concept of time, space, and energy control and also constitutes the basis of the original idea for the Siu Nim Tau level of knowledge and training.

More than three centuries ago, this control of time and space made Cheung Ng's Hung Fa Yi Wing Chun different from all other martial arts. It guarantees simultaneous defense and attack with pinpoint accuracy. It is the cold-combat equivalent of range detection and radar or sonar equipment in today's high-tech weaponry. Absolute precision in the positioning of body lines, coupled with equally precise control of distance between one's own body parts, allows the practitioner to use the hands and feet as space detectors. Similar precision focused on strategies and tactics designed to capitalize on structural flaws and motion occurring within six gates or zones of defense and attack becomes the practitioner's radar. Cheung Ng (and today's Hung Fa Yi practitioners) could fully express the complexities of simultaneous defense and attack through time and space control from the use of a single technique—the tan sau dispersing hand.

In Hung Fa Yi Wing Chun Kuen, Tan Sau is trained consistently at one single point in space and time in all skill development methodologies, including Saan Sau (separate hand) exercises, Chi Sau (sticking hand) drills, and applications training. A practitioner who uses Tan Sau at the wrong space would not be in a position for simultaneous attack and defense. A practitioner who uses Tan Sau at the wrong time would not deny an opponent the opportunity for challenge. Only one tan sau, applied at one specific point in space at one specific time, allows the practitioner to defend and attack while the opponent is denied the same. How, then, is this precision maintained in the chaos of combat? The answer lies in a disciplined structure that most efficiently enables employment of strategies and tactics developed from Hung Fa Yi Wing Chun's emphasis on the physics of three-dimensional space and the fourth dimension, time itself.

Hung Fa Yi discussions of space begin with an in-depth awareness of self. The word *begin* must be emphasized strongly here because Hung Fa Yi Wing Chun is a complete system for combat. Consequently, every aspect of the science of Wing Chun relates to every other aspect. Complete understanding of each individual part is impossible without an in-depth comprehension of the symbiotic relationship of all parts acting in concert. Purpose, techniques, structures, energetics, attributes, tactics, and strategies must all cooperate for any meaningful employment of space and time to occur. They affect even the description of time and space. For example, perfect alignment of one's body for the express purpose of horseback riding requires reference points in space that are distinctly different from those required for hand-to-hand combat alignment.

DEVELOPMENT OF MARTIAL AWARENESS

Hung Fa Yi examinations of space begin with an analysis of one's own body unity for the express purpose of engaging in hand-to-hand combat. Practitioners employ the precise structure of Wing Chun to develop innate awareness of the distances between each of their own body parts. Before any attempt can be made to precisely control an opponent's mass in motion while denying the time and space required to react, one must first possess absolute control over his own structure throughout its movement in space and time. This is known as development of martial self-awareness. It is what enables the Hung Fa Yi practitioner to maintain personal space while entering the space of another. In essence, the practitioner's body becomes a calibrated instrument capable of instantly measuring space. His structure becomes as effective as any modern day range detection instrument, enabling pinpoint accuracy in weapons employment.

Development of martial self-awareness occurs in three stages. The first stage involves attainment of maximum efficiency in structural unity by aligning one's own body parts to provide an optimum mix of balance, strength, and ease of use in relation to three-dimensional space. The second stage involves developing an awareness of an opponent's structures and flaws in relation to his own space. The third stage introduces the fourth dimension of time and involves movement of one's parts within defined space.

In the first stage, the practitioner examines the depth, height, and width of his own space in terms of the four elements of the Hung Fa Yi Wing Chun Formula: (1) the centerline (focal point), (2) two lines of defense (depth), (3) three reference points (height), and (4) the five-line concept (width). To define one's own precise space and the most efficient placement of one's own parts within it, one must be able to describe that space in all dimensions. These four elements of the Wing Chun Formula allow a practitioner to do just that.

The first element, centerline, provides a vertical reference line allowing for centering the depth, height, and width components of the practitioner's space.

The second element, two lines of defense, tells practitioners how far both hands need to be away from the body. This is the "depth" component of personal space. The height element, referred to as the three reference points, gives practitioners the proper vertical positioning for aligning each of their limbs. Lastly, the five-line concept provides a precise description of the width of one's space on a horizontal plane. Properly understood, these four elements allow practitioners to quickly align their body parts for optimum simplicity, efficiency, and directness in relation to their opponent when motion is introduced.

In the second stage, the opponent's structure is examined to determine one's own weapons alignment. The same four elements of the Wing Chun Formula are used to analyze the opponent's structure. Are his hands and feet at the proper distances from his torso? Are his elbows, hands, knees, and feet aligned according to the five-line concept? Are they at the correct height, or are they too low? All of these factors are taken into account because they will directly affect control of space and time.

In the third stage, time comes into play. This stage begins when the practitioner aligns his structure with his opponent's. Time can only be referenced when there is a second object to be interacted with in space. Optimum alignment allows the simultaneous use of offense and defense. It also requires the opponent to make adjustments in his own structure before employment of his own weapons. This gives the practitioner a time advantage over his opponent. He trains to align his structure so that his opponent is only able to use a fraction of his body and weapons against the practitioner's full arsenal. While the opponent is adjusting to bring all of his weapons into proper alignment, the Hung Fa Yi practitioner is in control of time and is already using it to advantage.

The basic function of time is to move forward in a linear progression. It never speeds up, nor does it slow down; it is a constant. However, in addition to the basic linear time progression, two other types of time exist in the same continuum. The first, cycle time, moves along the linear timeline repeating the events that are embedded in the measurements of time—a specific day of the week, monthly occurrences, annual holidays, or anniversaries. All of these events have been cycled and recycled throughout history and are projected far into the future. Practitioners have no control over the linear progression of time or the cyclical events that shape their history or their future.

The second type of time, matrix time, encompasses the realm in which a practitioner lives. A matrix by definition is something within which something else originates or develops. In relation to time, it is a time within time where all of a practitioner's actions are taken. It is within this matrix of time that a practitioner lives and performs all of his actions. The matrix of time is the here and now of his existence.

In relation to combat, a practitioner uses the time matrix to establish the length of time in which he will engage an opponent. Within the space configured by his six gates, he employs the minimum amount of matrix time to execute his techniques. Therefore, he uses the matrix of time to establish the length of time for combat, and within that time matrix he uses the speed of time to execute his techniques. The use of time within time by the Hung Fa Yi Wing Chun practitioner minimizes his use of time in combat.

Time is relative to space in this concept, for without space there could be no element in which to employ time. In combat, space is the precursor of time. It provides the area or volume within which time is used for combat engagement. Space not only provides the arena for combat, but also allows combatants to define their own individual space within that arena. Hung Fa Yi Wing Chun practitioners minimize the amount of space in their own arena, thus increasing their ability to use speed and conserve energy. The simultaneous minimization of both space and energy in combat allows for a more focused attack and defense while requiring less effort.

Within space, energy is expended to propel the execution of techniques. This energy, or life force, comes from within the combatant and is called *Qi* in Mandarin or *Hei* in the language of Wing Chun practitioners, the southern dialect of Cantonese. It is most important to recognize that energy employment must be properly harmonized with space and time. To focus on maximum power generation through unnatural motions (i.e., long throw kicks and punches, spins, jumps, etc., for the sake of generating greater-than-natural human power) without consideration of space and time constraints yields only an illusion of power projection capability. The proper control of hei and the knowledge of the universal concepts of time, space, and energy raise the Hung Fa Yi Wing Chun practitioner to a higher level of combat.

Hung Fa Yi practitioners train to recognize three different time frames in relation to combat. The first is called Fau Kiu (floating bridge). It represents a temporal window in space during which one has no control of either time or space. Any strikes landed during this time frame are considered nothing more than "lucky strikes" because the practitioner could not guarantee the outcome. In short, no part of the Wing Chun Formula is expressed in alignment or structure. The second time frame examined is called Saan Kiu (separate bridge). This time frame addresses the conditions and results of having time, but not space, or having space, but not time. The third time frame is called the Weng Kiu (everlasting bridge) time frame. It represents complete control of time and space, allowing simultaneous offense and defense.

These concepts of space and time relative to combat are foundational to the total comprehension and employment of Hung Fa Yi Wing Chun. By knowing what structures enable the quickest determination of when to act and where to act most efficiently, Hung Fa Yi practitioners are prepared to control space and time. They use the Wing Chun formula to recognize distortions in time and space, both their own and their opponent's. They train to remove their own distortions while amplifying those of their opponent. Coupled with strategies and tactics designed to capitalize on space-time distortions, they simultaneously disable an opponent's weapons while employing their own. Regardless of the type of attack (fast kicking, grappling, lunging, etc.), the common denominators in human structure form the basis of the technology that enables Hung Fa Yi practitioners to control and dismantle that attack.

The ability to explain these complex concepts in motion with a single technique, the tan sau, gave Hung Fa Yi Wing Chun's founder, Cheung Ng, his nickname, Taan

Sau Ng. When asked by Popular Wing Chun practitioners if it matters whether the tan sau is used to engage the opponent with one's front hand or back hand (the depth dimension of three-dimensional space), the Hung Fa Yi practitioner can employ the tan sau to clearly demonstrate that front hand usage denies attainment of simultaneous offense and defense because the back hand remains out of range for striking. The time required to bring the back hand within range following front hand engagement constitutes time the opponent could use for reaction. Clearly a time-space consideration is needed.

When Popular Wing Chun practitioners ask if it matters whether the tan sau is high (upper reference point level—the vertical or height dimension of three-dimensional space as expressed in the Hung Fa Yi Tan Sau) or low (shoulder level—the height dimension as expressed by Popular Wing Chun practitioners), Hung Fa Yi practitioners have another time and space–grounded answer. Dealing with an upper gate attack requires covering that gate. Upon contact, adjustment can be made. Making contact low and trying to adjust is dangerous. Leverage is insufficient. Making contact high provides sufficient leverage for adjustment with fast motion in time and space. In addition, it ensures proper range for simultaneous offense and defense. It is both structurally and temporally most efficient to use Tan Sau at the upper reference point level.

The last dimension of three-dimensional space is width. It is defined by proper application of the five-line concept of the Wing Chun Formula. To allow for simultaneous attack and defense, proper setup with the tan elbow on the yin line should result in application of the tan sau with the strongest structure and position.

Like their Si Jou (Cheung Ng) before them, Hung Fa Yi practitioners emphasize that there is only one most efficient way to use Tan Sau when time and space are taken into consideration. There is only one way to enable simultaneous attack and defense. Like their predecessor, they can express the entire system through this single hand.

Hung Fa Yi Wing Chun is a true martial science grounded in a realistic military heritage. Hung Fa Yi Wing Chun kung fu is the cutting-edge martial science of hand-to-hand cold combat, and was developed for actual life-and-death situations. It contains the total package of military scientific tactics and strategies as well as practical training methodologies. *It may well be the only combat system that reached maximum possible efficiency levels during centuries of warfare, regardless of continent or culture*. It reflects the Chan (Zen) view of practicality in dealing with combat. The paradigm shift that resulted in its creation was brought about by the collaboration of the Shaolin monks and the deposed military leaders who supported the Ming Dynasty. In their quest to develop a martial system that would counter all other fighting styles and address the immediate needs of the rebels in combat, they developed a new fighting system based on a new paradigm—the science of battlefield space, time, and energy management.

Hung Fa Yi is unique as a true military science in today's martial arts world. A true martial science is the highest level of martial activity and has its basis in the realities of the dimensions of time, space, and energy. Hung Fa Yi is not only a cutting-edge fighting system; it is also consistent with its Chan (Zen) philosophy of spontaneity, completeness, and practicality.

Wing Chun
Formula

三　點　一　線　定　元　神

sàam　dím　yät　sin　dihng　yùhn　sàhn

Three Points, One Line, Establish the Original Nature

五　道　六　門　化　乾　坤

ñgh　douh　luhk　mùhn　fa　kíhn　kwan

Five Ways and Six Gates, Influence the Universe

One of the earliest hou kuet, or oral idioms, in the Hung Fa Yi lineage dates back to the origins of the art in the Southern Shaolin Temple. The two phrases above express the key insight that led to the paradigm shift that gave birth to Hung Fa Yi Wing Chun.

Saam Dim Yat Sin (three points, one line) expresses the importance of the center of gravity in relation to heaven, man, and earth. This awareness incorporates both the vertical and the horizontal components of Hung Fa Yi and can extend to both internal and external training. Externally, it expresses proper alignment in body structure for striking. Internally, it expresses proper alignment of body structure for energy cultivation. In these two understandings (the trilogy of heaven, man, and earth, together with an awareness of body structure) is expressed the unity of both the vertical and horizontal planes.

Ng Dou Luk Mun is the five ways and six gates. The five ways refers to the five-line concept, an awareness of horizontal structure. The six gates is the Hung Fa Yi six gate concept. These two ideas are unique to Hung Fa Yi Wing Chun among the many Shaolin systems. Due to Ng Dou Luk Mun, Hung Fa Yi body structure stands out among Shaolin systems.

Together, Saam Dim Yat Sin and Ng Dou Luk Mun express the foundation that led to the realization of the Hung Fa Yi Wing Chun Formula. The Wing Chun Formula expresses the fundamental components of the human body to be mapped in time, space, and energy. This is the true jewel in the Hung Fa Yi Wing Chun crown.

The scientific information embodied in the Hung Fa Yi Wing Chun Formula has been maintained intact for more than three centuries. The information is based on physics and physiology that provide a foundation grounded in reality (time, space, and energy), as opposed to subjective interpretations based on personal style and experience alone. The essence of Wing Chun Kung Fu is simplicity, directness, and efficiency, yet this and following chapters describe great sophistication in the development of knowledge and skill. The inexperienced might consider this level of sophistication too complex for combat, without recognizing that simplicity, directness, and efficiency are born out of extensive knowledge and experience. A truly proficient practitioner can make any motion or application fluid and effective at the right time and space. The simplicity we find in a modern cell phone with extensive power at the touch of simple buttons provides a useful analogy. Underneath those buttons lies an extensive array of applied knowledge and scientific principles. The Wing Chun Formula forms the basis of such an array underpinning Hung Fa Yi Wing Chun's ultimate simplicity, directness, and efficiency.

The formula itself is, in essence, a window into the entire system of Hung Fa Yi Wing Chun Kung Fu. It gives every practitioner consistency of function throughout the chaos of combat. The information it provides was kept secret until this past decade and only revealed to those who took a blood oath. The formula ensured that the system remained intact throughout successive generations. Without the formula, the system would have been altered by personal expression within as little as a single generation.

As indicated in previous chapters, Hung Fa Yi was created out of military necessity. Numerous fighting styles and systems were employed throughout battlefield engagements during the Qing invasion of China. The amount of time required to train troops to learn all of these styles in order to defend against them was militarily infeasible. Revolutionary fighters needed one complete system that could address all possible attack strategies within the bounds of the human genetic code. Speed and power needed to be secondary to strategy and position. This drove an overarching emphasis on spatial and temporal control. This new system had to provide a road map of how to behave by finding one's harmony with space and time throughout all ranges of motion. At the same time, it had to provide the means of instantaneously detecting the opponent's loss of harmony and the ability to capitalize on that disharmony. To truly harmonize with energies in space and time, both hard and soft techniques needed to be trained; one is simply not complete without the other. Maintenance of one's own center of gravity and the simultaneous destruction of an opponent's center of gravity requires a balance between hard and soft techniques. In short, the Hung Fa Yi Wing Chun Formula is a blueprint of how to behave in the Wing Chun way. Ultimately, the goal is to find one's harmony with nature through the proper understanding and use of time, space, and energy.

The Wing Chun Formula scientifically expresses the dimensions of time, space, and energy through the employment of the practitioner's own body parts as precision measurement devices. Properly used, these same body parts demonstrate all of the concepts, principles, tactics, and strategies of Hung Fa Yi science. The formula is composed of six key components, each having its own function while simultaneously being related to the others. These components are (1) the centerline, (2) the two-line defense, (3) the three reference points, (5) the five-line concept, (6) the six gates, and (5) the five elemental battle arrays for facing and pursuit. The formula is numerically sequenced as 1, 2, 3, 5, 6, and 5. One (1) provides the core, two (2) identifies range, three (3) identifies height, and five (5) identifies width. Together these four components establish the fifth component called six (6) gates. These six zones constitute a three-dimensional plane that defines maximum efficiency for human anatomical combat formation. The first five components allow Hung Fa Yi Wing Chun practitioners to establish their identity. The sixth component, five (5) elemental battle arrays, gives practitioners the understanding of tactics and strategies for attack and defense. However, when any of these six components is out of position, there is a distortion in the time and space continuum. To understand the Hung Fa Yi Wing Chun Formula, one must explore each of the components and their individual concepts.

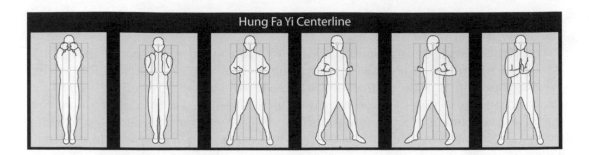

Hung Fa Yi Centerline

CENTERLINE (CORE)

The centerline, and its corresponding number one (1) in the Hung Fa Yi Wing Chun Formula, represents the core of the body and extends outward from the center of the body to infinity. Moving outward on the centerline, we become aware of time and space. The elements 2, 3, and 5 are contingent on the centerline, which is element one (1) and vertically divides the body into two halves.

Hung Fa Yi practitioners must not only have control of their centerline, but must also influence the centerline of their opponent. In a combat situation one's centerline must be maintained to keep one's balance. If one leans or moves off the centerline in any direction, one creates a distortion in at least one of the three dimensional realities, which ultimately affects the six gates. This distortion creates a domino effect that will allow an opponent to gain an advantage.

TWO-LINE DEFENSE (RANGE AND DEPTH)

The two-line defense, and its corresponding number two (2) in the Hung Fa Yi Wing Chun Formula, defines the extension of the centerline in two areas. The first is the inner gate (Mun Jong or Gei Jong), which is measured by the distance of one fist from the elbow to the chest of the inner arm and continues outward to the hand in the wu sau position. The second is the outer gate (Kiu Jong), which is measured by the farthest position of the extended elbow (striking point of Wu Sau) and continues outward to the hand in the kiu sau position. The spacing of the inner and outer gates is critical in defining the types of techniques that can be applied. When an opponent can touch his inner gate (Wu Sau), a practitioner can hit him with his outer gate (Kiu Sau) hand. In essence, the practitioner can simultaneously attack and defend.

Because this concept creates a dimension that exists on only one plane, the practitioner is using the centerline and extending outward through the inner and outer gates to create proper range and depth. As an example we can use the Saam Mo Kiu

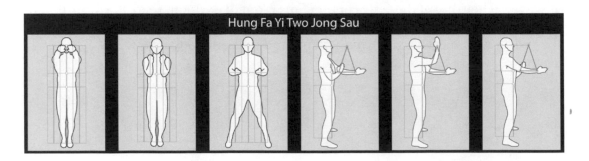

Hung Fa Yi Two Jong Sau

(three connecting bridges) philosophy to illustrate the reality of different time frames. The three stages constitute a progression that begins with Fau Kiu—a condition of not understanding range and time. Practitioners at the Fau Kiu stage have no concept of time and space and will telegraph their movements (drawing back a hand before a strike, for example). The second stage is Saan Kiu—a condition of understanding time but not being efficient with the use of range. In this stage practitioners may have some sense of distance and timing but have not developed the ability to use both range and time in a scientific manner. Therefore they depend on—and are required to use more—attributes such as speed and agility to compensate for the inability to determine the proper usage of range and time. The third stage is Weng Kiu. At this stage practitioners have developed an understanding of both range and time and can use them together in a scientific method and express them at will. Fighting at the Weng Kiu range allows the use of all four limbs without the need for readjustment of positions that cause the loss of time. At this stage a full understanding of the reality of three-dimensional space has matured, and practitioners know when to move and when not to move. Only in the Weng Kiu stage do practitioners have the ability to attack and defend simultaneously. This is sometimes referred to as the true Wing Chun time frame and range, whereas Fau Kiu and Saan Kiu represent distorted time frames and ranges.

THREE REFERENCE POINTS (HEIGHT AND VERTICAL)

The three reference points, and their corresponding number (3) in the Hung Fa Yi Wing Chun Formula, subdivide the centerline and the two-line defense into three vertical areas as follows:

Tan Jung—high reference point   From the top of the nose to the top lip
Yan Jung—middle reference point   The solar plexus
Daan Tin—lower reference point   Three fingers below the navel

The three reference points exist on this vertical three-dimensional plane. Again, the practitioner uses the centerline and extends vertically through the three reference points to create a second dimension, which is height. This dimension defines the height of the opponent's attack or defense.

To understand the three reference points, one must also consider the triangulations that are involved in the alignment of the hands, elbows, and body. When positioned in Leung Yi Ma (the two-element fighting stance) with the Kiu Sau (front hand) and the Wu Sau (rear hand) on the centerline of the body, the practitioner creates the inner and outer gates. A triangle is simultaneously formed vertically from the high reference point to the wu sau and down to the middle reference point. This is one of the triangles that provide the structure for the Hung Fa Yi Wing Chun Formula.

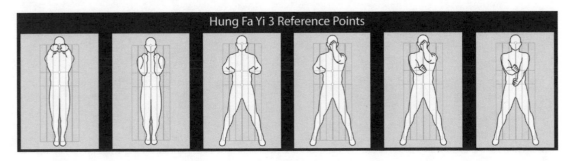
Hung Fa Yi 3 Reference Points

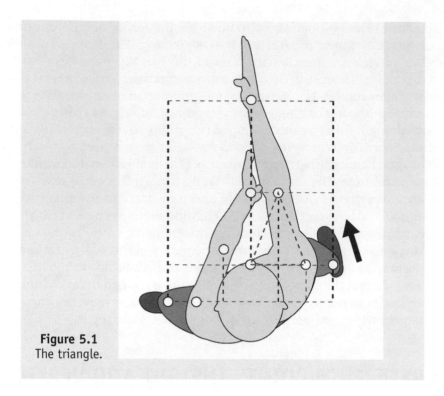

Figure 5.1
The triangle.

FIVE-LINE CONCEPT (WIDTH)

The five-line concept, and its corresponding number five (5) in the Hung Fa Yi Wing Chun Formula, combines the centerline, two-line defense, and three reference points concepts to create a two-dimensional plane of height and range. It then adds the width of the body from shoulder to shoulder to form a three-dimensional square existing in space, thus creating volume in space rather than on a plane. The five lines are composed of three vertical yang lines (the centerline and each shoulder line) and two vertical yin lines (the two nipple lines).

The five lines can be identified on the body from left to right as follows:

0	Left shoulder line	Yang
½	Left nipple line	Yin
1	Centerline	Yang
½	Right nipple line	Yin
0	Right shoulder line	Yang

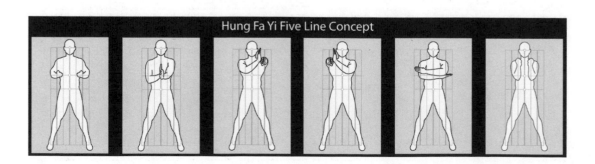

If one extends the arms out and brings the fingertips onto the centerline (1), this will identify the area that one must address straight on. By changing the horizontal angle of the arms to one side without rotating the waist, the range of the hand's motion covers the space from centerline (1) to nipple line (½) to shoulder line (0). This is true on either side of the centerline. The horizontal range of motion from shoulder to shoulder defines the five lines on a plane. If an opponent moves outside of a practitioner's five-line area and past the negative one half line (-½), the practitioner will not be able to address the opponent with both hands without adjusting his own body position.

In addition to a vertical triangle, a horizontal triangle is formed from the Wu Sau elbow at the Yin line to the Yang line at the shoulder and back to the Yang line of the centerline of the body. The horizontal and vertical triangles together form the locking position. The locking position (Wu Sau) is the strongest structural position and is sometimes referred to as the triangle theory.

When the practitioner raises his extended hands to the centerline at the plane parallel to the ground, all of his five lines run along that plane. He will use these reference lines to align his hands and elbows in Kiu Sau/Wu Sau positions for his offensive and defensive positions. Depending on the incoming energy exerted by the opponent's punches, hand position, and footwork, the practitioner can take the inside or outside path and destroy the opponent's structure. In a combat situation the practitioner's Kiu Sau and Wu Sau will travel along his five lines during the contact stage to gain a superior position over the opponent by creating a three-dimensional volume in the opponent's space.

SIX GATES

The six gates, and their corresponding number six (6) in the Hung Fa Yi Wing Chun Formula, represent the combat formation structure that is based on the human anatomical form. Hung Fa Yi Wing Chun is a scientific approach to combat and is designed for life-and-death situations. The six gates are used to determine the areas of attack and defense and to harmonize the human anatomy with the reality of the three dimensions of time and space. The use of time and space by the practitioner is

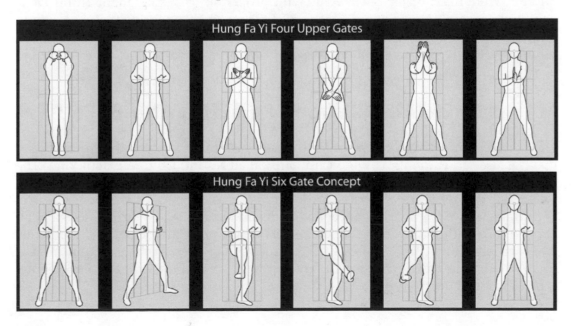

predicated on the opponent's position and movements. In combat one takes what is given. *Hung Fa Yi Wing Chun practitioners respect life and can use the element of control in combat because they have many options.*

Knowledge, translated militarily as intelligence, when properly employed through sound strategy and tactics, can be more powerful than conventional weapons. In conventional hand-to-hand combat, which is confined to control of one or two dimensions, a fighter must learn to attack and seize vast amounts of space in all directions. After the seizure is accomplished, the fighter must then expend considerable resources to maintain protective vigilance over the controlled area and prevent incursion and sneak attacks by the enemy. To physically control such a large space requires a significant arsenal of techniques and attributes to be employed at every range of combat. The size of a fighter's potential battlefield could grow to two or three times larger than his personal space as defined by the Hung Fa Yi six gate concept.

Scientific hand-to-hand combat, however, uses the four-dimensional volume in space and requires fighters to see and act on distortions in the space and time dimensions of the existing battlefield. Use of the improved intelligence provided by the Hung Fa Yi Wing Chun space and time concept can radically reduce the size of the potential battlefield. Hung Fa Yi Wing Chun fighters do not need to seize and control large amounts of space simply to protect from attacks. They have no imperative to structure their fighting mobility for the dissipation of their forces over a large area simply to engage and repel perimeter incursions. Their superior fighting intelligence, coupled with multidimensional strategy and tactics, enable them to concentrate their forces on key areas of range. The Mun Jong range covers all three vertical physical dimensions within the six gates and enables Hung Fa Yi Wing Chun fighters to keep their weapons delivery system, their limbs, mutually supported and reinforced for concentrated firepower. The surgical use of their firepower is triggered with maximum efficiency against the enemy. Conventional fighters are weakened through the dispersion of resources while maintaining a large battlefield. The size of their battlefield is mandated by the conventional approach to hand-to-hand combat.

Use of the six gates gives Hung Fa Yi practitioners the ability to analyze an opponent's structural weakness and identify potential threats to themselves. Through this awareness and assessment of potential challenges, they can minimize an opponent's offense while maximizing their own. With proper six gate alignment Hung Fa Yi practitioners can force an opponent to self-destruct by either luring the opponent to attack an area that is seemingly open or forcing the opponent to attack from a bad position, creating telegraphic motions.

FIVE ELEMENTAL ARRAYS FOR FACING AND PURSUIT

The five elemental battle arrays for facing and pursuit that apply to the concepts and theories used in Hung Fa Yi Wing Chun are called Ng Jan Chiu Min Jeui Ying. The elemental battle arrays, represented by the corresponding number five (5) in the Hung Fa Yi Wing Chun Formula, give the Wing Chun practitioner an instantaneous tactical and strategic awareness. The concept of five elements (wood, water, fire, metal, and earth) representing movements and energies permeates Chinese culture, medicine, and martial training from the early Taoist societies to present day. The nature and use of these elements is discussed in greater depth in chapter 7. The five elemental arrays are named as follows:

1. **Set Up (Baai Jong)** or the wood element (foundational energies and structures) maintains structure and position while identifying those of the opponent according to time and space.

2. **Intercepting or redirecting (Jit Kiu)** or the water element (how to penetrate in all directions) absorbs and steers an opponent's energy to gain an advantage, which is a superior structure and position.

3. **Sinking (Chum Kiu)** or the fire element (burning everything along the way) destroys an opponent's techniques, structures, and abilities to fight back.

4. **Pursuing (Jeui Ying)** or the metal element (cutting down structure and hacking it to pieces) continuously chases and dominates from a superior position.

5. **Recovery (Wui Ma)** or the earth element (absorbing energy) includes repositioning oneself in a spatially and temporally advantageous position that allows control of all energies.

At the first and simplest level, Hung Fa Yi Wing Chun fighters develop the capabilities that allow them to deny an opponent the free use of a given battle space. Fighters prevent an opponent from gaining an advantageous position by employing a long-range positioning called Chiu Min (facing the opponent's general direction) and a medium- to shorter-range positioning called Deui Ying (aligning to an opponent's anatomical structure and matching the opponent move for move). The use of these two concepts includes the simultaneous alignment of the three reference points and the six gates, and thus stations fighters in an advantageous position for addressing an opponent.

At the second level, Hung Fa Yi Wing Chun fighters have improved skillwise from denying the opponent battle space to controlling the battle space, thereby allowing them to operate within a given battle space without inordinate risks. At this level of fighting ability fighters can use specific battle space in pursuit of tactically limited goals. At this level Jit Kiu, the intercepting bridge, is employed at a range called Mun Jong (inner gate range) simultaneously with the two-line and five-line concepts.

At the third, and most demanding, level, Hung Fa Yi Wing Chun fighters have developed the ability to impose positive control over a given battle space and bring cohesive and concentrated power to bear against the centerline of the opponent's body structure. In so doing, fighters employ Chum Kiu, the sinking bridge, and destroy the opponent's techniques and ability to fight back.

Overall tactics and strategy constitute a random access application of the five elemental battle arrays that depends on the opponent's attack or defense. These arrays should not be viewed as sequential. Time, space, and energy determine the appropriateness of each array.

Siu Nim Tau Level of Science and Skill Development

The Chan Buddhism experience of reality occurs in three stages. Each stage serves to prepare the student for the next stage in the progression with the ultimate goal of enlightenment, or realizing one's true potentials through understanding and experiencing one's self-identity and true nature. In the first stage of the progression the goal is to develop and balance the body and mind for further training. Methods used to develop the body can include walking, standing, sitting, and reclining meditation. Different types of physical exercises such as punching, kicking, footwork, and stances to develop the connection between the body and mind are also employed. A third way to develop the body and mind connection is by using moving meditation called sets or forms to develop different feelings and strengths. With proper training in this first stage, the body is changed from weak to strong and becomes capable of enduring hardship, and the mind is changed from unfocused to disciplined and becomes capable of exacting focus with self-confidence, determination, optimism, peace, and stability. To use a teacup as an example, this first stage would be the manufacturing process of the teacup.

The second stage consists of two phases: understanding oneself (one's self-identity) and one's relationship to the larger world (one's true nature). In Chan Buddhism, the "Self" is called Siu Nim, meaning "Little Idea." To arrive at the stage of the "Little Idea" requires a strong sense of personal identity—not a small accomplishment. To attain the first phase of reality is to understand one's self-identity through experience, education, and reactions to influences from the outside world. The second phase involves understanding the surrounding universe. In Chan Buddhism, this understanding of the universe is termed Daai Nim, meaning "Big Idea." Through training, the student comes to understand and feel a connection to the universe. This awareness leads to a harmony with time, space, and energy, the fundamental layer of reality. Rather than seeing oneself as a limited, unchanging, and finite creature, one becomes united with the universe: limitless, changing, and infinite. While the world is continuously changing and moving, the change and movement occurs within time, space, and energy. When one realizes the "Big Idea," he fully realizes he is part of that changing energy moving within space and time. One continues to exist as a "Little Idea" with his own views and experiences of the world, but he also represents infinite potential. To continue the teacup example, this stage would be the realization of the sides of the cup and the impermanent nature of material objects. The sides of the cup are time, space, and energy, and the impermanent nature of the cup (i.e., the contents of the teacup change from moment to moment by such actions as heating and cooling or filling and draining) is the flow and change of time, space, and energy.

The third stage involves the realization of the true self to reach the stage of no self. By moving past the realization of oneself as being united with the universe, one reaches the point at which one becomes the universe. This is what is meant by the concept of no self: One ceases to think of oneself as separate from anything else that exists; instead, one becomes everything that exists. This experience is often described as a mystical union with the Buddha self. The manifestation of this experience will depend on your cultural heritage and experiences in life. This third phase is beyond thought or word and cannot be conveyed through speech. Chan Buddhism takes you to the realization of the world, beyond thoughts, feelings, or attachments. This realization of nonthought, nonfeeling, and nonattachment is called "Emptiness." This emptiness is not in the sense of a void. Instead, emptiness means the ultimate potential for any action. This is one's true nature: changing, dynamic, flexible, and adaptable. By not being attached to any particular thing, thought, or emotion, one is ready to respond to the situation at hand spontaneously, in a carefree manner, and with complete honesty and freedom. Returning to the metaphor of the teacup, its usefulness lies in the empty space it provides to hold the tea. This stage leads one to a realization of one's own total potential in any moment in time. This is Chan enlightenment.

THE SIU NIM TAU FORM: PHYSICAL DOCUMENTATION OF HUNG FA YI SCIENCE

Within the three-stage framework of Chan, the Siu Nim Tau form has two levels of understanding: mental and physical. Both must be fully understood to discern both the intent and the skill of this level of learning.

Siu ("Little")

Mental Understanding: The concept of "Little" has its roots in the Chan (Zen) concept of emptiness, which translates to "Dynamic, not fixed." In this case it gives rise to the concept of "Young." Young children are pure and open-minded; they are not "Fixed" by preconception or prejudice. Like the open-minded child, the practitioner must approach training with an empty teacup that can be filled with new knowledge. *Siu* in this sense means that practitioners must decrease the distractions in their lives to facilitate training. They must develop the ability to take things one step at a time and accept them for what they are, not what they would like them to be.

It is most important for practitioners to realize that Siu Nim Tau is all about building a martial identity based on time, space, and energy and full awareness of the true nature of that same time, space, and energy—that they are "Emptiness" in the Chan (Zen) sense. As such, they are not "Fixed." Nothing is permanent. *All Wing Chun techniques are motions in the process of becoming other motions. There simply are no static postures. The Wing Chun Formula allows the practitioner to be consistent in a nonpermanent reality.*

Physical Understanding: From a physical perspective, "Little" expresses the compact and efficient method of training and application. The goal in combat is to be efficient, thereby minimizing the movements, energy, and time needed to maximize results.

Nim ("Idea")

Mental Understanding: "Idea" in this context implies intent. This term asks the practitioner, "What are you here for?" The answer should be, "To acquire true knowledge." In mental training, this refers to consciously guiding one's intent and energy.

Physical Understanding: This refers to following the principles of science and the laws of physics, specifically by acquiring and comprehending the technical knowledge of the Wing Chun Formula and time, space, and energy. The name *Siu Nim Tau* itself implies the paradigm shift in combat thinking required to understand Hung Fa Yi's dimensional use of battlefield physics.

Tau ("Beginning" or "Head")

Mental Understanding: The brain is in the head. This refers to practitioners' intelligence, as well as to their control of accumulated knowledge. *Beginning* also refers to the start of a practitioner's training. The practitioner must understand the proper intent, have the right attitude, and know the time and space formula at the beginning of training. Learning to get over one's own ego, preconceived notions, prejudices, fears, etc., constitutes the first step to real training. It is a big thing to try to be small, to literally know one's proper time and space in the here and now. This is proper intent.

Physical Understanding: The techniques and concepts taught at the beginning of training serve as a foundation for further training. The human body does not have natural weapons such as large fangs or claws. The primary weapon for human beings is beyond a doubt their intelligence.

In ancient times, books couldn't be mass-produced. For this reason, forms served to contain information like a book. Likewise, on the battlefields of old where hand-to-hand combat meant literally being eyeball-to-eyeball with the enemy, books couldn't be employed for quick reference to strategies, tactics, concepts, and principles to counter threat and attack. By understanding what the form expressed, one preserved information into the next arena as well as into the next generation. To make the knowledge come alive, physical exercises existed to drill the body to maintain the human identity in time and space (as in Siu Lin Tau).

Hung Fa Yi is a practical system. As such, it contains few fixed forms. Forms are used solely for the purpose of describing the core of the science. Forms are literally the "periodic table" of Hung Fa Yi "chemistry." Forms give the practitioner the Wing Chun "DNA" with all body parts in the exact positions in which they will actually be deployed in combat.

SIU NIM TAU FORM

The photos on the next few pages reflect portions of the first section of the Hung Fa Yi Siu Nim Tau form. It is, in itself, a masterpiece of efficiency. Every motion describes the Wing Chun Formula while simultaneously describing a specific combat application. Each is consistent with the actual employment of that application. Unlike popular Wing Chun forms of today, there are no superfluous or transitional motions. Consistent with the nature of Hung Fa Yi science, there is no wasted space, time, or energy.

Building a Spatial and Temporal Model of the Battlefield With Siu Nim Tau

Siu Nim Tau gives Hung Fa Yi practitioners the ability to use their own body parts as precision measurement tools for drawing a complete spatial and temporal model of the battlefield. This model enables visualization of battlefield height, width, range, and time to target, as well as angles of attack—both incoming and outgoing. Six specific pieces of information are needed to build this model and must be described through the body to maintain precision and consistency. These body motions and geometries, in essence, become the common language of Hung Fa Yi Wing Chun. They are perceived and understood the same by all practitioners and are not subject to the nuances and varied meanings that mere words conjure.

To build a proper battlefield model (also called "the combat setup"), the first piece of information required is a vector to target. Without this information, practitioners don't know where the enemy's vital strengths and weaknesses are. Neither can practitioners make range and height determinations for employment of their own weapons. In short, everything crucial to the potential conflict at hand is contained within the battlefield boundaries surrounding this vector, which in Wing Chun is called a centerline. A vector, in simple terms, is a line in space with directional intent. To draw such a line, one must first determine where it will start and where it will end. Hung Fa Yi practitioners orient themselves in the direction of their attacker and then root. The process of rooting and describing a vertical self-centerline (center of gravity line) accurately describes gravity (by using the body structure as a plumb bob and sinking the weight perpendicular to the root) and provides the anchor point for the origination of the vector (or centerline) to target. The endpoint of that vector can then be determined by orienting the self-centerline to the shortest distance track to the attacker's center of gravity, as shown in the following drawing (figure 6.1).

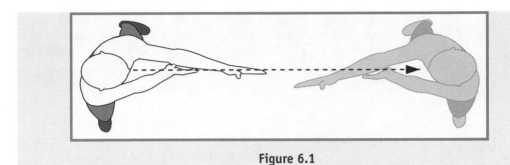

Figure 6.1

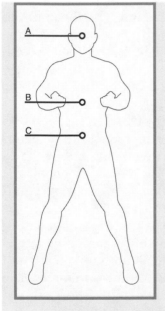

Figure 6.2

Additional battlefield information can now be efficiently discerned using the self-centerline and this centerline to target as a reference to the center of battlefield space. For instance, altitude can be determined by drawing the upper (called Yan Jung), middle (called Tan Jung), and lower boundary reference points (called Daan Tins) for weapons employment, as depicted in figure 6.2.

The maximum range of the inner gate is determined by crossing both hands at the wrist and extending them in a straight line from the middle bound to the outer lower boundary of the body centerline. Figure 6.3 reflects these structures.

The lower boundary is chosen for this description of range because it can be precisely described in space using the practitioner's own fist to describe the exact distance of the extended elbow from the body. Done this way, the full-range extension of the striking points also describes the distance from the body of the vertical plane in space called Mun Jong range, which represents the optimal starting point for firing range and the deployment of defensive forces. Hung Fa Yi always strives for simultaneous offense and defense. This means that the defensive hand must always be at mun jong range to retain simultaneous offense and defense. Additionally, the opponent's attack must be brought to Mun Jong range to facilitate simultaneous offense and defense. Any other positioning will leave one hand too long or too short for simultaneity.

The five-line concept using simple body motions like those expressed in figure 6.4 properly describes battlefield width and lateral positioning.

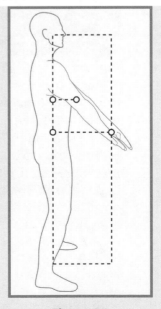

Figure 6.3

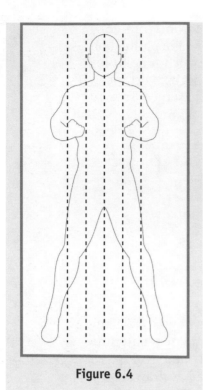

Figure 6.4

The five-line concept (explained in chapter 5) and pictured here is based on vertical lines that make precise lateral positioning on the battlefield possible. The drawings on page 80 depict these lines and their relationship to the upper and middle reference points and the upper gate. The lines themselves can be categorized as three Yang lines and two Yin lines. Two of the three Yang lines, also referred to as "zero lines," are located on the outer borders of the body at the tips of the shoulder bones. The third Yang line is called the "one line" or "centerline" and divides the body in half vertically. This line is considered the one true line of the body and covers many vulnerable vital points of human anatomy. The two Yin lines are located midway between the Yang lines and are sometimes referred to as the "nipple lines."

Hung Fa Yi also introduces the five-line concept in the opening of Wing Chun's first form, Siu Nim Tau. The arms are raised, fingers to eye level, palms down, on the centerline. This motion identifies the border of the body, which must be protected. Then, in a single motion, the fists are clenched and turned at a 45-degree angle, the elbow are aligned along the Yin line, and the knuckles are lowered to the locking position level. The elbows, pointing down, are kept one fist distance from the body and lined up with the Yin lines. When retracting the punch, Jang dai lik, or elbow sinking power, is developed by drawing the elbows back and out to the sides of the body, while never bringing the elbows closer than one fist distance from the body.

With centerline, altitude, range, and lateral references now clear, Hung Fa Yi's six gates (earlier described as the Hung Fa Yi equivalent of tactical radar) can be determined. These gates allow the practitioner to quickly map the opponent's line of attack, as well as structural strengths and flaws in terms of time and space. They enable the practitioner to literally read the opponent's attack and employ an appropriate counteroffense and simultaneous defense.

At this point, the practitioner's combat setup has offered a vector to target, critical altitude references, distance measuring information (range) for targeting, lateral references, and lines of attack information in zones that permit both interception of incoming forces and predictable results for the deployment of outgoing forces. The next crucial piece of information to be gleaned for a complete battlefield picture is initial weapons alignment (called Jong Sau, or "fighting hands").

Accurate alignment of weapons is now possible. Two initial alignments are possible: middle reference point Kiu Jong, with the hands aligned on the middle boundary (altitude reference) at the centerline (lateral reference), and locking point Kiu Jong, with the hands aligned on the locking position (altitude reference) at the centerline (lateral reference). In both cases, the horse (stance) must open to a side neutral posture incorporating the Yi Ji Kim Yeung Ma, Leung Yi Ma, and Lok Ma concepts referenced in chapter 9. The use of one rather than the other depends on the opponent's attack position and strategy, as well as the current elemental battle array for facing and pursuing (discussed in chapter 7).

The Kiu Jong complete the Hung Fa Yi practitioner's battlefield setup on the centerline. The practitioner has a position optimized for movement in all directions and which can most efficiently arrive at any of the six gates while maintaining a full range of response options. The practitioner is now ready to express the ability to move on the battlefield while retaining proper alignments that keep the battlefield picture intact.

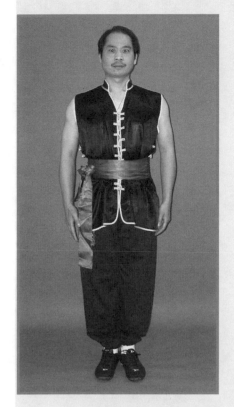

Neutral Stance

Kiu Jong on High Reference Point

Mun Jong / Triangular Position

Jaang Daai Lik

Yi Ji Kim Yeung Ma

Figure 6.5 Open horse.

Middle Reference point

Low Reference Point

High Reference Point

Triangular Position

Jaang Daai Lik

Figure 6.6 Drawing the height.

Wrist to Center

Triangular position

Yat Ji Chung Cheui

Chum Ging

Biu Ji Ging
Return to Triangular Position
(see above)

Jaang Daai Lik

Figure 6.7   Punching sequence on left side. Repeat the same on right side.

Taan Sau to Middle Reference Point, starting position

Taan Sau to High Reference Point

Huen Sau sequence

Huen Sau sequence

Triangular Position

Yat Ji Jeung

Figure 6.8 Taan Sau sequence. Repeat the same on the right side.

Wu Sau

Wu Sau to Middle Reference Point

Fuk Sau

Fuk Sau

Ching Gum Sau to Low Reference Point

Tahn Sau to High Reference Point

Figure 6.9 Wu Sau/Fuk Sau sequence one. Repeat the same on the right side.

Paak Sau

Fuk Sau

Tahn Sau

Gan Sau

Triangular Position

Yat Ji Jeung

Figure 6.10 Daai Huen Sau sequence one. Repeat the same on the right side.

Wu Sau to Middle Reference Point

Paak Sau

Yat Ji Jeung

Huen Sau Sequence

Huen Sau Sequence

Triangular Position

Figure 6.11 Ending sequence. Repeat the same on the right side.

(continued)

Figure 6.11 Jaang Daai Lik (ending sequence continued).

Basic Battlefield Movement

Stance, mobility, and footwork are emphasized next in developing offensive striking comprehension. The footwork of Hung Fa Yi Wing Chun never advances the practitioner to a position of being nose-to-nose with an opponent. Advancing straight forward (nose-to-nose) gives the opponent an equal opportunity to attack and oppose force with force, thereby creating a head-on collision of speed and power. For example, if the opponent extends both hands from his body to the centerline, his arms create a triangle surrounding his center space. Advancing straight forward without angulation would bring the practitioner directly into the tip of that triangle, the point of its greatest strength. Rather than take this approach, the footwork of the Wing Chun system advances through angulation. Closing on an opponent at an angle gives the practitioner control over his own timing and his opponent's five lines. At an angle the opponent's five lines are facing away from the practitioner. To provide the needed mobility, the practitioner maintains an equal weight distribution in his stance throughout his stepping and bracing to effectuate the angulation and subsequent advancement.

Summary of Battlefield Setup (Six Gate Fighting Stance)

The total setup described in the previous paragraphs should now describe a gridlike vertical plane in space at mun jong range. This plane is, in essence, a box that bounds the Hung Fa Yi practitioner's search for immediate knowledge. The practitioner seeks to know everything there is to know about what happens inside that box. Like Chu Hsi, who used a bounded approach to greater learning, the Hung Fa Yi practitioner uses this box to remain focused on the immediacy of combat and seeks total knowledge and control of all that is lethal, rather than "chase" that which is irrelevant to lethality.

OVERVIEW: HUNG FA YI'S TWO-TRACK TRAINING SYSTEM

The widespread practice of today's Popular Wing Chun has resulted in numerous discussions of the proper name for beginning level knowledge and training. Some families and lineages insist that proper Western translation demands that this level be referred to as "Little Beginning Idea," while others propose that it is more properly called "Little Beginning Drilling." In the Cantonese language of southern China, this level is specifically called Siu Nim Tau in some lineages, which literally translates as "Little Idea Head (system)." Others are adamant that the correct name is Siu Lin Tau, which literally translates to "Little Drilling Head (system)." From a Hung Fa Yi Wing Chun perspective, both are correct, yet both are incomplete in their expression because they do not refer to training in the same way; nor were they intended to.

When Shaolin Wing Chun left the temple, its survival depended on its employment and use in the efforts to restore the Ming Dynasty to power in China. That employment had to fulfill a military purpose, specifically in terms of guerilla type warfare and special operations of an insurgent nature. For most combatants, lengthy training times were not possible. Training of skills had to focus on specific threats and specific missions. Out of necessity, two different approaches to training were required. One fulfilled the needs of the actual trainers themselves, who required total knowledge across a broad spectrum of challenges, and the other addressed the needs of the trainees, each of whom may have required different skills and only those skills. Each represents a different approach to training with a specific military purpose attached to that approach. The Siu Nim Tau training track was employed to develop leaders who could reproduce combat warriors in whatever numbers were required. Out of military necessity, very few practitioners were trained to this level of knowledge. In contrast, Siu Lin Tau training was employed for the vast majority of practitioners who were expected to "produce" specific mission results on a battlefield that contained very specific threats. These warriors were expected to attain combat objectives, not "reproduce" fellow warriors. In truth, this is how military training has been approached for millennia by necessity. It is not a process unique to Chinese history.

The name given to the instructor's track of training was Siu Nim Tau. In essence, it focused on providing total technical knowledge of spatial, energetics, and temporal control of the hand-to-hand combat arena and was intended for leaders and reproducers of warriors. Included in the information constituting total technical knowledge were the philosophy of Saam Mo Kiu (three connecting bridges), representing the three stages of martial reality and the Wing Chun Formula with its one line (Baai Jong), two lines of defense (Jit Kiu), three reference points (Chum Kiu), five-line concept (Jeui Ying), five phases of combat arrays (Wui Ma), and six gate theories discussed in previous chapters of this text. Also included in the instructor's training track were additional principles of Yee Ji Kim Yeung Ma, Leung Yi Ma, Bun Yuet Ma, Saam Dim Bun Kuen, Saam Dim Yat Sin, Saam Dim Buen Geuk Jong, triangle theory, and numerous others that will be covered in this chapter. All constitute the technical knowledge base of Hung Fa Yi Wing Chun training. All build on one another to create a knowledge base that leads to the Weng Kiu (true focus) stage of martial reality. For example, the one-line concept gives the practitioner the core of human structure and balance. The two lines of defense, three reference points, and five-line concept theories give the practitioner three dimensions. Combined with Hung Fa Yi Wing Chun's triangle theory, all give rise to comprehension and efficient use of the six gates of offense and defense universal to human combat.

Although these principles, concepts, and methods are absolutely essential to training at the Siu Nim Tau technical knowledge level, they constitute an expense of human and time resources that cannot be militarily defended in terms of training guerilla tactics to combat special mission troops confronted with an express purpose and defined threat. Every troop does not need to know how to defend against every threat or every weapon. For example, on battlefields of 300 years ago, armies adopted the fighting style of their respective generals. Therefore, troops to be employed within the sphere of influence of any given enemy army needed strategies, tactics, and body skills tailored to the specific style or threat to be confronted. Likewise, troops engaged in guerilla activities required different skills than did troops engaged in large formation maneuvers with emphasis on specific weapons employment in support of other formations. A teacher with extensive technical knowledge could quickly create reaction drills and body mechanics drills that would counter specific threats without having to train troops for threats not anticipated in that same region or same mission objective. Since large numbers of troops are needed in a short time for production rather than reproduction, a simpler, more efficient training track is needed to produce effective fighters in four to six months.

Such a track is provided in Hung Fa Yi Wing Chun's Siu Lin Tau training. It was used 300 years ago to quickly train practitioners who did not require the knowledge to reproduce. It can be just as easily used in much the same way today. Siu Lin Tau employs body mechanics and reaction drills in conjunction with a clever structural heuristic called triangle theory to build true martial reality skills in warriors without having to train their mental awareness of how those skills were gained or could be replicated in others. It can be employed just as easily today to train effective self-defense regardless of the size or speed of the practitioner. That does not mean that speed and strength training are not needed. They will always enhance fighters' overall levels of confidence that allow them to remain calm enough to retain their structures and properly read the battlefield.

In summary, Hung Fa Yi's two-track training system fully addresses the military training imperatives of any specialized fighting force engaged in hand-to-hand conflict. Siu Nim Tau training provides complete technical knowledge for developing a few highly skilled and knowledgeable leaders and trainers. These leaders in turn can instantly assess the strategies, tactics, structures, and tools of the enemy and quickly develop or adapt body mechanics and reaction drills that build the necessary Weng Kiu skills into front line warriors. Siu Lin Tau training ensures that those same warriors are able to express the entire Wing Chun Formula in their bodies and weapons without the lengthy training time required to develop the in-depth knowledge possessed by their leaders and trainers. They are not, however, prepared to develop new drills or exercises to counter different threats. Nor are they prepared to reproduce other fighters. These abilities lie only within the grasp of the select few practitioners given full Siu Nim Tau track technical knowledge. Certainly, there are more advanced levels of Hung Fa Yi Wing Chun training (including the Chum Kiu and Biu Ji skill and knowledge levels addressed in the next three chapters of this book), but, under the guidance of skilled trainers, even Siu Lin Tau level fighters could be effectively employed in combat using weapons as well as hands and feet. This fact alone reflects the martial effectiveness and combat training efficiency of the Hung Fa Yi Wing Chun system. As such, it reflects the Chan (Zen) imperatives for reality, practicality, spontaneity, and completeness.

ONE SYSTEM TO COUNTER ALL THREATS

Before proceeding with Hung Fa Yi Siu Lin Tau drilling, it's time to answer the question, How can one system counter the threats from all other systems? The answer is not as difficult as it may appear at first glance. Orientation must shift from quantity to quality. The answer is not in the techniques. Any good fighter knows that techniques do not win fights. What enables a fighter to win is precision in timing and distance when employing a technique, regardless of which one it is. If two fighters throw simultaneous strikes—one a kick and the other a punch—and the puncher wins, good fighters do not automatically assume that a punch is superior to a kick. An experienced fighter knows that the puncher displayed a better sense of timing and distance awareness than the kicker. Hung Fa Yi practitioners describe this orientation as "directional." Without the six gate theory and the knowledge of the strategies and tactics for using it, the attributes of timing and distance awareness can never evolve to complete battlefield spatial and temporal control. They cannot become "dimensional."

The common denominators in any hand-to-hand conflict are time, space, and energy. The winner will always be the fighter who best controlled all three. Ultimately, directional fighters must always rely on speed and strength for success. Dimensional fighters, on the other hand, know how to alter space, time, and energy demands to control the speed and strength required. They also know that superior strength is irrelevant if a fighter refuses to engage it in the same plane in space that it is structured for. The six gates and the Wing Chun Formula enable dimensional fighters to alter battlefield time to jam and intercept from alternate planes in space. Likewise, these fighters know that superior speed is irrelevant if they refuse to travel the same path as their attacker. They know how to alter the shape of space so that the faster person travels greater distances to the target, thereby negating any speed advantage. Finally, since superior speed and strength are often encountered simultaneously, dimensional fighters know how to control both simultaneously. Hung Fa Yi's six gates and Wing Chun Formula give them the dimensional battlefield picture and alignment to accomplish this level of control. More important, these results can be duplicated on all attackers because the six gates and the Wing Chun formula are based on precise measurement of space and time, which allows for maximum force with minimum energy expenditure when weapons are released.

The information in the preceding paragraph is not new to military weapons designers. They are continually looking for ever more precise ways to measure the three dimensions of space and to alter it to provide the proper time for precision defenses and offenses. Martial artists have searched for centuries for ever-increasing control on the battlefield, but their orientation has most often been directional. As a result, their efforts have taken them down the path of developing greater strength, greater speed, and greater bone and tissue density. Prior to Hung Fa Yi development, they never approached the problem in the dimensional way modern weapons designers do. They never dreamed of dimensionally controlling space, time, and energy in the conflict arena. They assumed that such control could be had for a moment in time, but never retained throughout the conflict. This is precisely what is meant by the paradigm shift Hung Fa Yi's creators went through. They started believing that space, time, and energy control was not a matter of luck. It could be maintained throughout the conflict. They set about designing the structures, alignments, strategies, tactics, and drilling methods necessary to accomplish such control; Hung Fa Yi Wing Chun is the proof of their success.

SIU LIN TAU DRILLING

The express purpose of Siu Lin Tau's drilling is to give the practitioner three-dimensional awareness that is usable in combat. This purpose is achieved through repetitive drilling of basic motor functions followed by skill challenges or tests of the new motion's structural and temporal correctness. Proper drilling imprints the Wing Chun DNA blueprint on the practitioner, thereby enabling him to express the reality of three-dimensional space. For a teacher, this is done in two steps: receiving the idea (Nim) and then imprinting it with drilling (Lin). For the nonteaching practitioner, the process moves straight to drilling based on the triangle theory. Two general drilling concepts should be employed simultaneously for optimal results.

1. Drill for the proper cultivation of *Qi*.
2. Drill for the natural progression of learning, proceeding from conscious use of motion to subconscious response.

In the first drilling concept, practitioners develop their Qi through repetitious practice of Qi Gung exercises. Their internal prowess grows, thereby allowing them to move to a higher plane. They can experience a state of awareness above the normal realm of human experience.

When confronted with threat, three human responses are possible. The first is a constriction of response mechanisms due to "freezing." The second is to consciously think about the threat and generate a response triggered by conscious thought; this response is slow and predictable. The third is instant recognition of a threatening situation and a subconscious reaction resulting in immediate and proper response. The second drilling concept is oriented toward developing that third response.

Modern science gives us sufficient knowledge of the human brain and how it learns to enable us to appreciate why this type of drilling is the most efficient way to develop combat skill. Dr. Richard Chase, doctor of osteopathy and an avid Hung Fa Yi student, frequently emphasizes that humans can be thought of as having three brains: (1) physical, (2) emotional, and (3) intellectual. In Kung Fu philosophy, these are generally referred to as "body, spirit, and mind," respectively. The physical brain controls the body's internal environment and movement functions. The emotional brain represents the human equivalent of an alarm or warning sensor. It processes all sorts of external information that teaches the body how to get out of the way of danger. It responds the fastest of the three brains. The emotional brain learns by a process called conditioning. Fear is one of its output products. The third, or intellectual, brain is distinctly human. This brain can do what the others cannot—it can do things in a sequence, step by step. It enables humans to learn higher-order functions and things. Overall, the modern human brain learns by imitation. Watching and listening skills enable this imitation to occur. Martial arts employ these same input devices for imitation. With practice, the imitation becomes possible. With enough practice, the imitation becomes unconscious. In essence, it sinks from the intellectual brain into the physical brain. The conscious intellectual brain may now be turned to learning new imitations that can build on the previous ones.

The move from conscious brain response to physical brain response is quite important in the development of martial arts skill. The conscious brain is slow because it employs what is called serial processing—that is, one function is performed at a time and must be completed before another is begun. In contrast, the physical and emotional brains perform functions at a subconscious level. They employ parallel processing. In other words, multiple functions are performed simultaneously. These brains can even process information from the limbs about their position in space (called proprioception) simultaneously and without conscious thought, while generating immediate response. If no trained response is programmed into the physical brain, then, as Dr. Chase puts it, the default response is to freeze because of too much input from the emotional brain.

In essence, Hung Fa Yi practitioners learn a physical skill first consciously in the intellectual brain using step-by-step processing. With repetitive drilling, the basic movements become programmed into the physical brain and virtually immediate responses take over. The movements themselves are now freed from the slow intellectual brain processing and can be combined with other autonomic functions such as sensitivity to touch and release of energy. A much faster, coordinated response is now possible.

In light of the fact that the brain learns through imitation, there are inherent dangers to all involved in martial arts training. If a student watches incorrect motion in terms of time, space, and energy relationships or hears imprecise concepts or words, then the imitation will be flawed from the start. Similarly, the student can interpret what is seen or heard incorrectly, which will also result in flawed imitation. In most cases, bad imitations are a combination of both of these problems. The only real chance for creating good imitations of correct motions is through correct learning from proper face-to-face teaching. This is the essence of Hau Chuen San Sau. Knowledge in Hung Fa Yi Weng Kiu terms is only knowledge when it is exact and precise. Only then can the investment in drilling time be said to have paid off.

It now makes sense to identify some of the body mechanics drills employed by Hung Fa Yi Wing Chun's fourth-generation leader, Hung Gun Biu, to train combat troops. (As indicated earlier, the name Hung Gun means a high-level revolutionary leader given the responsibility for fielding fighters.) One example of Siu Lin Tau training under Hung Gun Biu began with finger, wrist, elbow, and punch structure development. The first exercise focused on moving the punching hand wrist from the centerline of the body to a reference point described by the triangle theory. An isosceles triangle is formed with the striking point of the fist forming the apex and the nose and diaphragm forming the root of the two equilateral sides of that triangle. Another triangle is formed by the elbow of the striking hand forming the apex with the two equilateral sides terminating at the centerline and the shoulder line on the striking hand side of the body. Once the reference point was mastered through drilling, the punching structure would be emphasized with the same drill, but the punch would extend beyond the reference point out to the upper gate (nose level) centerline.

The drills follow a logical progression from a stationary posture to an attack stance with the same structural drilling of the wrist-elbow-punch. This specific progression trains the body mechanics of moving into an opponent's space while maintaining proper risk management. Subsequent exercises incorporate the use of natural body weapons such as chain punches and strikes and, ultimately, exercises with partners to include Paak Da (redirect or punch), Gum Da (trap or punch), and so on. The nature of any technique or valid strategy or tactic can be trained through such drilling. For example, the nature of Hung Fa Yi Paak is to redirect up and down or left and right. All directions can be trained with this type of body mechanics drilling. Each exercise enables the trainer to drill the structural time frame of space into the body mechanics of the trainee without expending the time and resources needed to communicate and teach in-depth concepts, principles, and philosophies.

Following basic muscle motion through body mechanics training, tests are needed to ensure that true skill exists. For this purpose, teachers use skill and challenge exercises to determine whether trainees have reached the required combat skill levels. These drills employ specific counters to the strikes employed. These counters literally challenge the spatial and temporal control the strikes are supposed to exhibit. If spatial, energetics, and temporal control are real, the challenges fail. If the challenges succeed, then the trainee's use of space, energy, and time was illusory and unreal. Weaknesses are quickly identified and appropriate drilling is resumed to correct them. The ultimate tests of combat worthiness are the actual combat applications and their counters, and both are trained at every skill level in Hung Fa Yi Wing Chun. Because all exercises and drills reflect the reality to be employed in actual combat, retraining is not required and "deconditioning" of training methodologies is unnecessary. In essence, in Hung Fa Yi science, even the training methodologies must reflect an optimal use of space, energy, and time.

PROGRESSION OF SIU NIM TAU TRAINING USING SIU LIN TAU (DRILLS)

The following charts depict the matrix of drills employed to train the Siu Nim Tau skill level of Hung Fa Yi Wing Chun. Collectively, they constitute today's Siu Lin Tau program. When all three charts are arranged side by side, they form a completed matrix that supports training and development of each level building on the previous level in all directions. The matrix itself is a mastery of simplicity, efficiency, and directness in training composition. From the top down, the progression moves from long-range to short-range structures. From left to right, the matrices reflect a progression from beginning to advanced skill. For example, the Jong Sau hands and stance work in section 2 of the first level chart provide the base and structures necessary for training the concepts of the first elemental battle array, Baai Jong, referenced in section 2 of the second level chart. The exercises in the second level, in turn, develop the motion and structures for the live opponent training referred to in section 2 of the third level.

The Paak Sau section of each table provides another clear example of the matrix relationship between each corresponding exercise and learning level. The Paak Sau exercises first require the skill developed in section 2 of each table. They then provide a building block type of development for moving laterally across the tables. The Paak Sau exercises in the first table provide the groundwork for the paak sau exercises in the second table, but only after the previous sections of both tables have been properly employed.

Chart 1   HUNG FA YI WING CHUN KUEN
FIRST LEVEL—BLUE STAGE

I. Wing Chun (Dimensional Training)

1. Siu Nim Tau ("little idea in the beginning")—first section and applications
2. Jong sau
    a. Neutral stance (figure 6.12)
    b. Leung Yi Ma ("Two-element stance," figure 6.13)
    Three pairs: hip/hip, foot/foot, and hips/feet
    c. Bun Yut Ma ("Half-moon stance," figure 6.14)
3. Hei Gung
    Jaam Jong (standing structure)
4. Siu Lin Tau ("little drilling in the beginning")
    a. Stationary wrist, elbow, and punch
    b. Moving wrist, elbow, and punch with moving triangular theory
    c. Moving wrist, elbow, and triangle theory with lin waan kuen
    d. Moving wrist, elbow, and triangle theory, along with paak da (nature of paak and gum)
    e. Moving wrist, elbow, and triangle theory, and paak da above with partner
5. Jung Sin Paak Sau (applying your structure to outside, live elements)
    a. Punch and Paak, both partners
    b. One partner Paak, one partner punch
    c. Change from (b)—time factor introduced
    d. Change from (c)—time and space factors introduced
6. Fau Kiu Kiu Sau
    a. Kiu Sau facing, straight-arm touch (long bridge)
    b. Kiu Sau facing, bent-arm grab (short bridge)
    c. Kiu Sau facing, reaching for face (intercept)

Chart 2   HUNG FA YI WING CHUN KUEN
SECOND LEVEL—BLUE STAGE

I. Wing Chun (Dimensional Training)

1. Siu Nim Tau ("little idea in the beginning")—second section and applications
2. Jong sau with movement
    a. Chiu Min
    b. Deui Ying
    c. Chum Kiu

Figure 6.12 Leung Yi Ma

Figure 6.13 Bun Yut Ma (front view)

Figure 6.14 Bun Yut Ma (side view)

3. Hei gung and Siu Lin Tau Yi Sin Jong Sau (two-line structure hand)
    a. Faat Ging (releasing power)
    b. Yi Sin Jong Sau (two-line structure hand)
        i) Tan Sau, Biu Sau, Chin Gum Sau, Waan Gum Sau, Gan Sau
4. Kuen Jong (finding your own identity and applying your structure to an outside, dead element)
    a. Bun Yut Ma, stationary strikes (punch, palm, chop; see figures 6.15, 6.16, and 6.17)
    b. Leung Yi Ma stepping into Bun Yut Ma, strikes
    c. Jong Sau, moving strikes

Note: Kuen Jong exercises serve the same purpose as iron palm training.

5. Ng Sin Jong Sau and Paak Sau
    a. Chiu Min/Deui Ying
    b. Chiu Min/Jeui Ying
    c. Paak Sau skill challenge (from level one)
6. Chi Sau (standard Daan Chi Sau applying structure and getting feedback from an outside, live element)
    a. Harmony of three-dimensional space and striking point
    b. Striking testing
    c. Hung Jong
    d. Chi Jong
    e. Three reference points
    f. High gate challenge and single elbow challenge

Chart 3   HUNG FA YI WING CHUN KUEN
THIRD LEVEL—BLUE STAGE

I. Wing Chun

1. Siu Nim Tau ("little idea in the beginning")—third section and applications
2. Five elemental battle arrays for facing and pursuing
    a. Baai jong (first elemental battle array—setting up with live opponent)
        i) Chiu Min
        ii) Deui Ying
        iii) Chim Kiu
3. Hei Gung
   Sei Paai Da
4. Kuen Jong
    a. Po Jung Sau (setting up according to your opponent's structure and understanding the angle of attack)
5. Kuen Chuen kuen and Paak Sau
    a. Paak Sau (applying your structure to outside, live elements)
        i) Jong Sau / Paak Sau with Leung Yi Ma
        ii) Yat Ji Chung Cheui / Paak Sau with Leung Yi Ma
        iii) Yat Ji Chung Cheui / Paak Sau Alternating
    b. Baai Jong Paak Sau (close the distance)
        i) Yat Bou (Full Step)
        ii) Bun Bou (Half Step)
    c. Kuen Chuen kuen
        i) Punching Changes
        ii) Bak Fu Tiu Gaan – Huen Da
6. Saam Jin Bou (Three Battle Stance)
7. Chi Sau (dimensional daan chi sau applying structure and getting feedback from an outside, live element)
    a. Centerline
    b. Elbow line
    c. Shoulder line

When employing the preceding exercises, it is important to understand that each has a specific focus. A competent instructor will ensure that the student never loses this focus throughout the drills. The focuses of the first two levels of exercises are highlighted in the following two sections for purposes of illustration.

Focus of the Jong Sau Exercises

The focus of the Jong Sau exercises referenced in the preceding charts transitions through four key developmental stages. The first stage represents a Saan Kiu (awareness building) expression of Hung Fa Yi theory and upper body mechanics. As such, the exercises at this stage address only the upper four gates and employ only body mechanics for the arms.

The second stage also represents a Saan Kiu expression of Hung Fa Yi theory of whole body mechanics. The ability to change both footwork and handwork from the left side to the right side is emphasized in this stage. The Hung Fa Yi combat platform and fighting postures are studied in depth. This is where true knowledge of the concept of Leung Yi Ma (two-element stance) begins to take shape. Leung Yi Ma emphasizes the need to maintain both stability and mobility in close-quarter combat. Proper body root and weight distribution throughout the range of side-to-side combat motion are examined.

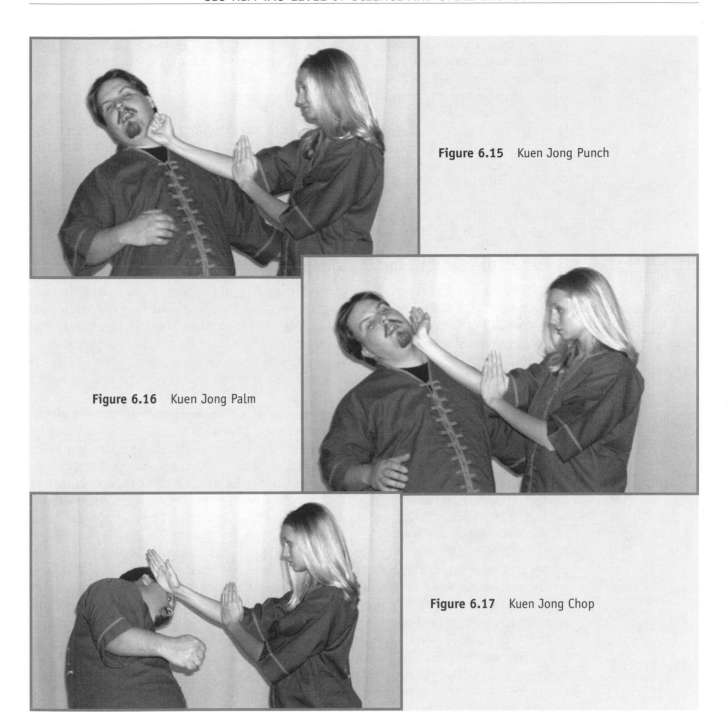

Figure 6.15 Kuen Jong Punch

Figure 6.16 Kuen Jong Palm

Figure 6.17 Kuen Jong Chop

The third stage of Jong Sau development focuses on building the ability to move forward while maintaining the six gates without spatial or temporal distortion. Both half-step (leading foot moves first) and full-step (back foot moves first) practice sets are employed. Ultimately, each is used in freestyle combination with a Biu Jong thrusting posture to intercept and break down an opponent's attack.

The final stage of Jong Sau represents a Weng Kiu (true reality bridging) of Hung Fa Yi theory through exercises focused on true skill challenges. This stage employs three distinct phases of progression. The first emphasizes knowing when to move and when not to move (based on distance awareness). The second phase focuses on total commitment (Biu Jong concept) to moving when the proper moment arrives. It ties energy, structure, and intent together. The third phase emphasizes retention of defense while simultaneously engaging in offense. It stresses the maintenance of the six gates structure while moving into combat space. Throughout these skill challenge phases, common mistakes are identified and corrected. Specific mistakes to watch for are (1) not penetrating far enough, (2) breaking formation (distorting the six gates), and (3) hesitating (a lack of total commitment). Overall development of physical and mental attributes properly applied in the right space at the right time should be the outcome of these skill challenge phases. To ensure optimum progression and results, the instructor should maintain the intensity levels of each drill for at least 30 to 60 seconds in each round. This intensity must be expressed both through body language and voice. At all times, personal focus must be on mental aggressiveness and determination. The practitioner is developing Hung Fa Yi's "heart of the tiger." A warrior does not give up!

Focus of the Siu Lin Tau Punching Exercises

Like the Jong Sau exercises just discussed, the focus of the Siu Lin Tau punching exercises progresses through several stages and culminates in a series of skill challenges that remove all illusion from the practitioner's awareness of true skill. The first five of these stages develop both body mechanics and technical knowledge. The sixth stage (skill challenge) develops physical attributes and provides experience with high-intensity, realistic challenges. It requires the practitioner to implement and integrate strategies and tactics with techniques.

The first stage of punch drilling focuses on developing proper wrist and elbow mechanics. Next, punch dynamics and "moving triangle theory" are examined by stepping with the body while practicing the drills. This is the same triangle theory that was examined in the discussion of Hung Fa Yi's two-track training system. At this same time, the concept of saam dim yat sin is emphasized. This concept reinforces maximum structural integrity by expressing the need to prevent the tailbone, elbow, and knee from intersecting on the same vertical plane in space when rooted.

The third stage of focus progression in Siu Lin Tau punching employs multiple punches (called Lin Wan Kuen or chain punching). Attention is targeted on developing and understanding the reactional power of punching. This stage is followed by the use of the Paak Sau in clearing the line. The intent of the line-clearing stage is to develop the ability to change and adapt structures and weapons in recognition of an ever-changing threat.

The fifth stage is called "fishing" (figure 6.18). The practitioner is literally trolling for an incoming attack. The exercise begins with a perceived threat from a single attacker requiring the practitioner to cover the gate from the outside. He trains to find the proper space and time for defense first while simultaneously setting himself up to launch an attack from a position of "high ground" (a position of structural and temporal advantage). The gate is cleared upon attack with the Paak Sau and simultaneously occupied with the opposite hand punch.

In truth, many "fishing" exercises and drills are employed in traditional Shaolin training that involve the use of arm energies to clear lines of attack to the body. These will be discussed in chapter 7 as the preparation stage for Chi Sau. These fishing drills and the attendant energetics training encompass a layer of learning and combat practice called Fau Kiu Kiu Sau, and are closely akin to the 18 Kiu Sau methods taught in Chi Sim Weng Chun.

The final stage involves two phases of skill challenges. In the first phase, three attackers assault the practitioner's defenses (one attacker at a time) from different

Figure 6.18 Maureen Mathews (right) and Tae Hayden (left) demonstrating the Fishing sequence.

angles. This develops a spatial and temporal understanding of where to position oneself in relation to multiple opponents. It also develops quick threat identification skills and reaction speed and structure to directional attack (involving one against three beginning from a neutral stance).

The second phase of skill challenge training involves dealing with three attackers simultaneously. This phase emphasizes the tactical importance of flanking and using an opponent as a shield. In essence, the superior force's attacking elements must be jammed so that full force cannot be brought to bear on a lesser force. It also stresses "all things in their proper time" by developing an understanding of when to move, when to strike, and when to grapple or throw. Finally, it develops an understanding of the differences among tactics, techniques, and the ability (an attribute) to change and adapt.

EMPLOYING THE TRIANGLE THEORY TO UNDERSTAND THE WING CHUN PUNCH

The triangle theory is a Wing Chun Formula derivative that makes Siu Lin Tau training possible. It enables total system effectiveness to be expressed in a single hand without having to train total system technical knowledge. Wing Chun Kung Fu is based on a system designed for one purpose—hand-to-hand combat! The revolutionary troops who used it, like today's elite special forces, had to be capable of defeating imperial soldiers possessing years of professional military training and combat experience. Only a complete martial arts system focused on human physiology and based on the principles of simplicity, efficiency, and directness—coupled with a fully integrated subsystem of training methodologies—could be expected to achieve these goals. Every movement of the hands and feet had to be coordinated with body unity and full body energy. At the same time, each movement needed to facilitate the direct application of fighting skills by enabling the fighter's ability to change and adapt. Consequently, every technique had to reflect the entire system by adhering to the same principles of simplicity, efficiency, and directness while contributing to the sole output product of the system—combat ability. The same can be said of the strategies and tactics needed to employ these techniques. The success of Shaolin Wing Chun as such a system is highly evident in one of its simplest, yet most elegant and effective, techniques, the Hung Fa Yi Wing Chun punch. This single technique clearly illustrates the principles of simplicity, efficiency, and directness. To fully understand this illustration, the underlying principles of body unity, the five-line concept, stance mobility and footwork, the triangle theory, and the six gate concept must be fully comprehended.

The Hung Fa Yi Wing Chun punch is considered by most experts to be the most effective hand-to-hand combat punch because it is the most direct (travels the shortest distance) and is supported by the entire body structure rather than just the arm and shoulder. In much the same way that a building is supported by a strong foundation, the body structure specified by the Wing Chun system provides the punch its maximal effectiveness. For this reason, prior to training for the development of speed, power, and sensitivity, Wing Chun practitioners first emphasize and train body structure and unity.

In forming the Wing Chun punch, the wrist is never bent. It is held straight so that the bones on the back of the hand are aligned with those of the wrist and forearm allowing for the strongest shock impact supported by the rest of the arm, body, and root. In contrast, a bent wrist engenders two major problems for a combat fighter: the risk of self-injury and the unintended dissipation of shock energy. The bent wrist is prone to impact-induced injury associated with the wrist bending back violently. Unintended dissipation of shock energy occurs when the bones are not fully aligned; upon impact, the energy from the punch travels in two different directions (one forward and one sideways). To further comprehend proper body structure and unity for supporting the punch, the practitioner must fully understand the five-line concept of Wing Chun. It is crucial to the execution of the punch.

The next important facet of Wing Chun punch comprehension is the use of the triangle theory in training for maximum effectiveness. Maximum power and support are generated via the alignment of body components in these inherently solid triangular formations. Multiple triangles are created in the opening movements of Siu Nim Tau. The first triangle is identified in the drawing on page 80. The points of this triangle extend from the tip of the shoulder to the elbow (on the Yin line) to the center (on the "one" line). The elbow must line up exactly between the tip of the shoulder and the one line.

By bringing the fists down and back along the centerline so that the knuckles line up at throat level, another triangle is created between the upper reference point and the middle reference point. The upper reference point is located between the nose and the upper lip. The middle reference point is located in front of the sternum. A third triangle is formed with the elbow, tailbone, and knee. Combined, these three triangles describe a properly held fist. When a force is applied to such a fist, the elbow, hip, and root support it.

The Siu Nim Tau form teaches the practitioner to keep the tailbone tucked in while punching so as to avoid leaning into the punch. The second point of support is the knee. The hip on the punching side is tucked in, and the toes of the same side foot point to the target, the opponent's center. The toes of this foot must parallel the fist's line to target so that the knee bends in such a way as to have the most effective support from the heel.

Testing the Punch Structure

The correct structure of the Wing Chun punch can be easily assessed. To test your own Wing Chun punch structure, have your partner start by having one palm over her other palm against your fist. Next, she should lean with all her weight so that she is on her toes and her back is straight. Any distortion in your punch structure, such as an outward turned toe (on the same side as the punch) or the elbow drifting outside the triangle, will result in an inability to support your partner's weight.

In throwing the Wing Chun punch (or open hand strike), the practitioner always attacks the upper gate, even in practice. The upper gate is also identified in the Siu Nim Tau form. The wrists are crossed like an × at the upper reference point (between the nose and the upper lip). The space above the elbows represents the upper gate.

Before the punch extends in Siu Nim Tau, the wrist is lined up in front of the sternum. The fist is held so that the bottom three knuckles create the striking surface. This initial position protects the centerline. If an opponent intercepts the punch early in its travel, the practitioner has two options. A stronger practitioner can overcome an opponent's weaker energy, while a smaller practitioner must adjust with footwork.

As the punch extends, it continues to the upper gate position (knuckles between the nose and upper lip). As this extension occurs, the entire forearm travels in a straight line, followed by constant direct support from the elbow. The elbow is continually lined up on the Yin line but never fully extended. By keeping one's elbow on the Yin line, one can easily intercept an opponent's inside attack with one's own forearm, no matter how fast that attack develops.

A smaller practitioner punching a larger opponent's body may not be as effective as desired. But the cheekbones, jawbones, and carotid artery, located at or around the upper gate, are fragile. A strike to the eyes will disable the opponent, resulting in an inability to see and, therefore, an inability to fight. A properly thrown Wing Chun punch to the cheekbone will collapse it into the sinus cavity, also causing loss of vision and mental focus. If a smaller practitioner punches low, the larger opponent protecting the upper gate can counter with a Saat Gang Sau (knife hand to the throat). Attacking the upper gate keeps the opponent occupied. The opponent cannot ignore the fact that an attack is aimed at his face. This keeps him on the defensive, and the practitioner retains the offensive advantage.

Executed properly, the Wing Chun punch allows even the small practitioner maximum punching effectiveness because it is supported by her entire body structure. The structure of the punch gives the opponent difficulty in countering with such common techniques as Biu Sau (thrusting hand) or Paak Sau (slapping hand). An opponent applying Biu Sau would have to uplift the practitioner's entire body weight to effectively break her structure.

The Wing Chun vertical punch is harmonious with the efficiency of symmetrical structures throughout nature. From simple elements (such as snowflakes and crystals) to highly evolved living beings, nature tends to create symmetry for maximum strength and efficiency. The Wing Chun vertical punch retains symmetry throughout its range of motion. Proper Hung Fa Yi footwork and body alignment enable perfect simultaneous employment from either hand with the least amount of motion and maximum impartation of shock energy.

From the initial emphasis on body structure, the Wing Chun practitioner advances into concepts dealing with time and space factors. With an understanding of time and space factors, speed and power become secondary considerations.

In Shaolin Wing Chun, as practiced and passed on to us by the Hung Fa Yi, techniques become an expression of the application of the system's concepts, principles, and theories. The precision of that expression is constantly evaluated using the sciences of physics and physiology in conjunction with body structure, and ultimately weighed against the all-encompassing principles of simplicity, efficiency, and directness. Thus we come full circle back to where we started. Such is the nature of any journey through a true system or any of its properly functioning subsystems. Wing Chun Kung Fu is based on the science of fighting and the absolute sciences of physics, physiology, and kinetics. It is supported by a highly structured training methodology that ensures that the practitioner derives maximum development of attributes from these sciences. Properly adhered to, the Hung Fa Yi Wing Chun system can replicate elite fighters who can readily demonstrate that the Wing Chun punch has the entire system behind it!

JONG TERMS AND CONCEPTS

The term *Jong* has many meanings and inferences throughout Hung Fa Yi training. Jong itself simply implies "pillar." A pillar is something with strong structure or substance. Jong takes on more specific meaning when used with other terms. Prior to beginning our discussion of Jong training, it is necessary to distinguish between the different terms associated with Jong.

Hung Jong (meaning "empty hand") specifically refers to motion and the attendant energies trained by oneself. Hung Jong is trained from three different types of experience. The first experience comes from initial Qi Gong training called Jaam Jong. It develops internal energy. The second experience comes from Faat Ging exercises that train how to properly release energies. The third experience comes from Sei Paai Da, which incorporates faat ging (whipping energetics) and Laap Da (jerk or punch) training. It specifically teaches how to react to energies—how to absorb and disperse them and how to give them back to the attacker. Hung Jong also incorporates shadow motion training. Simple Jong Sau and Kuen Jong exercises provide two such examples. Hung Jong Daan Chi Sau is yet another example.

Kiu Jong describes the setup of the hands and body lines at the first phase of combat. It reflects placement of the hands on the centerline and either the middle boundary or locking position depending on the opponent's position. Attendant with the Kiu Jong concept is the concept of Gei Jong.

Gei Jong represents mechanical ability (called Gei Nang) and reaction ability (called Fan Ying). For our purposes, they represent the motion and reaction ability to mobilize the hand. It is important to note that Gei Nang Fan Ying only happens at Mun Jong range. This gives rise to another important concept called gei fah luk mun, describing the result of training Gei Nang Fan Ying—that is, the ability to dissolve what comes into the six gates. By way of example, Daan Chi Sau is a Gei Jong training method. It should be noted that both Kiu Jong and Gei Jong employ the two-line theory—the concept of maintaining two simultaneous lines of attack and defense.

Mun Jong was expressed extensively in chapter 5. Mun Jong represents the distance of the "box" from the practitioner's body. Specifically, it is the range that allows simultaneous offense and defense. All incoming strikes and attacks are brought to this range for absorption, dispersion, redirection, or destruction.

Biu Jong represents the trigger point in the first phase of combat. It is the shooting out of the hands and footwork in the time frame between the Kiu Jong of Baai Jong (the first elemental battle array) and the Mun Jong of Jit Kiu (the second elemental battle array). Biu is translated as "shooting out with speed," and jong is translated as "structure." The purpose of shooting out with speed is to cover up the telegraphing motion often associated with bridging the gap between the practitioner and the opponent. Biu jong occurs when the space between the practitioner and the opponent reaches one palm distance between their respective asking hands when properly extended. This space allows for the most effective execution of biu jong because it allows for the practitioner's footwork and hands to be exactly positioned for economy of motion.

To bridge the gap between the practitioner and the opponent, Biu Jong is applied with the knee brought high to cover the middle and lower gates. Before the forward leg lands, it explosively attacks the opponent's lower gates, shooting in at an angle to minimize the opponent's ability to counter. Simultaneously, it sets up a flanking position.

The reader is advised that there are many more uses of the term Jong. Only those necessary for our purposes have been covered here.

KNOWLEDGE WITHIN KNOWLEDGE; METHODS WITHIN METHODS

Within the two-track training approach of Siu Nim Tau and Siu Lin Tau, Hung Fa Yi training can be further tailored from three different approaches. This is possible because the systems perspective of Hung Fa Yi reality enables the teacher to focus training on the unique mental and physical abilities of each student upon approaching initial training. Ultimately, this enables teachers to train troops quickly with specific backgrounds for specific missions.

The triangle in figure 6.20 reflects the three approaches that can be employed within the two-track training system. All three approaches lead to full system expression in the Siu Lin Tau–trained fighter and full system awareness in the Siu Nim Tau–trained teacher or leader.

The triangle is an excellent example of the Chan (Zen) belief that there are many roads to the same goal. In fact, Damo taught that enlightenment could be reached through many different activities leading to self-awareness and, ultimately, enlightenment. Specific to our purpose here, each point on the triangle in figure 6.20 represents a different entry point into Hung Fa Yi training, thereby permitting the Weng Kiu–level teacher to tailor the curriculum to each student's unique mental and physical abilities, as well as military imperatives. For example, a skilled martial artist with real military fighting experience would benefit most by approaching Hung Fa Yi training from the perspective of the five elemental battle arrays and strategy and tactics orientation. In contrast, a skilled grappler would sooner profit from the energetics and bridge control training of the layered Chi Sau progressions. Lastly, a person familiar with Saan Sau training, such as that found in Jeet Kuen Do, or a person frequently engaged in cross-training, might profit most from Saan Sau exercises designed to bring out Hung Fa Yi space, time, and energy control through body mechanics drills.

JONG CONCEPTS AND THEIR USE

The following section will present one of many examples of the System Approach from the five elemental battle arrays as approached through Jong Sau training in the Baai Jong or wood elemental array. The triangle chart in figure 6.20 references three Jong concepts employed within the systems approach. They are as follows:

1. Hung Jong (empty jong or energy self-development). Within this concept are three exercises: jaam jong (for qi gung development), faat ging (for energy release), and sei paai da (for qi gung reactional ability development—that is, lop da).
2. Kiu Jong (setup exercises, i.e., jong sau exercises)
3. Gei Jong (gate exercises, i.e., paak sau exercises)

The use of these jong sau in a systems approach is referred to as *Baai Jong Faat* (meaning "setting up methods").

Baai Jong Faat—Hung Jong

The first stage of training baai jong faat is hung jong. This is the stage of initial energy training. In essence, it is treated as a tool to develop the energies needed to protect one's own space while progressing to greater awareness of combat reality. Hung Jong training is also approached in three different stages: 1) Jaam Jong, 2) Faat Ging, and 3) Sei Paai Da. Jaam Jong is a standing Hei Gung exercise that awakens the Hei in the

Heaven

Man

Earth

Figure 6.19 The three postures of Jaam Jong shown by Allen Kong.

Dan Tin and begins circulating it throughout the body. Faat Ging takes the Hei Gung energies awakened in Jaam Jong and trains how to whip them through the hands.

The Sei Paai Da exercise represents the third experience of Hung Jong training. Its focus is on being able to withstand incoming energies while simultaneously releasing one's own attack. It represents the Hung Fa Yi equivalent to "Iron Shirt" training. When techniques such as Laap Da (jerking and striking) are added, Sei Paai Da summarizes a practitioner's ability to express power in combat under fire. The photos in figure 6.21 depict a Sei Paai Da exercise.

Systems Approach

Five Elemental Arrays
(Strategy and Tactics Approach to Learning)

- Hung Jong Exercises
  Three Experiences
  1. Jaam Jong Exercises
  2. Faat Ging Exercises
  3. Sei Paai Da Exercises (with Laap Da)

- Kiu Jong.... (i.e. Jong Sau Exercises)
- Gei Jong.... (i.e. Pak Sau Exercises)

Weng Kiu

Hung Fa Yi Skill
and Knowledge

Kiu Sau—Chi Sau—Saan Da

(Energetics approach to learning. This represents the entry point for total systems learning)

- Kiu Sau. (i.e., Hung Jong) Begins from any stance and becomes side neutral for redirection and counter. Trains both single- and double-arm bridge energies.

- Sup Ming Dim Chi Sau. (ten points of enlightenment). Incorporates 5-line, 3 reference points, and triangular theories with striking point technology.

- Joy Yeng Saan Da. Incorporates Chu Meen, Doi Yeng, and Chum Kiu.

Saan Sau

(Philosophic approach to learning; *not* system format)

Application oriented. Training applications within the Saam Mou Kiu philosophic framework without reference to Chi Sau's levels of development or the Five Battle Arrays of Combat.

Note: This particular training method gave rise to many of the Saan Sau systems that came later in history.

Figure 6.20 One example of the Systems Approach.

Figure 6.21 Fundamental training combining both Iron Skin and Faat Ging, simultaneously. 6.21*a* shows the set up, 6.21*b* shows the timing. The Dan Tin must be struck at the same time as the hands contact the partner's bridges.

Baai Jong Faat—Kiu Jong

The second stage of training in the Baai Jong Faat is Kiu Jong. This is the stage of initial battlefield awareness development. It involves setting up a position of maximum mobility and stability. It also involves stealing the opponent's time and space through proper angulation and structural alignment before he even attacks. If advance warning does not exist, combat could begin in the fifth elemental time frame of combat, Wui Ma, meaning recovering horse and position. Wui Ma involves protection of one's space and time while proceeding from a totally Fau Kiu battlefield posture to a Saan Kiu posture, and ultimately a Weng Kiu one (all of which could involve flowing to any or all of the other elemental time frames of combat). Below is one example of a Kiu Jong training scenario.

Advance Warning of Attack (Opponent Announces Intent Outside Bridge Range)

In this example, an opponent has taken a fighting posture. Baai Jong Faat training for action initiated outside bridging range involves footwork and hand alignment training that set up a position of maximum mobility and tactical advantage while giving the opponent as little information as possible about one's own abilities and strategies. This training focuses on gathering intelligence and using it while denying the opponent the same. Two kinds of footwork are employed to maintain mobility and tactical advantage. Chiu Min footwork, used outside bridging range, involves facing movements that enable risk management without announcing one's own intent. As the opponent nears bridging range, the second footwork, Deui Ying footwork, is used to keep facing correct by matching the opponent's positional adjustments, thereby denying him the opportunity to flank one's position.

Crucial to success at this stage of combat is the timely recognition of "Biu Jong" (go point or firing point). The Hung Fa Yi practitioner trains the precise moment in time to move so that simultaneous offense and defense are possible. Both Kiu Jong and Gei Jong exercises support this training. The photos in figure 6.22 depict Chiu Min and Deui Yeng footwork and positioning.

Figure 6.22 Setting up in Chiu Min facing and adjustment for different angles as shown by William Elliopulos and Jeremy Roadruck.

Baai Jong Faat—Gei Jong

The third stage of training in the Baai Jong Faat is Gei Jong. This is the stage of initial reactional combat skill training, also referred to as "Gei Ling Fan Ying" meaning "ability to react." One example of this training is the Jung Sin Paak Sau exercise. Step one of Jung Sin Paak Sau begins with each partner alternating Punch and Paak referred to as "Daan Paak Sau." The focus initially is on centerline and elbow position, learning to sink the elbow when encountering incoming energy. This focuses on learning proper structure and positions.

In step two of Jung Sin Paak Sau, one partner punches continuously, called Lin Waan Kuen, while the other partner applies only Paak Sau. This step addresses the issue of time. If a Paak redirects the punching hand downward, the second Paak hand immediately becomes a punch. The original punching partner must immediately convert his punches to Paak Sau and the exercise continues with each partner's roles reversed.

In step three of Jung Sin Paak Sau, called "Jeui Ying Paak Sau," both time and space are addressed. The set up is the same as in Step Two. However, as a Paak redirects the punching hand downward, the Paak Sau turns into a Punch. This application steals both the time and space of the person originally punching, allowing no time to counter the second partner's punch. At advanced levels, skill challenges are added to each of the above steps.

At the conclusion of Siu Nim Tau training, the Hung Fa Yi practitioner should have a true sense of self-identity. The Wing Chun Formula should be comprehended to a degree that the practitioner can effectively identify spatial and temporal needs from structural, positional, and energy perspectives. From the combination of exercises drilled, the practitioner should possess the experience necessary to engage in real battle and prevail. The foundational identity required for transition to the next level of system knowledge should be well established.

Fau Kiu Kiu Sau and the Five Elemental Battle Arrays for Facing and Pursuing are discussed in greater detail in the intermediate stage of learning (Chum Kiu) that follows in the next chapter. One final note is needed here. None of the above can be properly explained or comprehended without Hau Chuen San Sau ("one-on-one" or "face-to-face" teaching and real first-hand experience). The concept of "Bun Jyun" (a teacher instructing a disciple or true indoor student) is most important. "Who" the Bun Jyun "is" remains vitally important. His comprehension and communicative skills make the "experience" what it ultimately becomes.

Chum Kiu Level of Science and Skill Development

According to Hung Fa Yi Wing Chun lore the original term for the form (and level of learning) known today as Chum Kiu was *Ng Jan Chiu Min Jeui Ying*. The term *Chum Kiu* first came into use at the time of the Red Boat Opera. It was introduced by Hung Fa Yi leader Hung Gun Biu to known Red Boat players such as Wong Wah Bo and Leung Yi Dai. *(Note: Hung Gun Biu, himself, was not a member of the Red Boat Opera. He was an active leader of the Hung Gun Boxer Society. His contacts with the Red Boat were presumably for the purpose of fomenting and coordinating revolutionary activities. Many Red Boat Opera players were also active revolutionaries.)*

The original name Ng Jan Chiu Min Jeui Ying was replaced with Chum Kiu because it connotes much less meaning than the original term. For public use, only the "seeking the bridge" information implied by the term Chum Kiu was opened to public awareness. The deeper meanings of Ng Jan Chiu Min Jeui Ying remained hidden in the secret societies still engaged in revolution.

As noted in previous chapters, Siu Nim Tau is focused on developing one's own identity in terms of time and space, while simultaneously developing energies via Qi Gong training (called Hei Gung). In contrast, Chum Kiu (in its original Ng Jan Chiu Min Jeui Ying form) focuses on proper application of energy in accordance with strategies and tactics appropriate for current space and time. Ng Jan Chiu Min Jeui Ying provides the communicative tools for discussing and relating all three factors of time, space, and energy.

The term *Ng Jan Chiu Min Jeui Ying* is made up of two distinct phrases. *Ng Jan* refers to five time frames (Baai Jong, Jit Kiu, Chum Kiu, Jeui Ying, and Wui Ma) that make up the time factor of the time, space, and energy equation. It also refers to five elemental energies (wood, water, fire, metal, and earth) highlighted in a previous chapter that make up the energy factor. Chiu Min Deui Ying and Chiu Min Jeui Ying make up the space factor. In short, there are space considerations associated with each of the five time frames, and space is defined using the Kuen Kuit unique to each time frame. The coupling of a time frame, a space consideration, and an energy (along with proper strategies and tactics) constitutes an array. The arrays form the Ng Jan portion of Ng Jan Chiu Min Jeui Ying.

The second part of the term, *Chiu Min Jeui Ying*, deals with facing and pursuing. In short, Deui Ying and Jeui Ying develop according to the changes in energies or the Ng Jan portion. Overall, understanding Ng Jan Chiu Min Jeui Ying requires maintaining focus on the true intent of both halves of the whole term. They represent the true meaning and intent of what we have come to know as Chum Kiu.

Prior to beginning an examination of Hung Fa Yi Chum Kiu science, a basic concept of combat operations must be established. Several ground rules are delineated for this purpose. The first ground rule is: Never engage the opponent in the same plane in space in which he is structured to release weapons. If an opponent's energies at the bridge are forward in nature, then they may be redirected sideways or up and down, either directly via redirection or indirectly via the shape of one's own interception or attack. If the opponent's energies are sideways in nature, then they may be redirected up or down, again either indirectly or directly. Finally, if the opponent's energies are up or down in nature, then they may be controlled either forward or back, also either directly or indirectly depending on whether one's own action is defensive (redirection) or offensive (interception, jamming, or attack). This ground rule is often referred to in Hung Fa Yi as "efficient use of energy."

The second ground rule of combat operations is: Always assume the opponent's forces are bigger, stronger, and faster than one's own. This leads to "risk management" in military terms. Combat without risk management is nothing more than lucky strike release of weapons with the winner generally determined on the basis of biggest, strongest, or fastest. Proper risk management involves accurate battlefield depiction, correct threat identification, proper threat evaluation, and strategies and tactics designed to sweep threat from attack corridors, thereby permitting accurate and safe employment of one's own forces.

The third ground rule of combat operations is: Every stage of combat training must address risk management, and every stage of actual combat must employ sound risk management strategies and tactics. Every stage of Hung Fa Yi training incorporates extensive risk management strategies and tactics into each exercise drilled. In truth, the entire Wing Chun Formula represents the culmination of close-quarter combat risk management and battlefield control. The six gates themselves depict the relevant corridors of attack. Proper use of these gates enables accurate assessment of the attacker's strategies and tactics, ultimately allowing the Hung Fa Yi practitioner to literally take apart an incoming attack while simultaneously releasing lethal strikes to the attacker. This represents risk and battlefield management at their best. This ground rule is often referred to in Hung Fa Yi Wing Chun as "efficient use of space."

The fourth ground rule of combat operations is: Understand that all weapons are range dependent. No weapon is ever employed because it is a "favorite." To do so would imply that the opponent could be forced into a posture of cooperating with the exact space and time required to use that favorite weapon—an assumption only possible if the opponent were weaker, slower, or more gullible. This is a dangerous assumption to make on a battlefield. It lacks core requirements for risk management. Weapons are chosen only because they are the right tool for the right job, at the right moment in space and time. In any close-quarter fighting, four distinct ranges for weapons deployment can be identified. Table 7.1 depicts all four.

In addition to knowing the ranges of combat, a true fighter must also understand five basic laws for using ranges of combat. They are as follows:

1. Mobility gets you to the right place at the right time to apply the right technique.

2. Mobility does not occur in a vacuum; it has a reference—distance.

3. Range of combat determines the appropriateness of the technique—right distance; right technique; right time, space, and energy.

4. In hand-to-hand combat, a technique is finished when one makes contact with an opponent in the first two stages (kicking and striking range).

5. In the third and fourth ranges, technique begins on contact (trapping and throwing range).

Comprehension of these basic ground rules for combat operations allows a logical progression to begin examining the Chum Kiu level of Hung Fa Yi science and application. Said examination begins with an overview of Chum Kiu's purpose.

OVERVIEW OF HUNG FA YI CHUM KIU'S PURPOSE

Siu Nim Tau training stresses knowing one's identity by understanding space, time, and energy through one's own body and within one's own space. In conjunction with Siu Nim Tau identity, Chum Kiu puts that identity in motion with properly applied strategies and tactics within the greater arena of the total combat environment. That

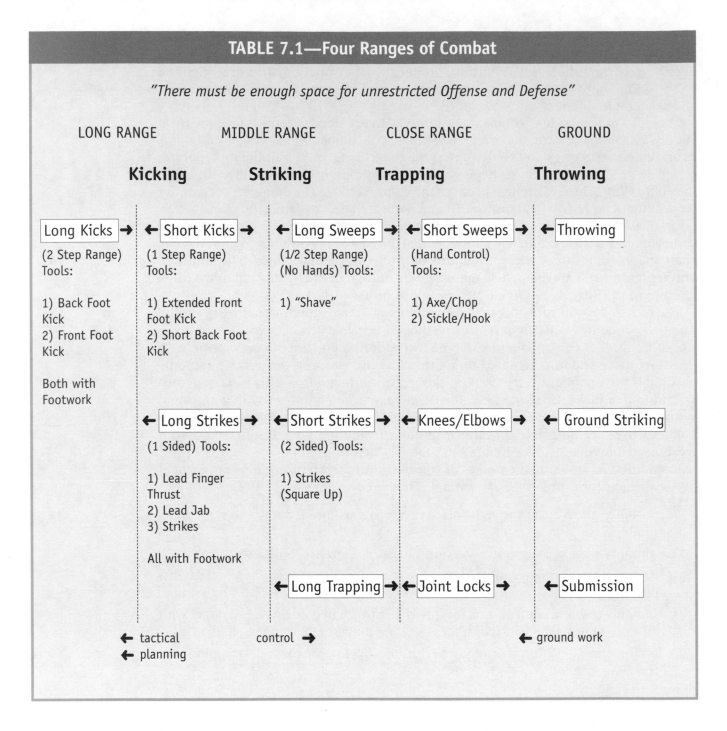

TABLE 7.1—Four Ranges of Combat

"There must be enough space for unrestricted Offense and Defense"

LONG RANGE	MIDDLE RANGE	CLOSE RANGE	GROUND
Kicking	**Striking**	**Trapping**	**Throwing**

Long Kicks →	← Short Kicks →	← Long Sweeps →	← Short Sweeps → ← Throwing
(2 Step Range) Tools:	(1 Step Range) Tools:	(1/2 Step Range) (No Hands) Tools:	(Hand Control) Tools:
1) Back Foot Kick 2) Front Foot Kick	1) Extended Front Foot Kick 2) Short Back Foot Kick	1) "Shave"	1) Axe/Chop 2) Sickle/Hook
Both with Footwork			
	← Long Strikes →	← Short Strikes →	← Knees/Elbows → ← Ground Striking
	(1 Sided) Tools:	(2 Sided) Tools:	
	1) Lead Finger Thrust 2) Lead Jab 3) Strikes	1) Strikes (Square Up)	
	All with Footwork		
		← Long Trapping →	← Joint Locks → ← Submission

← tactical   control →   ← ground work
← planning

environment includes one's own space, one's opponent's space, and shared space. Chum Kiu–level learning introduces and helps one master the footwork and combat strategies necessary to engage in bridge location and destruction. There are major differences between modern day Popular Wing Chun and Shaolin Wing Chun in terms of accomplishing these tasks. Popular Wing Chun is directional in nature with all emphasis on chasing and collapsing the opponent's centerline. Side-to-side and circular motions are, at best, greatly restricted. Consequently, footwork is primarily limited to short, powerful bracing motions. Shaolin Wing Chun footwork is far more complex because it must support both directional and dimensional natures.

Hung Fa Yi Chum Kiu trains six distinct footworks that allow the Hung Fa Yi practitioner to express and control the Six Gates of the Wing Chun formula throughout all five elemental battle arrays. They are (1) Yi Ji Kim Yeung Ma, (2) Leung Yi Ma, (3) Bun Yut Ma, (4) Wui Ma Deui Ying, (5) Wui Ma Jeui Ying, and (6) Ding Ji Ma. These footworks and stances are guided by concepts described earlier, such as Yi Ji Kim Yeung Ma, Leung Yi Ma, Bun Yut Ma, Lok Ma, Saam Dim Yat Sin, etc.

Overall, there are three main strategies for employing the Chum Kiu level of skill. All three directly affect the integrity of the opponent's centerline. The first involves attacking the five lines, or destroying the opponent's left–right orientation. This strategy is referred to as line destruction. In essence, it approaches the job of destroying the opponent's facing from a dimensional point of view. The second strategy involves attacking the opponent's three reference points, or destroying the opponent's up–down centerline orientation. It is referred to as center-of-gravity destruction. It approaches the task of destroying the opponent's body bridge from a structural point of view. The third strategy employs the concept of Loi Lau Heui Sung (retain what comes in and send off what goes—when pushed, pull; and when pulled, push) to attack the opponent's energetics, thereby directly affecting both mobility and stability. It is referred to as "destruction through cooperation of energies." Here the concept of "empty hand, continuous form" must be fully understood and fluidly trained.

Chum Kiu has two meanings derived from the same phonetic sound for Chum. Specifically, Chum can mean either "sinking" or "seeking." The main meaning of Chum Kiu (also properly called Man Kiu) is "seeking the bridge" with the opponent. Two important concepts are employed to train the footwork for "seeking." The first is called Yi Sau Daai Geuk (meaning "feet follow the hands"). It employs a "probing" hand to find a position of advantage before final positional setup for bridging. This concept emphasizes using the hand strike going into the battlefield with properly supporting footwork. An initial strike leads the body, and a second strike is delivered following proper repositioning of the body from the first hand's probe.

The second concept for properly training footwork is called Yi Gerk Daai Sau (meaning "hands follow the feet"). This concept employs the foot to probe for a position of advantage before taking a final position for bridging. As such, it trains employment of kicks or steps leading the body, followed by properly supporting hands. Correct angulation following the footwork is of utmost importance. The foot never lands where a kick started and never lands in the opponent's center. It lands such that the opponent's structures and weapons are always flanked. It should be noted that these two footwork concepts ultimately give the Hung Fa Yi practitioner a sense of focus on the battlefield.

"Sinking the bridge" is the second major meaning of Chum Kiu–level training and employment. This meaning falls within the context of the Five Elemental Battle Arrays for Facing and Pursuit called Ng Jan Chiu Min Jeui Ying. Within the concepts of "seeking" and "sinking" the bridge are 36 tactics for getting the job done. In other words, there are 36 methods of Chum Kiu. They are derived from six specific footworks employed differently for each of the 6 Gates.

Hung Fa Yi teaching varies according to the student's experience, performance and abilities, and different times and places. These variations were created to help different students. Many skillful methods are used with reference to practice (San Sau), principles (Hou Chuen), or both (Hou Chuen San Sau).

Many beginners can't integrate the multi-dimensional reality of Hung Fa Yi training in time, space, and energy and therefore feel uncertain or hesitant. An appropriate method of teaching in this case is Fau Kiu to Weng Kiu through progressive training by such means as introducing time without relation to space or time/space without relation to energy. Only when time, space, and energy come together in teaching and training is it considered Weng Kiu.

Although the teaching methods are many, all are interconnected. The different teachings start out as different approaches but each arrives at the others. The Hung Fa Yi three-track (chapter six) approach is an example of this nature.

Chum Kiu training can be approached with similar methods. For example, in only addressing the five time frames of combat, which is the time factor of Ng Jan Chiu Min Jeui Ying, the training is considered Fau Kiu. The five time frames are (1) Baai Jong (set up a position of maximum mobility), (2) Jit Kiu (intercept the bridge), (3) Chum Kiu (sink or destroy the bridge), (4) Jeui Ying (chase or pursue the collapsing bridge), and (5) Wui Ma (recover position/horse for further destruction if required).

When you can integrate and implement the information in the following table, only then are you said to be training at a Weng Kiu level for Ng Jan Chiu Min Jeui Ying.

Table 7.2 Ng Jan				
Time	Baai Jong	Jit Kiu	Chum Kiu	Jeui Ying	Wui Ma
Space	Chiu Min Deui Ying Chiu Min Jeui Ying				
Energy	Wood	Water	Fire	Metal	Earth
Kuen Kuit	• Mou Ying Da Yeng • Yau Ying Da Ying	• Chi Kiu • Fong Kiu • Laap Kiu	• Jung Sin • Ng Sin • Chum Jaang • Jaam Ma	• Lin Waan Kuen • Saat Geng Sau • Biu Ji Jin Bou	• Loi Lau Heui Sung • Bou Bou Jeui Bik • Kin Kwan Taai Heui, Lau Yam Fa Ming

Note: Most of the above Kuen Kuit have been explained elsewhere in the book. The following new terms are translated below.

- Fong Kiu: close of the bridge or jam the bridge.
- Chum Jaang: sink the elbow.
- Jaam Ma: destroy the knee.
- Jin Bou: challenge footwork in battle.
- Bou Bou Jeui Bik: continue pressing the opponent's footwork.
- Kin Kwan Taai Heui, Lau Yam Fa Ming: within the change of space and time, harmonize the yin and yang to regain superior position.

The many paths and adaptations of Hung Fa Yi Chan teachings, the different levels of difficulties (Saam Mo Kiu), and the doctrinal interconnections are usually ignored by people outside the Hung Fa Yi Wing Chun Family. Instead, people without clear information tend to make generalizations and think that all teachings are the same.

Since the teachings are similar, some think one particular way is the same as others. Therefore, some think that they don't need to study and practice extensively, which leads them to failing to grasp Hung Fa Yi completely. In Chan, this type of thinking is referred to as "abandoning the truth and taking only what one prefers, thinking that what one prefers is the truth."

On the other side, some praise a doctrine, a method, or a style thinking that the object of praise is the ultimate. They think they have everything and need nothing more. If this type of thinking is applied to Hung Fa Yi, the system will become narrow and dead.

In essence, those that are unable to integrate and organize Hung Fa Ying systematically will make the mistake of taking the parts for the whole. Those who understand and practice should guard against being confused or biased.

SECTION THREE OF HUNG FA YI CHUM KIU

The following photos depict a portion of section three of the Hung Fa Yi Chum Kiu form. They give the reader a flavor of the merger of footworks, energies, and tactics employed in the Chum Kiu time frame of combat.

Figure 7.1 Yi Ji Kim Yeung Ma

Figure 7.2 Gan Sau Yat Ji Jeung Leung Yi Ma

Figure 7.3 Gan Sau Yai Ji Jeung Leung Yi Ma

Figure 7.4 Faht Sau Leung Yi Ma

Figure 7.5 Go Laap Sau Wui Ma

Figure 7.6 Dim Geuk

Figure 7.7 Dim Geuk

Figure 7.8 Chum Sau Wui Ma

Figure 7.9 Go Kwan Sau
Leung Yi Ma

Figure 7.10 Go Laap Sau
Leung Yi Ma

Figure 7.11 Go Kwan Sau
Leung Yi Ma

Figure 7.12 Go Laap Sau
Leung Yi Ma

Figure 7.13 Go Kwan Sau
Leung Yi Ma

Figure 7.14 Go Laap Sau
Leung Yi Ma

Figure 7.15 Go Laap Sau Wui Ma

Figure 7.16 Laap Da Lok Ma

Figure 7.17 Turning Paai Jaang

Figure 7.18 Chum Jaang Dim Geuk

Figure 7.19 Chum Jaang Dim Geuk

Figure 7.20 Noi Jyut Sau

Figure 7.21 Tok Sau Dim Geuk

Figure 7.22 Tok Sau Dim Geuk

Figure 7.23 Bong Sau Waang Geuk

Figure 7.24 Jong Sau Leung Yi Ma

Figure 7.25 Faht Sau Wui Ma

Figure 7.26 Faht Sau Wui Ma

Figure 7.27 Gum Sau Yat Ji Jeung Bun Yeut Ma

Figure 7.28 Huen Sau Sau Kuen

Figure 7.29 Sau Sik

Figure 7.1 reflects the opening posture of the third section of the Hung Fa Yi Chum Kiu form. Figures 7.2 and 7.3 reflect the proper use of Gaan Sau and Gum Sau with appropriate footwork to enable a lower gate interception. Figure 7.4 reflects the proper use of Faat Sau and Paak Sau to enable a high gate interception. Figures 7.5 through 7.7 show the appropriate use of grappling immediately following the high gate interception with accompanying footwork and lower gate attack. Figures 7.8 through 7.14 depict movement from Deui Yeng facing to Jeui Yeng pursuit bu employing Bong/Laap while turning. Figures 7.15 through 7.17 show the proper use of the hip at close range while employing Jiang Dai Lik energy in a slicing elbow attack called Pai Jing. This elbow strike comes from a side angle to capture center via a 180-degree body rotation. Figures 7.18 and 7.19 follow the elbow attack with Paak Geuk and Dim Geuk kicks to the lower gate breaking the opponent's body and leg structure. Figures 7.20 through 7.22 demonstrate the correct use of Toc Sau to destroy an opponent's balance by breaking the arm while attacking the lower gate with a Dim Geuk kick. Figure 7.23 shows how to follow up the lower gate attack by chasing the opponent's position with a side kick. Figures 7.24 through 7.27 demonstrate the use of Faat Sau from an outside position to clear body lines through one's own opposite shoulder, then recapturing bridge energies back to center to enable a devastating palm strike. Figures 7.28 and 7.29 reflect the finish of this portion of the Chum Kiu form.

These motions actually reflect only one half of the third section of Chum Kiu. To complete this section, these same motions would be repeated in the opposite direction so that these applications are trained on both sides of the body. In all, there are five distinct training sections in the completed Chum Kiu form—each in turn repeating moves both left and right.

FIVE ELEMENTAL BATTLE ARRAYS FOR FACING AND PURSUIT

In Siu Nim Tau training, a myriad of three dimensional space and time tools were identified and trained. Chum Kiu takes these tools and merges them into five arrays (called Ng Jan Chiu Min Jeui Ying) that incorporate energies needed to support proper strategies and tactics for combat. The energy factor of the time, space, and energy equation is represented by the Five Elemental Energies (Ng Hang) of Chinese classical internal medicine (wood, fire, earth, metal, and water). Each of the five energies is represented by the element that most closely resembles its nature and function. Focus remains on the energy and its transformations. It must be emphasized that these arrays are not necessarily linear or sequential in nature. A Weng Kiu skilled person could proceed from any array directly to any other as time and space dictate.

First Elemental Battle Array: Baai Jong

In the elemental battle array, Chiu Min Facing is used to prevent lateral flanking by one's opponent. This type of facing involves squaring up on an opponent's leading foot while setting up the asking hand (Kiu Jong) with the opponent's changing hand positions (called Sau Ying Bin Fa). In contrast, Deui Ying matching is used to cut an opponent off from sideways attack when approaching the reactional time frame of battlefield space and time. A famous Wing Chun expression describes the focus at this time: Dik But Dung Ngo Dung, Dik Dung Ngo Dung Sin; meaning, "The opponent doesn't move, yet I move; the opponent moves, yet I move first." This really means that the practitioner recognizes the Biu Jong Go point and is prepared for immediate reaction.

In terms of energies, wood is strong and stable, yet capable of bending and swaying without overreacting or reacting too quickly. This is the foundational nature of combat in the time frame prior to bridging. It is a time frame for setting up positional advantage without giving away too much information to the opponent about one's intents or abilities.

To properly set up in the Baai Jong elemental array, one must first understand Kiu Jong (asking hand) and Mun Jong (guarding hand). Kiu Jong and Mun Jong are about knowing one's own identity before setting up. Ultimately, Kiu Jong is used for Deui Ying (matching), and Mun Jong is used for Jit Kiu (intercepting the bridge). Kiu Jong range involves searching or seeking, whereas Mun Jong range involves sinking the opponent's structure.

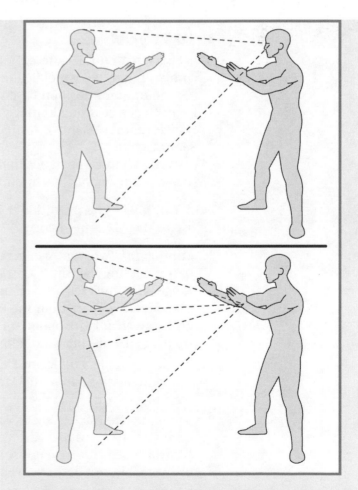

Figure 7.30 Top: Eyes watch the whole body; Bottom: The hands guard Heaven, Man, and Earth.

Kiu Jong has a saying: Kiu Sau Saam Gwan. It means, "The asking hand guards the three gwan." The three Gwan are the reference points: high, middle, and low.

Mun jong has a saying, Gei Fa Luk Mun, meaning that during the intercepting stage, one must have the ability to dissolve any incoming attack at any of the six gates.

In the first elemental battle array, the practitioner uses Chiu Min Facing to prevent lateral flanking and Deui Ying matching to prevent circular flanking. Some exercises for this stage can be done alone, and some require a partner. Exercises done alone are called Chiu Min/Deui Ying footwork. Exercises done with a partner are called Chiu Min Baai Jong and Deui Ying Baai Jong.

In accordance with the Chiu Min concept, the practitioner squares up on the opponent's front foot and sets up his asking hand to deal with his opponent's Sau Ying Bin Fa (changing hand positions) as follows:

1. Face the opponent's leading hand if it is on center. Face his leading elbow if his leading hand is off center.

2. If the opponent's hand goes higher, align your asking hand to the locking position. If the opponent's hand drops below the locking position, lower your asking hand to the middle reference point. Don't follow the opponent's hand lower. Don't chase his hand. Defense at the Kiu Jong range creates a distortion in time and space that leaves you too far away for a simultaneous strike and gives the opponent time to apply a fake.

3. Footwork:

   a. Use side neutral stances. Don't commit to any particular footwork outside of combat range. Stay mobile.

   b. Line up your position based on the closest structure presented by the opponent. Regardless of whether you use a closed stance (cross hands) or an open stance (parallel hands), form a triangular foot placement and apply Kiu Sau Saam Gwan.

   c. Parallel hands (open position) are good for defensive positions. If you are not sure of your opponent's intentions, it is safer to intercept from an open stance.

Deui Ying takes the practitioner into the reactional time frame. As a concept, it gives rise to the Six Gate theory.

1. Timing: *Dik But Dung Ngo Dung* is important here. It emphasizes the importance of not missing the Biu Jong trigger time frame. When you move into Deui Ying range, you must set yourself up to react immediately. The correct distance is one extended leg apart from the opponent's body. When this distance is reached, do not wait for the opponent to move. Attack first. Always keep your hands up in the Deui Ying time frame.

2. Applying Gei Fa Luk Mun: This means that you must not lose Mun Jong range or awareness of where the Mun Jong hand is. Likewise, be sure to maintain a scan of all six gates and sweep whichever gate indicates incoming motion.

3. Saam Mo Kiu can be used as a tool to analyze the current situation in relation to time and space. In Fau Kiu, you are either lucky or unlucky because you have control of neither time nor space. In Saan Kiu, you have control of either time or space, but not both. In Weng Kiu, you have control of both time and space.

4. When closing the gap, don't just pick up the leg and go in. Use a powerful kick when closing the gap.

Second Elemental Battle Array: Jit Kiu

The second elemental battle array is called "intercepting bridge" or Jit Kiu. In Popular Wing Chun, intercepting the bridge implies contact with the opponent. This is not the case with Hung Fa Yi. Intercepting the bridge from a Hung Fa Yi perspective implies the ability to both intercept and simultaneously occupy proper combat space, time, and energy. This only occurs when the opponent's arm bridge, leg bridge, or facing bridge is broken, and proper angulation results from the interception. It requires the right technique at the right moment in time. If the wrong technique is employed, Jit Kiu does not occur. In other words, "contact" is not Jit Kiu. It may merely represent the first phase of Jit Kiu. This phase is still considered "seeking," despite the initial bridge destruction, because the pressure from the opponent's arm or leg is being used in a second phase to determine and facilitate the Hung Fa Yi practitioner's own proper position in relation to space, time, and energy. In contrast to the first phase, in a second phase the opponent's body parts are now being used as precision measuring tools for further weapons alignment information. The third phase for employing "seeking" tactics is called the "positional bridge stage."

Jit Kiu requires footwork to engage. Specifically, the angle-in concept is employed. A practitioner should never Jit Kiu when squaring up (i.e., when nose to nose with an opponent). Jit Kiu requires adaptation and change of position to maintain center orientation while gaining a superior position. This phase of combat makes use of the Wing Chun idioms Loi Lau Heui Sung and two-line defense. The six footwork patterns of Wing Chun and Kiu Sau Bin Faat are also employed. Under Kiu Sau Bin Faat (bridge hands changing methods) are two additional concepts: (1) Sau Faat Bin Fa (change at the hand position, i.e., Paak to Tan) and (2) Jaang Daai Lik Bin Fa (change at the elbow position, i.e., tan to Bong). All of these concepts are employed as follows:

Figure 7.31 Jit Kiu

1. Chiu Min Jit Kiu / Sei Mun Chuen Sau— meaning, "hand through four doors."

a. The outside/inside parallel stance and outside/inside cross stances are both represented in single-hand Chi Sau exercises.

b. Chin Geuk: front kick. Once interception occurs, one checks one's position with this foot. If one can kick and punch with either hand, the positioning is correct.

2. Deui Ying Jit Kiu: One has to be able to sense another's energy and intent through vocalization or body language. In reference to the Five Elemental Battle Arrays for Facing and Pursuit, one can Jit Kiu before making contact. If one senses hostile intent, one does not stand directly in front of the potential attacker. Instead, one automatically moves to the attacker's side. This constitutes a Jit Kiu before the potential attacker has an opportunity to do anything and incorporates the above referenced three phases simulta-

Figure 7.32 Grand Master Gee demonstrating Chum kiu.

neously. It also serves as the best example of the energy dominating this time frame—that of "flowing." The water element is associated with this array because water's nature is to flow around obstacles and/or undermine them.

Third Elemental Battle Array: Chum Kiu

Within the third elemental battle array, there are five bridges that can be broken. Often the destruction of one results in the simultaneous destruction of one or all of the remaining bridges as well. These five bridges are as follows: (1) arm, (2) leg, (3) body, (4) centerline (center of gravity out, or shifting the opponent's attack to the upper or lower reference point with receiving energies, thereby stealing the opponent's stability and mobility), and (5) dimension (facing or five-line concept, which gives one the ability to select targets).

This array is most closely associated with the element of fire. Fire rages and consumes while destroying everything in its path. In a technical sense, this moment in time and space is not about exchanging techniques. It is about destroying an opponent's ability to use techniques from any position. Fire leads to metal in the destruction cycle.

Fourth Elemental Battle Array: Jeui Ying

This stage focuses on chasing and dominating a superior position on the battlefield. Jeui Ying capitalizes on any given moment following bridge destruction when an opponent presents a target wide open and signifying a position of weakness. Jeui Ying means to immediately chase that position of weakness.

Figure 7.33 Jeui Ying

This array is represented by metal. Jeui Ying proceeds to cut and hack an opponent's structure (metal cuts wood). Jeui Da is another term used for Jeui Ying when the pursuit involves hitting. It is generally employed when the opponent's center is forcefully broken allowing simultaneous pursuit and hitting.

Fifth Elemental Battle Array: Wui Ma

This elemental battle array involves repositioning the horse to regain Weng Kiu alignment and position. Practitioners who are caught off guard or in a bad position must recover their own space and time while maintaining safety. It is a tactical mistake to fight from a weak position. Wui Ma teaches that entrenchment is not viable from a tactically vulnerable position. Escape and recovery must be quickly employed instead.

Loi Lau Hoi Sung, Bo Bo Jeui Bik is an important idiom for the footwork of Wui Ma. It translates as follows: energy comes, make it stay, step by step press and pursue (energy). The earth element represents this array because earth absorbs energy. In this time frame, the Hung Fa Yi practitioner must be able to absorb incoming energy while regaining proper position and time frame.

It is important to note that some popular Wing Chun practitioners have suggested that there are five stages or progressions to combat. To translate Ng Jan Chiu Min Jeui Ying as Five Stages of Combat is to miss the essential nature of Ng Jan. Ng Jan is about proper tactics arrayed with proper time, space, and energy. The word *stage* denotes levels in a progressive sequence followed in an assumed order moving towards a higher level. In contrast, an array is a positioning or placement in an overall schema with a sense of overall order that does not denote sequential employment. Awareness of the five arrays is a tool to return to the reality of the moment rather than focusing on the illusion of a predetermined cycle. When training within the tactics and strategy track of Hung Fa Yi Wing Chun, movement and moment of a given exercise is guided by the five elemental battle arrays.

CHI KIU TRAINING

Chi Kiu represents the combined training of Kiu Sau and Chi Sau in Hung Fa Yi Wing Chun. They actually represent a separate training track for Hung Fa Yi Wing Chun. As such, they are not necessarily restricted to the Chum Kiu level of learning. They are presented in this chapter because they logically flow from the manner in which this information has been presented. The various forms of Chi Sau practiced throughout the last three centuries share some similarities, but also reflect significant differences, dependent upon which Wing Chun lineage a practitioner trained in. For example, Popular Wing Chun contains some of the technology present in Hung Fa Yi's striking point Chi Sau, but shares none of the Kiu Sau knowledge. In contrast, Chi Sim Weng Chun possesses all of the Kiu Sau knowledge, but shares none of the striking point technology. This is because striking point Chi Sau represents the militarization of Southern Shaolin Wing Chun's arm bridges for battlefield employment. It was created specifically to enable reduction of arm bridge circles (at specific time and space) to their smallest point of travel and to allow straight line action and interaction at the proper moment of space and time for ultimate efficiency in combat. Striking point Chi Sau does not negate the use or need for Kiu Sau. It augments Kiu Sau effectiveness at the proper space and time.

It should be noted that all southern Shaolin styles employ some form of Kiu Sau training. However, the other southern Shaolin systems flow logically from Kiu Sau to Kam Na (capture and control or grappling). This limits options on the battlefield because it ties up the hands and body and forces focus on a single attacker. In sharp contrast, Hung Fa Yi Wing Chun flows from Kiu Sau to Chi Sau first. This provides the Hung Fa Yi practitioner the opportunity to deal with a grappler by countering the grab rather than prolonging conflict by grappling in turn. It allows the Hung Fa Yi practitioner a much broader spectrum of immediate options and reduces risk by not limiting the practitioner to ground tactics. This is not to say that Hung Fa Yi does not possess Kam Na capability. In truth, it possesses very lethal Kam Na, but it may be employed at the proper time and place—that is, when the threat of multiple attackers is nonexistent or Kam Na may be applied with the speed and effectiveness of a lethal strike.

Employment of Kiu Sau, along with the presence of internal and external Hei Gung training and Chan (Zen) philosophy, explains why Chi Sim and Hung Fa Yi identify with southern Shaolin roots. Because Popular Wing Chun does not employ a majority of southern Shaolin footwork and Kiu Sau training (or Hei Gung or Chan philosophy training), it is easy to see why many modern day Wing Chun practitioners appropriately deny Shaolin roots.

In truth, the creation of the Hung Fa Yi Wing Chun Formula drove the creation of the three forms: Siu Nim Tau, Chum Kiu, and Biu Ji. It also drove the creation of striking point dimensional Chi Sau. Likewise, it is at all times reflected in the strategies and tactics employed in combat.

In short, centuries of arm bridge (Kiu Sau) training gave the monks a mastery of Kam Na (grappling), but when it came time to fighting on a battlefield, subduing an opponent was no longer desirable. Thus, striking point control science (Chi Sau) was created in such a way that Kiu Sau could lead directly into Chi Sau if one's Kiu Sau could be challenged. Grappling was no longer the next resort.

Within Hung Fa Yi Wing Chun, Chi Sau represents a complete evolutionary process that trains the practitioner to deal with energetics from the point of contact through all phases of combat to the point of sophisticated battlefield control. As with all Hung Fa Yi training methods, Chi Sau employs the Saam Mo Kiu concept throughout all phases of evolution. Kiu Sau (arm bridge) concepts are trained, as are single-hand, double-hand, and cross-hand concepts. All play a specific role in progressing from Fau Kiu to Weng Kiu skill and knowledge. Chi Sau itself incorporates three major stages (and many substages or layers) of development that, in essence, build the skill necessary for employing the energetics of all five elemental battle arrays. They include (1) Kiu Sau, (2) striking point Chi Sau, and (3) Jeui Ying Saan Da (the fighting stage of Chi Sau dealing with intermittent bridge contact—i.e., the strike becomes the bridge). It should be remembered that Hung Fa Yi employs both Kiu Sau and striking point Chi Sau training throughout the Siu Nim Tau and Chum Kiu levels of training.

KIU SAU TRAINING

As indicated earlier, the "wandering bridge" of Saam Mo Kiu philosophy is represented by Fau Kiu Kiu Sau. As such it represents the first of many layers of bridge training with an opponent. In truth, there are five major stages of Kiu Sau training, with Fau Kiu Kiu Sau representing the first stage. The other four stages are Deui Ying Kiu Sau,

Bong Laap Kiu Sau, Kwan Sau Kiu Sau, and Saan Da Kiu Sau. Kwan Sau Kiu Sau and Saan Da Kiu Sau represent live training with no prearranged sequence. This live training is not discussed here since it would require several chapters in and of itself.

Kiu Sau in Chinese means "bridge arm." Specifically, it focuses on the area from the wrist to the elbow. Hung Fa Yi Kiu Sau traditionally was developed against animal systems and to counter grappling systems. From a Hung Fa Yi three-track systems perspective the members start with the Kiu Sau and progress to Chi Sau and Saan Da. Hung Fa Yi makes a clear distinction between Kiu Sau and Chi Sau, whereas other systems do not. Other styles or systems of Kiu Sau have different meanings. Some Kiu

Figure 7.34 Kiu Sau training shown by Sifu Mike Mathews and Sifu Wayne Schulz.

Sau are used as a form of forearm conditioning. Some are primarily motions related to the techniques. Hung Fa Yi Kiu Sau is based on concepts and strategies. Kiu Sau ultimately relates to the employment of the Jit Kiu Elemental Battle Array. The Jit Kiu battle array deals with the time frame before hitting or sinking the structure of the opponent. During this time one can intercept or neutralize by redirecting.

The Saam Mo Kiu philosophy must be followed to efficiently develop the skills necessary to properly employ Kiu Sau. Initial training must focus on lau (flowing). The purpose of training at this stage is to develop the ability to deal with energy outside the box, in terms of both delivery and response. Footwork and structures are not defined at this point; gaining experience from sensing and flowing remains the sole focus of the exercises at this level. Once that experience is gained, focus changes to examination and drilling of proper body mechanics (footwork and structures). Following the experience gained from body mechanics drilling, skill challenges are employed to develop Weng Kiu–level knowledge of Kiu Sau. These skill challenges consist of attempts to grab, tackle, hold, push, pull, strike, etc. Ultimately, Kiu Sau enables the practitioner to bridge the gap with an opponent while simultaneously providing the first line of defense against surprise attack strikes, grapplers, and the employment of Kam Na (capture and control) techniques. Upon successful completion of skill challenge training, practitioners should be able to contain surprise attacks outside the box until they are ready to move inside the box. Kiu Sau should now enable practitioners to move inside the box at will where they begin to apply Chi Sau skills for destruction of their opponent's bridges.

Fau Kiu Kiu Sau

The first stage of Kiu Sau, Fau Kiu, reflects that moment in combat when the practitioner still has no available knowledge of elbow and yin line orientation. It happens outside the "box" defined by the Wing Chun Formula.

Fau Kiu Kiu Sau focuses on proper forearm energetics and shoulder-to-shoulder protection via mobility and motion. Three principle Fau Kiu Kiu Sau exercises are used in initial Fau Kiu Kiu Sau training and are referred to as the three time frames. Each represents a separate nature, or Kiu Sau in a distinct time frame. These exercises all start from the side because they represent the Fau Kiu nature of the attack scenario. In essence the attacker is coming from a blind side, so no battlefield picture has yet been drawn. Time, space, and energy awareness at this moment are nonexistent for the defender. Kiu Sau (arm bridge) offers a bridging hand for contact while maintaining distance for establishing the structure and footwork needed to build a proper battlefield picture via the Wing Chun Formula. In essence, Fau Kiu Kiu Sau constitutes a safety measure that gives the practitioner a "sense of reality" while building a complete awareness of combat reality (as defined by time, space, and energy).

Two of the most basic concepts are facing (the unknown) and position and structure (time and space). Kiu Sau means "arm bridge." Table 7.3 shows the original Kuen Kuit for Kiu Sau.

Table 7.3			
無	形	打	影
mou	ying	da	yeng
no	shape	hit	shadow

Mou Ying ("no shape") refers to possessing improper space or improper Fau Kiu facing. This means that no form or facing is in front of you. The direction of the attack or energy is coming from an unknown point of view. For example, you see it coming through the corner of your eye.

Da Yeng ("hit shadow") refers to the fact that if you don't have facing (i.e., there is no shape), you must find it. Da Yeng, in essence, is finding the proper space. Once you have Kiu Sau contact, you must align your Kiu Sau arm to the corner of your eye, much like sighting a gun. This is the proper space or angle that you are supposed to enter through. Da Yeng, or hitting the shadow, in this context refers more to hitting the mark of proper space as opposed to actually striking something physically.

Fau Kiu Kiu Sau, in essence, teaches proper positions and facing. It also identifies proper actions using the three techniques (Faht Sau, Gan Sau, Biu Da). For example, when someone grabs you, do you react with Faht Sau or Gan Sau? The Fau Kiu Kiu Sau progression teaches you to go from having no facing to having the proper space and facing.

The first Fau Kiu Kiu Sau exercise is called Faht Sau Kiu Sau. This time frame is from the touch (contact but no control) of an extended arm (longer distance) using Faht Sau as the proper action. The key is using the proper angle and extension of the elbow to hit the opponent's elbow, and engaging with both hands in the outside position.

The following photos depict Faht Sau Kiu Sau. In this case, the attacker's elbow is high. The defender recognizes the attacker's elbow position by feel rather than sight. The high extended elbow of the attacker exerts a pushing motion on the defender's shoulder (rather than a pulling sensation that would result from a bent and sunken elbow energetic). Defense involves long arm sweeping of the attacker's elbow, followed by setting up the body and footwork to allow Gan Sau sweeping shoulder to shoulder with the other hand. No initial attack or strike is possible yet because time and space (in this case, "range") are wrong. This particular exercise indirectly trains the "both hands on the outside" motion needed later for two-handed striking point Chi Sau.

Touch from the side

Faht Sau (Buddha Hand)

Gan Sau

Gan Sau on the other side

Roll to opposite side, one partner inside/
one partner outside

Figure 7.35 Fau Kiu Kiu Sau—Faht Sau against shoulder touch from the side. (Sifu Benny Meng demonstrates with Sifu Andy Kalish)

The second Fau Kiu Kiu Sau exercise is called Gan Sau Kiu Sau. This time frame is from controlling through grabbing with a bent arm (close distance) using the Gan Sau as the proper action. The key is when one's opponent is grabbing and pulling, one defender must establish a six gate structure to support a Gan Sau sweep of space to protect from a potential incoming strike. Another reason for using the Gan Sau is that the opponent has a bent rather than extended elbow that must be challenged with the defender's elbow also in the sunken position. The practitioner ends up engaging with an inside hand and an outside hand position. This time frame is more urgent than the first because of the control the opponent is starting to exhibit from initial contact.

Urgency demands that the the attacker's (opponent's) forearm is met with a shoulder-to-shoulder Gan Sau and swept to the low reference point while simultaneously striking with the second hand. The defender's strike is possible because time and space are correct. The attacker counters with a Gan Sau sweep of his own, setting up a rolling motion with each partner having one hand inside and one hand outside. Again, both are indirectly training the "one hand inside, one hand outside" motion required later for striking point Chi Sau training.

Grab from the side

Gan Sau while stepping out to Six Gate facing

Gan Da

Return to Kiu Sau rolling with switch

Figure 7.36 Fau Kiu Kiu Sau—Gan Sau against shoulder grab from the side.

The third Fau Kiu Kiu Sau exercise is called Biu Da Kiu Sau. This occurs when an opponent's arm or energy is coming in. One's Biu Da is employed as the proper action. The key is to establish the two elbow positions in front of the body supported by the Saam Dim Yut Sin structure. Reaching forward or overextending during the Biu Da is incorrect. The focus is not to hit the opponent, but rather to establish one's identity with proper space and time. One ends up with both hands on the inside position. This time frame is the most urgent. The action requires simultaneous attack and defense. In this exercise, the attacker has not yet made a bridge. The practitioner detects the attacker's motion via peripheral vision and executes a Biu Da from Bun Yeut Ma footwork. The attacker responds with Gan Sau sweeps from shoulder to shoulder. The end result is a rolling motion with the initial defender having both arms inside of the attacker's. This indirectly trains the "both hands inside" motion required for striking point Chi Sau training.

Attack from the side

Facing the threat with Biu Da

Kiu Jong engagement

Returning to the Kiu Sau flow

Figure 7.37 Fau Kiu Kiu Sau—Biu Da against sudden attack from the side.

(continued)

Switch to the other side

Figure 7.37 Fau Kiu Kiu Sau—Biu Da (continued)

During the three Kiu Sau exercises the time factor involves development of the physical attributes of timing and shifting (mobility). The footwork (angle) of Leung Yi Ma represents the time travel during shifting. The space factor is proper position and structure. The energy factor focuses on forward energy and projecting it to the opponent's center.

Deui Ying Kiu Sau

Deui Ying Kiu Sau takes place when an attack originates from a better position of awareness. The practitioner is already facing the opponent and has some awareness of the direction and severity of the attack. With proper facing, the practitioner focuses on how to enter the battlefield and bridge with the opponent. Here, we introduce a new concept often referred to as nose-to-nose facing.

Table 7.4			
有	形	打	形
Yau	ying	da	ying
Have	shape	hit	shape

Yau Ying Da Ying (see table 7.4) means that when one possesses facing, one should maintain it. One must learn how to enter with a six gate position and with both arms forward. This allows for the simultaneous application of attack and defense. Depending on the opponent's facing, one enters with a single or double arm. If one's opponent is facing with an open stance, a single arm entry may be used to engage the bridge. If one's opponent is facing with a closed stance, a double arm entry is required to engage both arms simultaneously.

Deui Ying Kiu Sau exercises teach proper use of stances and footwork. They drill entry with the front foot going from neutral stance to Bun Yeut Ma and Leung Yi Ma. Once proper entry and footwork is trained, then tactics are introduced with Bin Ma array for single-arm entry and Ji Ng Ma for double-arm entry. Deui Ying is complete when the tactics are combined with the proper entry and footwork. For the purpose of this exercise the person who is entering finishes with both arms on the outside.

Sequence One—Parallel Arm

Dead Side facing

Hitting the Shape on the Dead Side

Sequence Two—Cross Arm

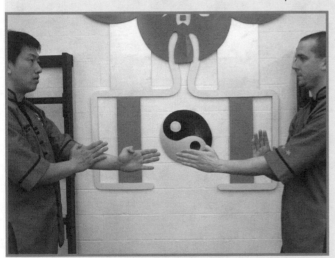

Live Side facing

Hitting the Shape on the Live Side

Kiu Sau Engagement

Figure 7.38 Deui Ying Kiu Sau demonstrated by Sifu Benny Meng and Sifu Jeremy Roadruck.

Bong Laap Kiu Sau

Bong Laap Kiu Sau follows the Deui Ying Kiu Sau. In other words, the exercise begins with the contenders already in a Kiu Sau posture. This exercise is primarily divided into two parts. The first part teaches the concepts of Deui Ying and Jeui Ying through three training steps. The first step refines the Kiu Sau skill of protecting one's inside space. This falls into the Saan Kiu level of experience because one already possesses the skill from the previous Kiu Sau training.

The second step involves moving from an inside position to an outside one. The outside position is obtained by going to Bong Sau. Once this happens, both partners must change to Bin Ma positioning to apply proper tactics. Having the proper position with tactics provides the proper conditions for the Deui Ying concept. Focus is on the mechanics of Bong Laap with the Deui Ying concepts. During the Laap the hands should not be too low because that creates a distortion and leaves the practitioner open for challenge. The centerline must be maintained.

Kiu Sau in Leung Yi Ma

Bong Laap in Bin Ma (both partners in front stance)

Other partner flows with the Bong Laap Sequence

Figure 7.39 Bong Laap Kiu Sau demonstrated by Sifu Benny Meng and Sifu Chango Noaks.

The third step focuses on the Jeui Ying concept. This means that practitioners are applying forward energy with their Bong Sau or their Jong Sau with Jaang Daai Lik. If Jeui Ying is successful, then it corresponds to the Chum Kiu Elemental Battle Array. Jeui Ying must advance with the front stance structure, which is Saam Dim Yat Sin. Another technical detail is that the distance must be maintained within the Kiu Sau position. If it is too far, the practitioner will be open to challenges with kicks.

The skill challenge develops the ability to have the proper Deui Ying to Jeui Ying. In Hung Fa Yi, this point in training is used to develop the skill to engage energy head on by meeting it with structural force. This is the ability to express Jeui Ying with force. The second ability required at the end of part one training is to be able to steal an opponent's time and space.

The challenge at this point is to do the following:

1. If the Bong Sau is under the opponent's arm, then extend to use Biu Sau.

2. If the Jong Sau is on top of the opponent's arm, then continue to press the advantage with a punch.

The second part of Bong Laap Kiu Sau focuses on the five-line concept and the change of dimensions. The exercises that make up the second part of Bong Laap Kiu Sau are as follows.

1. **Paak and punch to upper gate:** This teaches the use of the Paak Sau to change the line from shoulder to shoulder. One applies Paak and then punches an opponent with the same hand. The opponent covers the high gate with a Bong Sau. This step is referred to as line-to-line change.

Paak to Wrist

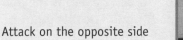

Attack on the opposite side

Figure 7.40 Bong Laap Kiu Sau Line to Line Change

2. **Recovery when Bong is lost or given up**: This begins when partner A applies Laap to the low reference point, taking away partner B's Bong Sau. Partner B then releases the Bong Sau structure while adjusting body position with footwork. At the same time, partner B brings the other hand up to Paak the upper gate through the shoulder line to protect against a punch to the upper gate. At this point partner B is expressing Yi Sau Daai Geuk (using the hand to lead the legs). Opening the hip is the key to proper footwork. Partner B applies a punch with the Paak Sau hand to partner A's center immediately. This is referred to as a dimensional change (from left to right, or high to low).

3. **Closing the sequence**: Partner B turns Paak Sau into Low Gum Sau (instead of applying the punch as described in step 2). Partner B uses the Low Gum Sau against partner A's low Laap Sau to finish the exercise and go back to two-handed Kiu Sau.

Laap to Low Reference Point, covered by Paak Sau

Punch to Upper Gate, covered by Bong Sau

Figure 7.41 Bong Laap Kiu Sau Dimensional Change

The second part of Bong Laap Kiu Sau develops the ability to have the proper Deui Ying to Jeui Ying movement. In Hung Fa Yi, this point in training is used to develop the skill to engage energy by redirecting it with line-to-line changing or dimensional changing, rather than meeting it head on. This also represents the ability to express Jeui Ying.

Table 7.5 describes the exercise sequence for training the Deui Ying to Jeui Ying movement and attendant energies. The concepts trained in each phase of motion are outlined. As all Kiu Sau exercises involve specific training in energies, they must be learned under the direct guidance of a competent instructor.

Table 7.5 Bong Laap Kiu Sau Dimensional Changing				
#	Steps	Concepts	Technique	Skill Challenge
	Part A			
1	Starts from Kiu Sau position	a) Yau Ying Da Ying b) Maintain proper distance	Bong / Kwan	Protect inside gate
2	Going into Bong / Laap	a) Inside Gate changing to Outside Gate b) Leung Yi Ma changing into Bun Yuet Ma tactics c) Creating a Deui Ying condition d) Deui Ying focus on proper structure supported by Five-Line concept and Saam Dim Yat Sin	Bong / Laap	Bong / Laap skill
3	Applying forward energy, chasing with front stance	a) Jeui Ying concept b) Good chasing creates Chum Kiu 1) Lose balance 2) Over Bong to Attack 3) Under to Biu or Attack		a) Jeui Ying to Chum Kiu b) Energy with energy
	Part B			
4	Paak Sau Chong Kuen	a) Line to Line change (change of dimension) give up Bong Sau b) 2 Positions 1) Line to line—Paak and punch, maintaining the upper gate 2) Dimensional change—Laap down and use the hands to lead the foot c) Not fighting force with force	Paak, punch footwork	a) Shift line and dimension b) Steal time and space
5	Finish or go back to Kiu Sau	Huen Sau going up or other partner too low Bong Sau		

Sap Ming Dim Chi Sau

Following Fau Kiu Kiu Sau training, Chi Sau training proceeds to the striking point technology alluded to earlier and enters the realm of Saan Kiu knowledge and skill development. Hung Fa Yi Chi Sau's formal name is Sap Ming dim Chi Sau, meaning "ten points of enlightenment sticking hands." The name itself is of Chan Buddhist origin. The words Ming Dim directly translate to "bright points" in Chan Buddhism and represent ideas or concepts that lead to enlightenment.

Daan Chi Sau (single-hand) teaches proper syllables (techniques) and body structures while developing proper energetics. Luk Mun Chi Sau (double-hand) teaches how to deal with five lines and six gates while simultaneously developing sensitivity. Saam Sin Chi Sau (three line) uses the high, middle, and low reference points to teach when to move and when not to move. Its primary focus is on learning the proper time frame in which to react. Jit Kiu Chi Sau (seeking bridge) teaches how to "move first."

Sap Ming Dim Chi Sau focuses on the five-line concept, the three reference points, and the two triangles employed in identifying the upper and lower locking positions on the centerline. Think of these 10 points of enlightenment as checkpoints for training. In essence, Sap Ming Dim Chi Sau is a concept that exists in everything a Hung Fa Yi practitioner does because it is the Wing Chun Formula in action. When viewed in this context, it is referred to as Kin Kwun Chi Sau ("becoming one with nature"). This layer of Chi Sau represents the "lab homework" learning that every practitioner must progress through. Ultimately, the goal is to express the harmony of space and time at every checkpoint throughout all ranges of combat motion. This lab homework is subdivided into three primary stages with many substages of training. The first (called Daan Chi Sau progressions) has three substages that teach how to deal with energies on the centerline (directional) and on the five lines (dimensional). The first substage is somewhat similar to the single-hand Chi Sau set reflected in today's Popular Wing Chun, but it places a much greater emphasis on striking point structures and employs some techniques not included in Popular Wing Chun. The second substage has no counterpart in Popular Wing Chun, nor has the third. To properly study and train requires face-to-face contact with the teacher. All three substages of Hung Fa Yi Daan Chi Sau are described in some detail here solely for the purpose of comparison with the simple Daan Chi Sau exercise employed today in Popular Wing Chun.

Daan Chi Sau Progressions

Stage I

Trains Tan, Bong, and Fuk structure and how to deal with side-to-side energies. It begins with the hands expressing harmony of three-dimensional space while each partner's hand shares the centerline of attack.

STEP 1

- The Tan Sau is held in locking position (halfway between the middle and high reference points).
- Both partners' hands are on the centerline, and their elbows are on the Yin line.

STEP 2

- Partner 1 gives forward energy toward the high reference point with a palm strike.

- Partner 2 responds by taking it down to the low reference point with Jat Sau.
- Upon completion, both partners' hands will be on the lower reference point (same orientation). The hands will be straight vertically with half points down and thumbs up.
- The elbows will be on their Yin line.
- The energy between the hands is balanced.

STEP 3 (FIGURE 7.42)

- Partner 2 now makes a fist and punches from the elbow, trying to scrape up into the other partner's boundary.
- Partner 1 responds by bringing an arm up into Bong Sau at the high reference point (wrist at the top lip, elbow at eye level).

STEP 4 (FIGURE 7.43)

- To shut the line back off, partner 2 transitions his punch to a Fuk Sau.
- Partner 1 reacts by changing his Bong Sau to a Tan Sau at locked position.
- The process is back to the original positions and now repeats.

Stage II

Trains elbow position—how to deal with forward energies. Five-line elbow.

STEP 1 (FIGURE 7.44)

- Partner 1 starts in Tan Sau, and partner 2 covers it with Fuk Sau.
- The Tan Sau is held in locking position (halfway between the middle and high reference points).
- Both partners' hands are on the centerline, and their elbows are on the Yin line.

Figure 7.42 Stage I, Step 3

Figure 7.43 Stage I, Step 4

Figure 7.44 Stage II, Step 1

149

Figure 7.45 Stage II, Step 2

Figure 7.46 Stage II, Step 3

Figure 7.47 Stage II, Step 4 shown by Sifu Savi Kruoch and Sifu Jason Walz.

STEP 2 (FIGURE 7.45)

• Partner 2 punches forward along the centerline from Fuk Sau.

STEP 3 (FIGURE 7.46)

• Partner 1 feels the incoming energy and responds by running to the outside.

• As partner 1 runs, he extends out to Kiu Jong range toward the opponent's elbow and then cuts back to center at Mun Jong range (horizontal dimension).

• Partner 1 then continues down to the low reference point with Jat Sau (vertical dimension).

(Note that after partner 1 runs, he is really catching partner 2 with his elbow, bringing the elbow back to Mun Jong range, and then bringing the hand down to the low reference point.)

STEP 4 (FIGURE 7.47)

• After partner 1 brings the hand down to the low reference point, he then makes a fist and punches from the elbow, trying to scrape up into the other partner's boundary.

• Partner 2 responds by bringing an arm up into Bong Sau at the high reference point (wrist at high reference, elbow at eye level).

STEP 5 (FIGURE 7.48)

• To shut the line back off, partner 1 transitions his punch to a Fuk Sau at locked position.

• Partner 2 responds by changing his Bong Sau to Tan Sau at locked position as well.

STEP 6 (FIGURE 7.49)

•From these positions, partner 1 can take a turn punching with partner 2 providing the appropriate horizontal and vertical response, or they can just continue the flow of the basic Daan Chi Sau exercise.

Stage III

Trains wrist position (maintaining contact point). Learn to move as soon as harmony is lost.

STEP 1

- Partner 1 starts in Tan Sau, and partner 2 covers it with Fuk Sau.
- The Tan Sau is held in locking position (halfway between the middle and high reference points).
- Both partners' hands are on the centerline, and their elbows are on the Yin line.

STEP 2

- Partner 1 takes Tan Sau to the high reference point on the centerline and then takes Tan Sau to the Yin line, still at the high reference point.
- Partner 1 turns the hand out and makes contact with the half point and takes the half point out to the Yin line at the locking position.
- Partner 2 stays relaxed in Fuk Sau and continues to cooperate with partner 1's energy.

STEP 3

- Partner 1 then strikes to the high reference point with the half point.
- Partner 2 continues to keep stick and Gan Saus to the Mun Jong high reference point with half point contact.

STEP 4

- Partner 2 takes half point to Mun Jong Jat Sau at the low reference point.
- Partner 1 relaxes and flows to Mun Jong Chum Sau at the low reference point.

STEP 5

- Partner 2 now makes a fist and punches from the elbow, trying to scrape up into partner 1's boundary.
- Partner 1 responds by bringing an arm up into Bong Sau at the high reference point (wrist at the top lip, elbow at eye level).

STEP 6

- To shut the line back off, partner 2 transitions his punch to a Fuk Sau.
- Partner 1 reacts by changing his Bong Sau to a Tan Sau at the locked position.
- Both partners are now back to their original positions and the whole series of motions repeats.

Figure 7.48   Stage II, Step 5

Figure 7.49   Stage II, Step 6

From a Saam Mo Kiu perspective, these Daan Chi Sau progressions represent the Fau Kiu level of Sap Ming Dim Chi Sau training.

Daan Chi Sau Initials (Challenges)

The Saan Kiu level of Sap Ming Dim Chi Sau training is reflected in the second major stage of training, called Daan Chi Sau initials. This is the level at which initial testing of energetics and striking point structures occurs. In concert with its Chan (Zen) roots, Hung Fa Yi Chi Sau allows no room for illusion. From a logic perspective, initial testing is best represented by ones and zeros. One either has control of time and space completely, or one doesn't. It is totally objective. Popular Wing Chun trains Chi Sau in a linear fashion that progresses in the manner of a, b, c, d, e, and so on. It is subjective in nature as to its success. No such subjectivity is allowed in the reality of Hung Fa Yi training.

The flowcharts on the following pages depict the many layers of Sap Ming Dim Chi Sau initials training.

The final stage of Chi Sau training uses both single-hand (in the form of cross-hand) and double-hand exercises employed within a "touch and go" framework. This level is referred to as Jeui Ying Kiu Sau. It employs all of the structures, energetics, and footwork learned previously to move toward the Weng Kiu stage of Saam Mo Kiu philosophy. For purposes of illustration and comparison, the charts on pages 153 through 163 depict single-hand cross-hand exercise flowcharts.

Again, these detailed flowcharts are not presented with the intent of teaChing the reader how to train Sap Ming Dim Chi Sau in the absence of face-to-face contact with a qualified teacher. They simply give the reader an opportunity to compare the depth of space and time knowledge and expression present in Hung Fa Yi Daan Chi Sau—a depth that is not present in Popular Wing Chun.

Fuk Sau Daan Chi Sau Initial Testing:

1. Noi Jat sau/reaction with High Bong Sau (initial energy going side to side)

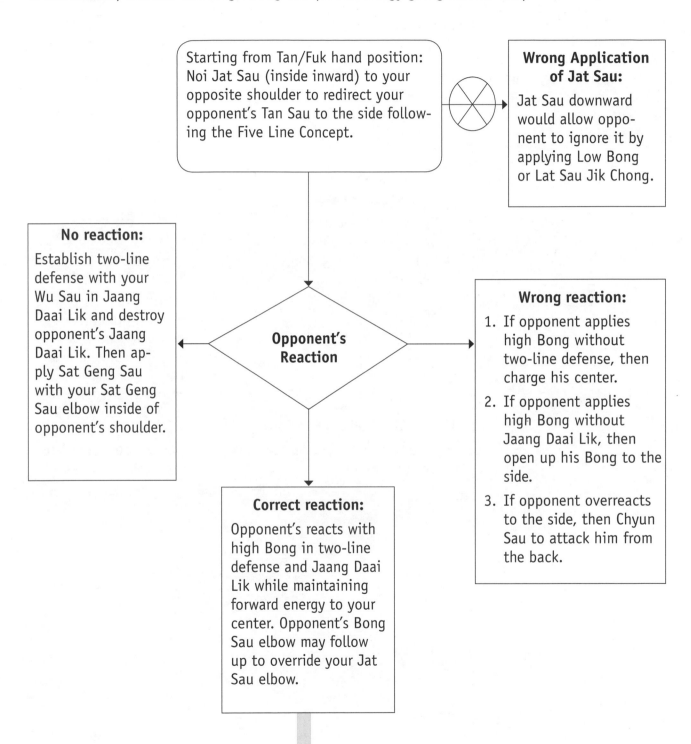

Starting from Tan/Fuk hand position: Noi Jat Sau (inside inward) to your opposite shoulder to redirect your opponent's Tan Sau to the side following the Five Line Concept.

Wrong Application of Jat Sau:

Jat Sau downward would allow opponent to ignore it by applying Low Bong or Lat Sau Jik Chong.

No reaction:

Establish two-line defense with your Wu Sau in Jaang Daai Lik and destroy opponent's Jaang Daai Lik. Then apply Sat Geng Sau with your Sat Geng Sau elbow inside of opponent's shoulder.

Opponent's Reaction

Wrong reaction:

1. If opponent applies high Bong without two-line defense, then charge his center.

2. If opponent applies high Bong without Jaang Daai Lik, then open up his Bong to the side.

3. If opponent overreacts to the side, then Chyun Sau to attack him from the back.

Correct reaction:

Opponent's reacts with high Bong in two-line defense and Jaang Daai Lik while maintaining forward energy to your center. Opponent's Bong Sau elbow may follow up to override your Jat Sau elbow.

Your Reaction?

No reaction:

Opponent will charge your center with his high Bong Sau in Jaang Daai Lik and override your Noi Jat Sau elbow.

Correct reaction:

Relax your hand and bring your elbow down to maintain Jaang Daai Lik, while maintaining contact with the back of your hand.

Go back to single-hand Chi Sau flow:

Opponent changes high Bong Sau to Tan Sau. Go back to Tan/Fuk.

Wrong reaction:

1. If your elbow is low as with Fuk Sau, opponent could react with Biu Jong to override with his Bong elbow.

2. If your hand is not maintained in a Fuk position, your opponent could open you up with Biu Sau.

3. If no two-line defense or foward energy, opponent's Bong Sau can charge your center.

4. If you try to open up opponent's Bong Sau to the side while he has Jaang Daai Lik, he can borrow your energy to apply Biu Sau or Hok Bong (with forward energy to your center) to open you up instead.

Fuk Sau Daan Chi Sau Initial Testing:

2. Downward Gum Sau/reaction with low Bong Sau (initial energy going downward)

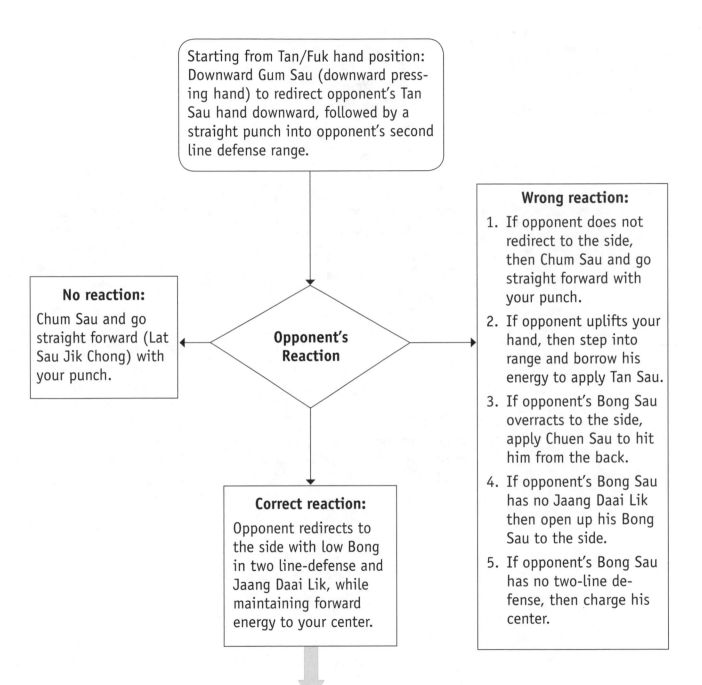

Starting from Tan/Fuk hand position: Downward Gum Sau (downward pressing hand) to redirect opponent's Tan Sau hand downward, followed by a straight punch into opponent's second line defense range.

Opponent's Reaction

No reaction:

Chum Sau and go straight forward (Lat Sau Jik Chong) with your punch.

Correct reaction:

Opponent redirects to the side with low Bong in two line-defense and Jaang Daai Lik, while maintaining forward energy to your center.

Wrong reaction:

1. If opponent does not redirect to the side, then Chum Sau and go straight forward with your punch.

2. If opponent uplifts your hand, then step into range and borrow his energy to apply Tan Sau.

3. If opponent's Bong Sau overracts to the side, apply Chuen Sau to hit him from the back.

4. If opponent's Bong Sau has no Jaang Daai Lik then open up his Bong Sau to the side.

5. If opponent's Bong Sau has no two-line defense, then charge his center.

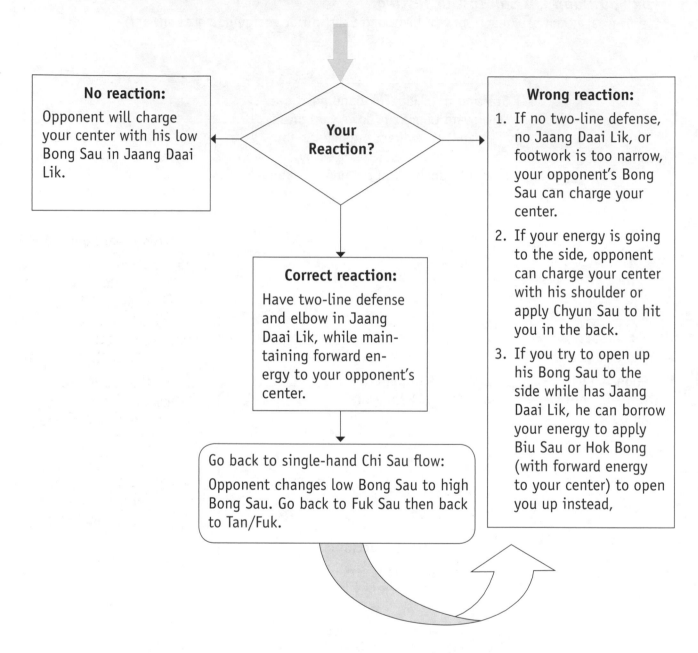

Your Reaction?

No reaction:
Opponent will charge your center with his low Bong Sau in Jaang Daai Lik.

Correct reaction:
Have two-line defense and elbow in Jaang Daai Lik, while maintaining forward energy to your opponent's center.

Go back to single-hand Chi Sau flow:
Opponent changes low Bong Sau to high Bong Sau. Go back to Fuk Sau then back to Tan/Fuk.

Wrong reaction:

1. If no two-line defense, no Jaang Daai Lik, or footwork is too narrow, your opponent's Bong Sau can charge your center.

2. If your energy is going to the side, opponent can charge your center with his shoulder or apply Chyun Sau to hit you in the back.

3. If you try to open up his Bong Sau to the side while has Jaang Daai Lik, he can borrow your energy to apply Biu Sau or Hok Bong (with forward energy to your center) to open you up instead,

Bong Sau Daan Chi Sau Initial Testing

Jaang Daai Lik Daan Chi Sau

Biu Ji Sau Jaang Daai Lik/reaction with Fuk Sau Jaang Daai Lik
(Jaang Daai Lik Chi Sau—Bong Sau Jaang Daai Lik and reaction with Fuk Sau Jaang Daai Lik)

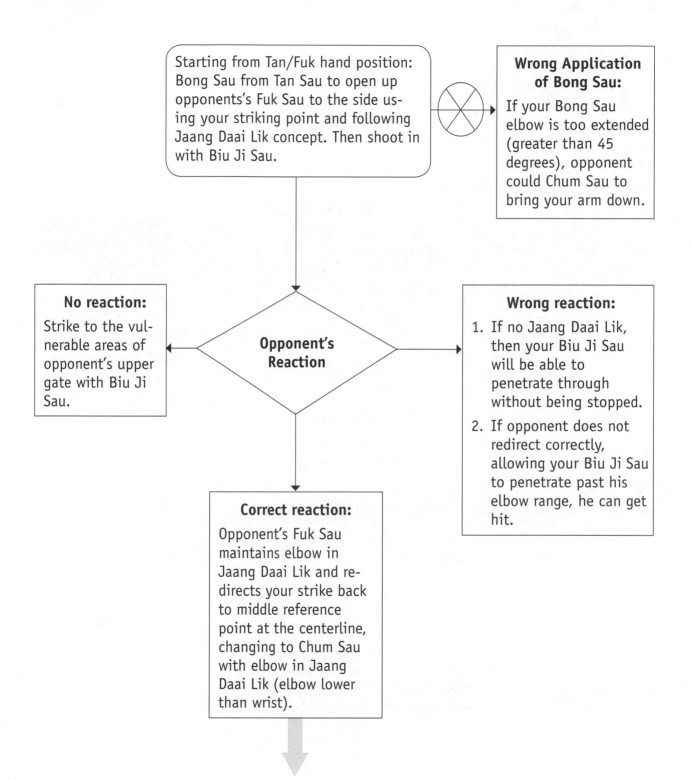

Starting from Tan/Fuk hand position: Bong Sau from Tan Sau to open up opponents's Fuk Sau to the side using your striking point and following Jaang Daai Lik concept. Then shoot in with Biu Ji Sau.

Wrong Application of Bong Sau:

If your Bong Sau elbow is too extended (greater than 45 degrees), opponent could Chum Sau to bring your arm down.

Opponent's Reaction

No reaction:

Strike to the vulnerable areas of opponent's upper gate with Biu Ji Sau.

Wrong reaction:

1. If no Jaang Daai Lik, then your Biu Ji Sau will be able to penetrate through without being stopped.

2. If opponent does not redirect correctly, allowing your Biu Ji Sau to penetrate past his elbow range, he can get hit.

Correct reaction:

Opponent's Fuk Sau maintains elbow in Jaang Daai Lik and redirects your strike back to middle reference point at the centerline, changing to Chum Sau with elbow in Jaang Daai Lik (elbow lower than wrist).

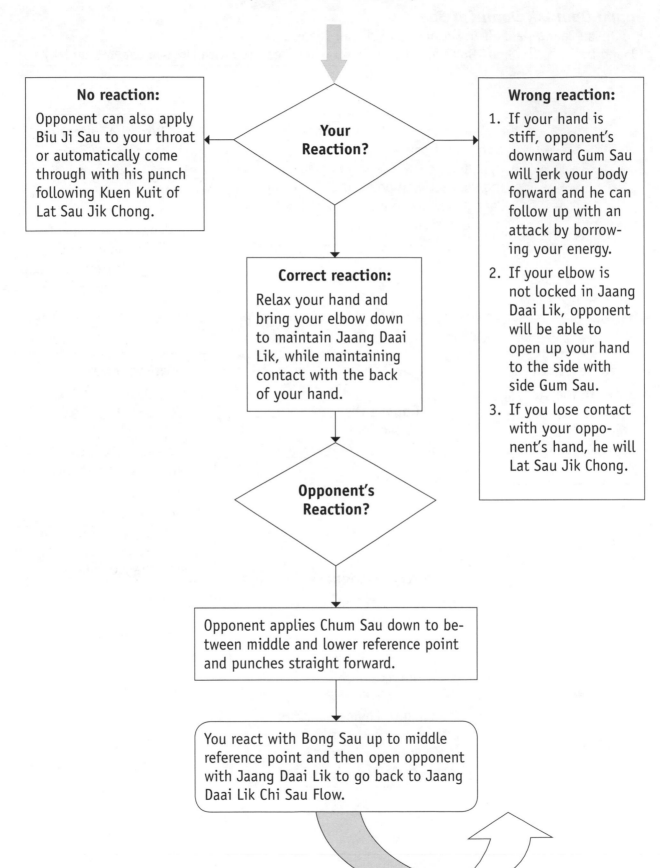

No reaction:

Opponent can also apply Biu Ji Sau to your throat or automatically come through with his punch following Kuen Kuit of Lat Sau Jik Chong.

Your Reaction?

Wrong reaction:

1. If your hand is stiff, opponent's downward Gum Sau will jerk your body forward and he can follow up with an attack by borrowing your energy.

2. If your elbow is not locked in Jaang Daai Lik, opponent will be able to open up your hand to the side with side Gum Sau.

3. If you lose contact with your opponent's hand, he will Lat Sau Jik Chong.

Correct reaction:

Relax your hand and bring your elbow down to maintain Jaang Daai Lik, while maintaining contact with the back of your hand.

Opponent's Reaction?

Opponent applies Chum Sau down to between middle and lower reference point and punches straight forward.

You react with Bong Sau up to middle reference point and then open opponent with Jaang Daai Lik to go back to Jaang Daai Lik Chi Sau Flow.

Tan Sau Daan Chi Sau Initial Testing:
Ngoi Jat Sau/reaction with redirecting in a different dimension (initial energy goes forward)

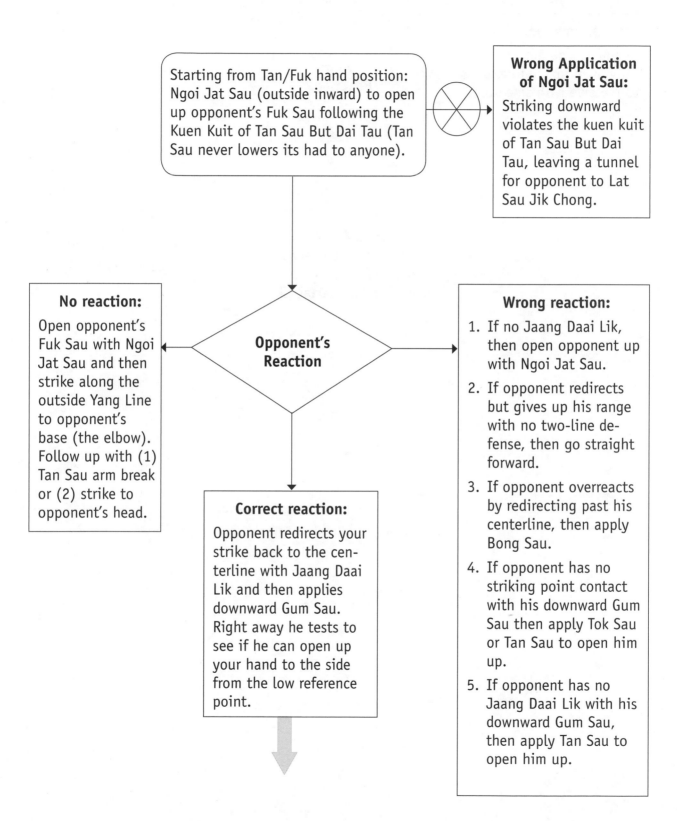

Starting from Tan/Fuk hand position: Ngoi Jat Sau (outside inward) to open up opponent's Fuk Sau following the Kuen Kuit of Tan Sau But Dai Tau (Tan Sau never lowers its had to anyone).

Wrong Application of Ngoi Jat Sau:

Striking downward violates the kuen kuit of Tan Sau But Dai Tau, leaving a tunnel for opponent to Lat Sau Jik Chong.

No reaction:

Open opponent's Fuk Sau with Ngoi Jat Sau and then strike along the outside Yang Line to opponent's base (the elbow). Follow up with (1) Tan Sau arm break or (2) strike to opponent's head.

Opponent's Reaction

Correct reaction:

Opponent redirects your strike back to the centerline with Jaang Daai Lik and then applies downward Gum Sau. Right away he tests to see if he can open up your hand to the side from the low reference point.

Wrong reaction:

1. If no Jaang Daai Lik, then open opponent up with Ngoi Jat Sau.

2. If opponent redireects but gives up his range with no two-line defense, then go straight forward.

3. If opponent overreacts by redirecting past his centerline, then apply Bong Sau.

4. If opponent has no striking point contact with his downward Gum Sau then apply Tok Sau or Tan Sau to open him up.

5. If opponent has no Jaang Daai Lik with his downward Gum Sau, then apply Tan Sau to open him up.

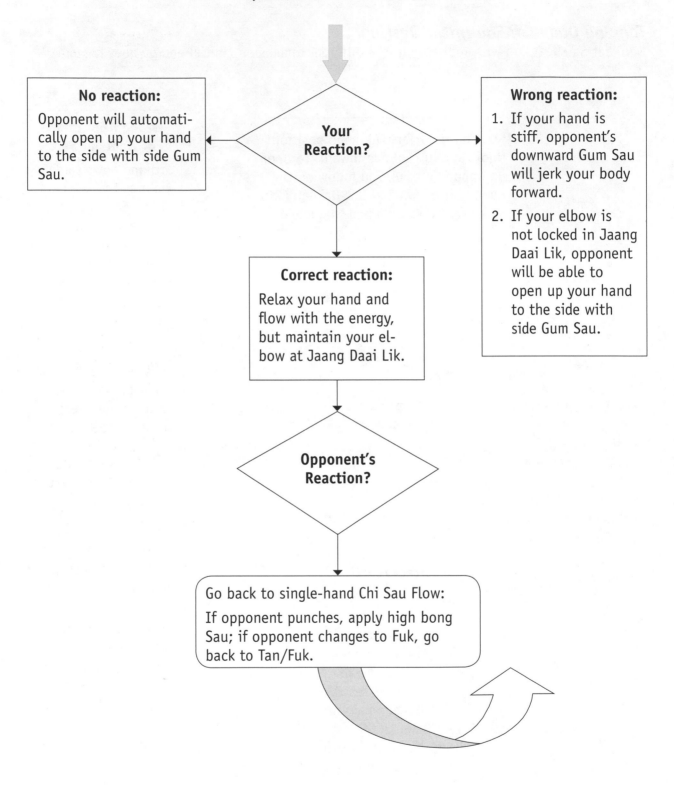

No reaction:
Opponent will automatically open up your hand to the side with side Gum Sau.

Your Reaction?

Wrong reaction:
1. If your hand is stiff, opponent's downward Gum Sau will jerk your body forward.
2. If your elbow is not locked in Jaang Daai Lik, opponent will be able to open up your hand to the side with side Gum Sau.

Correct reaction:
Relax your hand and flow with the energy, but maintain your elbow at Jaang Daai Lik.

Opponent's Reaction?

Go back to single-hand Chi Sau Flow:

If opponent punches, apply high bong Sau; if opponent changes to Fuk, go back to Tan/Fuk.

Biu Sau Cycle

■ = Partner #1

□ = Partner #2

Wrong:
Overreact, then opponent will Faht Sau to the inside

Wrong reaction:
Elbow not in Jaang Daai Lik, then opponent will open you up with Chuen Sau

Biu Sau with forward energy:
Potentially follow up with Gan Sau

Wrong:
In Deui Ying Ma, opponent can potentially apply high Paak Da or low Paak Da

Reset to high gate:
Saam Dim Yat Sin concept, forward energy, elbow in with Jaang Daai Lik

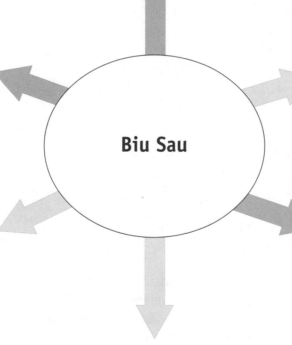

Biu Sau

Noi Bong Sau (inside Bong Sau):
Chiu Min Ma

Reset to high gate:
Saam Dim Yat Sin concept, forward energy, elbow in with Jaang Daai Lik

Laap Sau to open up opponent:
No stopping motion so opponent cannot Laap Saat Geng Sau

Tan da:
Deui Ying Ma

Laap Sau Cycle

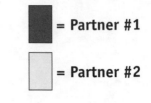

= Partner #1

= Partner #2

Wrong reaction:
Elbow not in Jaang Daai Lik, then opponent will open you up with Chuen

Laap Sau:
Maintain range, lop downward to the side

Reset to high gate:
Saam Dim Yat Sin concept, forward energy, elbow in with Jaang Daai Lik

Huen Jat Sau:
Turn your forearm, maintain your center, Chiu Min Ma, then Biu Sau

Laap Sau

Reset to high gate:
Saam Dim Yat Sin concept, forward energy, elbow in with Jaang Daai Lik

Gan Sau in Gate position:
Follow up with Biu Sau

Counter Gan Sau Huen Sau:
Outstretch opponent's arm with Gan Sau, Huen Sau should be able to stop both opponent's arms

CROSSING SINGLE HAND CHI SAU

Tan Sau Cycle

= Partner #1

= Partner #2

Wrong reaction:
Elbow not in Jaang Daai Lik, then opponent will open you up with Chuen Sau

Punch to high gate:
Saam Dim Yat Sin

Tan Sau with Deui Ying Ma in Gate Concept:
Six gates, five lines, attack range, Leung Yi Ma, Huen Jong, forward energy

Reset to high gate:
Saam Dim Yat Sin concept, forward energy, elbow in with Jaang Daai Lik

Tan Sau

Palm strike:
Saam Dim Yat Sin, striking point control

Reset to high gate:
Saam Dim Yat Sin concept, forward energy, elbow in with Jaang Daai Lik

Beginner level—Tan Sau with Chiu Min Ma in Bridge Concept:
Range defense

Advanced level—Tan Sau with Deui Ying Ma in Gate Concept:
Six gates, five lines, attack range, Leung Yi Ma, Huen Jong, forward energy, elbow tucked in

Wrong reaction:
Run away (no forward energy), tucked hip too far away then you cannot attack with low palm strike; open hip too far away, then you cannot attack with high palm strike

Tan Da:
Possible attack with low palm strike or high palm strike

If you overreact, then opponent will counter with Laap Saat Geng Sau

Biu Ji Level of Science and Skill Development

PURPOSE OF BIU JI

From the perspective of Saam Mo Kiu philosophy, Biu Ju represents Weng Kiu–level skill. It is here that everything trained comes into complete focus. Likewise, everything on the battlefield (including strategies, tactics, weapons, techniques, space, time, and energy) comes into complete focus. In short, Biu Ji brings the following three new layers of knowledge and skill to the practitioner's arsenal:

1. The proper use of 10 different elbow striking techniques in the upper gates and two also employable in the lower gates
2. Vital target and pressure point strikes
3. The ability to select specific target areas by destroying an opponent's dimension

Biu Ji exists specifically for developing the ability to employ both devastating power (i.e., elbow strikes) and precision strikes (i.e., thrusting fingers) with the least expenditure of resources. Training at this level requires that practitioners already possess the ability to recognize proper space and time for precision strikes. They must also be capable of breaking down an opponent's strongest defenses to enable precision striking. Possessing a fully realized self-identity from Siu Nim Tau training and the ability to destroy an opponent's attack strategies and structures from Chum Kiu, practitioners can now afford to focus on "the kill."

The Hung Fa Yi Biu Ji practitioner can identify the proper time of day for each strike, the proper striking point, and the proper energy required, and knows precisely what damage will be done to the opponent. This depth of knowledge and skill is frequently referred to as Dim Mak (meaning "death touch") in the Kung Fu world at large. Humans are highly evolved with very extensive neural networks that enable the use of higher-order intelligence. This is man's greatest strength and also one of his greatest weaknesses. Simply put, man's incredibly complex neural network cannot withstand the shocks that lesser-order life forms with less complex neural nets can handle. A single shock (via pressure point strike) to a complex neural net can immediately turn it off, either temporarily or permanently, depending on the net and the manner in which it is shocked. The knowledge of striking point science can fill a book in itself. Consequently, we will not deal with it in this broader text. It is sufficient for the reader to note at this time that Hung Fa Yi Wing Chun does incorporate extensive striking point science at this level of training.

HUNG FA YI BIU JI'S DEADLY ELBOW STRIKES

Hung Fa Yi Wing Chun is a complete combat system that fully employs all of the weapons of the human body, including fingers, knuckles, hands, forearms, elbows, knees, shins, heels, and feet. Hung Fa Yi is a science that fully understands human structure and trains to use each of these weapons with maximum efficiency and effectiveness. Table 8.1 depicts the 10 elbow striking methods of Hung Fa Yi Biu Ju training. The first four target the limbs specifically, while the remaining six deal with destroying the head or body structures, bones, and organs (figures 8.1 to 8.5).

	10 Methods	English Translation	Detailed Description
旋	syùhn	Inward turning	A horizontal spinning elbow strike from the outside to inside that targets the limbs
翻	fàan	Outward turning	A horizontal spinning elbow strike from the inside to outside that targets the limbs
壓	ngaat	Pressing	Normally employed as an arm break applied with continuous pressing force employing the upper forearm as the contact surface
撞	johng	Hitting	Explosive strike to the limbs employing the elbow bone as the striking surface
批	pài	Slicing	Horizontal hit to the body
橫	wàahng (side)	Side	Used specifically to hit bony areas of the body with the intent of crushing the targeted bone
摽	biu (also called Ji Ngh Jaang)	Forward centerline thrust	Elbow striking the centerline with forward energy
頂	díng	Backward centerline thrust	Elbow striking with reverse rotation
扱	käp	Downward hitting	Vertical downward striking to the body
提	tàih (raise)	Upward hitting	Vertical upward striking to the body

Table 8.1 Hung Fa Yi Elbows

Hung Fa Yi's 10 elbow methods contrast sharply with those of modern day Popular Wing Chun, which teaches and employs only three. Those three are employed laterally, vertically, and diagonally.

Figure 8.1 Limb Destruction

Figure 8.2 Head Destruction

Figure 8.3 Body Structure Destruction

Figure 8.4 Bone Destruction

Grand Master Gee demonstrates Biu Ji's elbow strikes with Daid Escarcega.

Figure 8.5 Organ Destruction

HUNG FA YI'S LETHAL THRUSTING FINGERS

Five different finger strikes are employed in Hung Fa Yi Biu Ji to engage a target from Hung Fa Yi's 10 dimensions. The first explodes downward employing whipping energy to hit a striking point from above (figure 8.6). The second explodes upward with whipping and thrusting energy. It is used to attack a striking point from beneath. The third is sideways and can be used from either inside or outside. The fourth is derived from the Bong Sau and thrusts inward for throat penetration. The fifth and final finger strike is generated from a Huen circle to the practitioner's opposite shoulder and is released downward to the opponent's center.

The first section of the Biu Ji form demonstrates the five finger strikes of Hung Fa Yi (figures 8.7 to 8.24).

Figure 8.6 One example of Biu Ji (downward energy).

Figure 8.7   Neutral Stance

Figure 8.8   Mun Jong/
Triangular Position

Figure 8.9   Jaan Daai Lik/Yi Ji Kim
Yeung Ma

Figure 8.10   Middle Reference Point

Figure 8.11   Low Reference Point

Figure 8.12   High Reference Point

Master Benny Meng demonstrating the first section of the Biu Ji Form.

Figure 8.13 Triangular Position

Figure 8.14 Jaang Daai Lik

Figure 8.15 Wrist to center

Figure 8.16 Yat Ji Chung Cheui

Figure 8.17 Biu Ju Downwards (#1)

Figure 8.18 Biu Ju Upwards (#2)

Figure 8.19 Biu Ju Sideways (#3)

Figure 8.20 Bong Sau Biu Ju (#4)

Figure 8.21 Huen Sau to Downward Biu Ju (#5)

Figure 8.22 Huen Sau to Downward Biu Ju (#5)

Figure 8.23 Face center with Triangular Position

Figure 8.24 Jaang Daai Lik

It should be noted that Hung Fa Yi also employs the single-finger phoenix fist for delivering strikes to vital pressure points.

HUNG FA YI COMBAT DOCTRINE

Combat doctrine provides a common set of understandings on which fighters base their decisions. It codifies accumulated wisdom and experience and provides a scientific framework for planning, training, and conducting combat operations. Doctrine must be both enduring and flexible. Hung Fa Yi doctrine meets all of these requirements. It constitutes a body of enduring principles and general scientific truths that provide guidance and a sense of direction regarding the most effective way to develop, deploy, and employ hand-to-hand combat skills.

Outline of Hung Fa Yi Combat Doctrine

I. Know oneself

A. Know one's space and train to maintain it (emphasizes range and simplicity).

1. The space one occupies
2. The distance from one's opponent
3. The environment

B. Know one's focus and train to keep it (six gates).

1. Continuously scan the corridors of attack
   a. Six gates
   b. Two-line offense and defense, three reference points, and five lines (three-dimensional perspective)

C. Know one's motion and train to control it (emphasizes centerline and directness).

1. Identify shortest distance to target when opening
   a. Centerline
   b. Straight line

II. Strategies and tactics (combat applications)

A. Five elemental battle arrays (Ng Jan Chiu Min Jeui Ying)

1. Prepare and set up (Baai Jong)
2. Surprise and intercept (Jit Kiu)
3. Destroy the enemy's ability to fight (Chum Kiu)
4. Pursue (Jeui Ying)
5. Reposition or recover (Wui Ma)

B. Thirty-six combat strategies of Chum Kiu

1. Six footwork patterns
2. Six gates
   (The above combine for 36 specific strategies.)

C. Battle array wooden dummy

III. Empty hand (Hung Jong) training (without partners or equipment)

A. Little beginning idea and drilling (Siu Nim Tau)

B. Seeking and sinking the bridge (Chum Kiu)

C. Master striking point science and the energies to use it (Biu Ji)

D. Twelve saan sau (Sap Yi Mo Kiu)

E. Incorporate all preceding knowledge into weapons employment

IV. Outside element (Chi Jong) training

A. Arm bridge (Kiu Sau)

B. Sticking hand (Chi Sau)

C. Sparring (Saan Da)

D. Green dragon or white tiger dummy (Ching Lung Baat Fu Jong)

E. Leg dummy (Geuk Jong)

F. Weapons training

   1. Double butterfly swords (Yi Ji Wu Dip Dou)
   2. Killing staff (Hung Mun Saat Gwan)

V. Hei gung and complementary training

A. Siu Nim Tau breathing sets

B. Heaven, Man, and Earth set (Hei Gung)

C. Whipping energy methods (Faat Ging)

D. Iron palm (Tit Sa Jeung)

E. Iron vest (Gum Gong Wu)

VI. History, philosophy, principles, and concepts

A quick scan of the preceding doctrinal outline clearly shows that all material covered up to this point clearly falls within Hung Fa Yi doctrine. It also gives the reader a perspective on how and where the material covered in the final chapter fits into the system.

Hung Fa Yi Wooden Dummy and Weapons

OVERVIEW: TYING EVERYTHING TOGETHER WITH APPLICATIONS TRAINING

Each of the subjects discussed in this chapter—the dummy (Muk Yan Jong), pole (Gwan), and swords (Dou)—could fill an entire volume. This chapter provides sufficient historical background and basic technical descriptions to gain appreciation for their origination and depth.

The Muk Yan Jong, Dwan, and Dou forms demonstrate the combat applications of Hung Fa Yi techniques. Training drills for both the Gwan and Dou also use the wooden dummy as a representation of a true opponent. At this stage of training it is most important to understand how the accumulated knowledge and skill gained from Saam Mo Kiu training is arrayed in combat. By the time practitioners reach this point in their development, they no longer view footwork as footwork. They no longer see principles and concepts in isolation. Instead, they see the relationship of each concept to another and understand their interconnectedness within the scope of properly applied strategies and tactics.

At the foundational level, students often think that Yi Ji Kim Yeung Ma, Leung Yi Ma, and Bun Yut Ma are stances, and the movements into them are thought of as Geuk Faat (footwork). In reality, they are descriptive terms depicting geometric structure and motion. For instance, Leung Yi Ma does not express a side stance, but rather the concept of the knee occupying the yin line during rotation. Bun Yut Ma does not express a forward stance, but rather the occupation of centerline during advancement and proper angulation at the completion of bridging. As such, they constitute dynamic concepts expressed through the employment of specific body mechanics. When coupled with all other Hung Fa Yi principles and concepts, and arrayed properly with strategies and tactics (Jan Faat), they become something greater than stances and footwork. They evolve into battlefield alignments that have a specific purpose (strategy) in a specific space and time supported by a specific use of energy.

New terms are needed to describe these alignments. The first is Ji Ngh Jung Sin Ma. It describes Yi Ji Kim Yeung Ma, Leung Yi Ma, and Bun Yut Ma relationships to the concept of Deui Ying (matching) and the maintenance of self-centerline while applying the Wing Chun Formula during rotation within specified tactics and strategies. The second and third terms needed to describe battlefield array alignments are Bin Ma (edge alignment) and Ji Ng Ma (closed alignment). The diagrams in figure 9.1 depict Bin Ma and Ji Ng Ma.

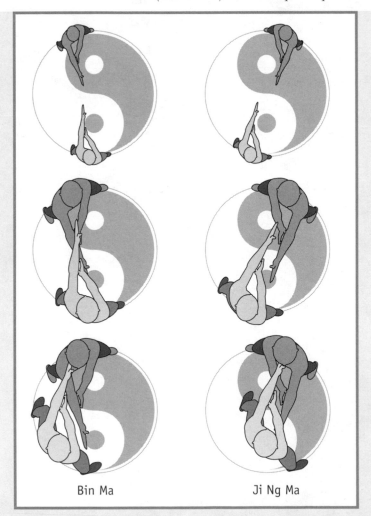

Bin Ma   Ji Ng Ma

Figure 9.1 Jan Faat.

Use of these alignments is tied directly to strategies and tactics. As different strategies become necessary, different alignments become appropriate. The specifics of these (and other) alignments and attendant strategies could fill a volume in themselves. Consequently, in-depth discussion is reserved for a future work. Before proceeding with our wooden dummy (Muk Yan Jong) discussion, two additional terms must be noted. These terms describe the process of communicating, training, and employing certain strategies and tactics. They are Bin Ma Baai Jong, and Ji Ng Ma Baai Jong. These terms help the practitioner understand that footwork and handwork in and of themselves are just that—footwork and handwork. When arrayed for combat with proper strategies and tactics, they become part of a whole that is greater than the sum of its parts. This is the only way a system can be properly described and understood. To get to this level of communication, the philosophy of Saam Mo Kiu must be applied throughout training. The student gains knowledge through experience at the Fau Kiu stage. Focus is on gaining experience rather than on the details such as body mechanics. Experience leads to development of physical and mental attributes and the training of details at the Saan Kiu stage. Ultimately, full focus and awareness of how the pieces fit together (in terms of space, time, and energy) with cohesive strategies and tactics happens at the Weng Kiu stage.

MUK YAN JONG: LEARNING POSITION, FOOTWORK, AND TACTICS

The traditional Hung Fa Yi dummy is referred to as Ching Lung Baak Fu Jong, meaning "green dragon/white tiger jong." The name itself is an attestation to Hung Fa Yi's Shaolin roots; the green dragon and white tiger are the original warrior symbols of Shaolin kung fu. Historical legends of the Southern Shaolin Temple allude to the existence of a Wooden Man Hall. A monk was deemed qualified to represent Shaolin to the world at large if he could pass all of the tests in this hall.

In a traditional sense, Hou Ling chanting (called oral command) was employed to teach students how to use the dummy in their training. It served two specific purposes. First, it represented spiritual chanting (called Sau Yan, meaning "hand print"—in this case a reference to being the hand print of Taoist martial roots). This Hou Ling was addressed to four guardians (also emanating from Taoist martial roots): the tiger, dragon, bird, and tortoise. Together they refer to four directions: dragon—left, tiger—right, bird—front, and tortoise—rear. These guardians have direct correlation to time, space, and Qi Gung applications. High-level descendents of Hung Fa Yi Wing Chun were taught this ritual and attendant knowledge. They used it as late in history as the Boxer Rebellion.

In Popular Wing Chun, movements on the dummy are repeated virtually the same to both sides. In other words, they represent training the left side motions and then the right. In contrast, the Hung Fa Yi dummy sets are best described by the term Leung Yi Jong, meaning "both sides are different but remain in harmony." If one side teaches the concept of inside, then the other side teaches the concept of outside. When one side teaches close range, the other teaches long range. Attendant with the changes from inside to outside alignments and close-range to long-range alignments are strategies and tactics changes. All require efficient foot and body alignments coordinated with the time, space, and energy requirements employed. In essence, while the two sides of the dummy are played differently, they do complement each other. They are balanced. It should also be noted that both Chi Sim and Hung Fa Yi dummy sets address attacks from ground fighters—something not covered in most Popular Wing Chun wooden dummy versions seen today.

Muk Yan Jong demonstrates the application of the techniques learned using the wooden dummy as the representation of a true opponent. In Hung Fa Yi, the Muk Yan Jong has two levels of depth in learning. The first variation of the Muk Yan Jong focuses on an eight-directional concept. This variation is often referred to as "directional dummy," but its correct name is Ching Lung Baak Fu Jong. This variation of the dummy represents the beginner's level of dummy training. As such, it emphasizes the use of angulation for gaining and maintaining a superior position. It deals with footwork from a facing perspective by referring to the four corners of the box described by the Wing Chun Formula. It does not delve into the details of dimensionality or how the footwork relates to that dimensionality. The eight directions are depicted in figure 9.2.

The second variation is for advanced stages of learning Muk Yan Jong. It is focused on time and space strategies with more than 150 moves as skill progresses. This variation is often referred to as "dimensional dummy," yet its correct name remains Ching Lung Baak Fu Jong. It employs the eight directions shown in figure 9.2, but the perspective has changed from directional movement to dimensional shifting. In addition, the directions of top and bottom are added and also trained dimensionally.

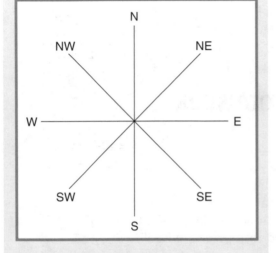

Figure 9.2   Eight directions.

In Wing Chun Muk Yan Jong training, the number 108 has always been significant. Popular Wing Chun teaches that 108 signifies the number of movements in the dummy form. Some popular lineages also teach that 108 is properly divisible by three, further emphasizing Popular Wing Chun's emphasis on training triplets of motions throughout the Siu Nim Tau, Chum Kiu, and Biu Ji forms. In Hung Fa Yi Wing Chun the number 108 has a completely different meaning. Hung Fa Yi Wing Chun space, time, and energy control focuses on ten dimensions and eight directions. The number 108 is emphasized on the dummy to remind the practitioner to pay attention to each dimension and each direction when employing techniques and tactics. It also complies with the Saam Mo Kiu philosophy of employing Saan Kiu–level training with the eight directions to provide the experience necessary to comprehend the details covered in the Weng Kiu–level dimensional training.

For purposes of illustration, the following photos depict some of the movements from the third section of Hung Fa Yi Ching Lung Baak Fu Jong. Along with the photos is a detailed description of the third section of the Jong. In total, there are 10 such sections for completion of the dummy form. This section was chosen because it clearly highlights both inside and outside concepts, as well as close-range and long-range concepts. It also shows the efficient footwork and body alignment needed to support them.

Third Section of Ching Lung Baak Fu Jong (Green Dragon/White Tiger Dummy)

1.   This section begins with three inside Paak Sau—right hand inside paak, then left hand inside paak, then right hand paak. Emphasis is on stepping so that the knee rotates on the Yin line with Leung Yi Ma footwork. This movement teaches how to mobilize with shoulder-to-shoulder clearing of the gates employing an inside gate technique.

Figure 9.3 Three inside Paak Sau (a, b, a). Grand Master Gee demonstrates the third section of the Jong.

2. A left-hand outside Paak Sau with a right-hand Chuen Sau is executed. This movement teaches how to Paak on the shoulder line. This is the realized application of the shoulder Paak Sau reflected in the third section of the Siu Nim Tau form. The Chuen Sau allows Jeui Ying facing while redirecting and flanking the opponent at close range. Upon turning back to Deui Ying facing, the three reference points are read to determine which of the gates are open and available for offensive attack. If the turn was done properly, all three reference points should be exposed, and all gates (high, middle, and low) should be open.

Figure 9.4 Left-hand outside Paak Sau.

3. The next movement teaches how to attack the open gates. A Saat Geng Sau is executed to the upper gate while employing a simultaneous Laap Sau to keep the gate open throughout the strike. It is followed up with a left-hand Jat Sau to the middle reference point and a simultaneous right-hand strike (punch) to the gate. Again, the Jat Sau keeps the gate open throughout the strike.

Figure 9.5 Attacking the open gates.

4. A Laap/Dim Geuk is performed next, setting up a Faat Sau to enable interception and redirection of an open-hand attack. The redirection itself begins with a right-hand Jat Sau at long range and advancing footwork that becomes Bin Ma (triangulated on the dummy's knee and emphasizing Lok Ma Jong) with a left-hand Chuen Sau and long-range Jeui Ying facing. This footwork and body angulation specifically teaches how to change the opponent's dimension when turning back to Deui Ying. Again, the three reference points are read to determine which of the gates are open and available for offensive attack. If the turn was done properly, all three reference points should be exposed, and all gates (high, middle, and low) should be open.

Figure 9.6 Laap/Dim Geuk followed by Faat Sau, then Jat Sau with Bin Ma alignment.

5. A right-hand Saat Geng Sau is executed to the high reference point while keeping the gate open with a left-hand Laap Sau. This is immediately followed by flowing to a low reference point strike with a left-hand punch, while keeping the gate open throughout the strike via a right-hand Jat Sau.

6. Gan/Jaam and Leung Yi Ma are executed next, followed immediately by a right-hand Huen (with Ji Ng Ma foot alignment) and an upper gate palm strike with the right hand, all while simultaneously stepping to rotate with the knee on the Yin line. Here, too, middle gate control is retained while the upper gate is struck.

Figure 9.7 Right-hand Saat Geng Sau.

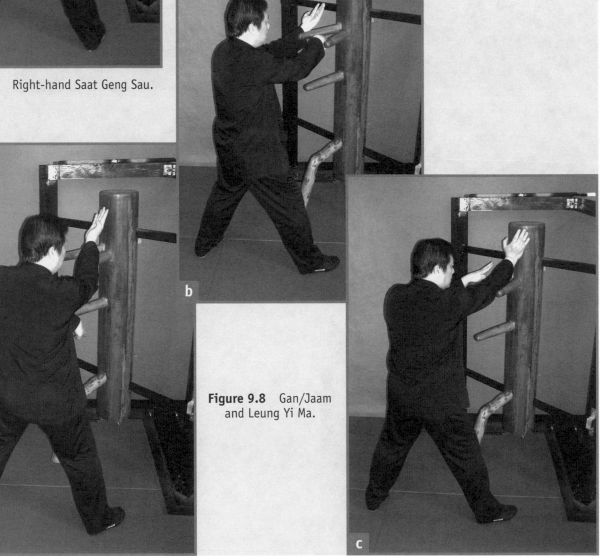

Figure 9.8 Gan/Jaam and Leung Yi Ma.

7. The section closes with a long-range Huen Sau and a right forward stance Seung Tok Sau (a Kam Na arm break).

In conclusion, it is important to reemphasize that the focus in the previous steps of dummy training is on proper angulation and proper use of energetics during angulation to apply the combat techniques with optimal power while safely controlling an opponent's gates.

HUNG FA YI GWAN FAAT: POWER AND PRACTICALITY IN POLE WEAPONS TRAINING: ROOTS OF THE SOUTHERN SHAOLIN STAFF

Three distinct sources of martial arts contributed to the formation and development of the southern Shaolin pole: the monks, the Chinese military, and the Ming royal family. As indicated previously, the warrior monks populating the Southern Shaolin Temple transferred there from the northern temple at Song Shan. At the same time, remnants of the Ming military officer corps also took shelter at the southern temple. Finally, members of the Ming royal family intermittently sought shelter and sanctuary there as well. The source of the northern Shaolin monks' martial arts was previously highlighted beginning with Ba Tuo.

Figure 9.9 Long-range Huen Sau and right forward stance Seung Tok Sau.

The second contributory source to the development of the southern Shaolin pole, the military, developed its martial knowledge over many centuries practicing and refining Taoist originated systems. The Ming military corps in southern China consisted of elite troops and highly trained officers placed there earlier to counter frequent coastal incursions by Japanese pirates. This southern Chinese military corps was quite famous for its skill in the use of 13 highly developed spearing principles. These principles ended up at the Southern Shaolin Temple and are reflected in all of the southern Shaolin systems and many derivatives that came after these systems left the temple. They contributed equally to the development of the Hung Fa Yi pole since all 13 principles are reflected in its tactics and applications.

The third source of knowledge for the development of the southern Shaolin pole, the Ming royal family, also possessed its own martial arts system called Chu Ga. Their talent merged with those of the monks and soldiers in the creation of pole fighting methods renowned for over three centuries. There is a saying that the southern Shaolin pole consists of 70 percent spear and 30 percent pole. The name given the southern Shaolin pole was Luk Dim Sap Saam Chueng, meaning "six points, thirteen spears." Many of today's southern Shaolin derivatives retain this name for their pole form, training methods, and applications.

Following the destruction of the Southern Shaolin Temple and the dispersal of the southern Shaolin systems to the revolutionary societies, the southern pole took on the complexion and mission purposes of the systems that employed them in actual combat. Hung Fa Yi's pole took on the name Hung Mun Saat Gwan. It is important to note that the term *Hung Mun* used in this context does not refer to a specific secret society; here it refers to all secret societies in general. The correct contextual translation is "secret legions' killing staff." After more than a century and a half of employment within the various secret societies, the pole reappeared to the public as Luk Dim Bun Gwan, meaning "six-and-a-half-point pole." This name is virtually universal among modern versions of Wing Chun, but its expression is significantly different for each modern lineage.

HUNG FA YI HUNG MUN SAAT GWAN

The Hung Fa Yi pole consists of two versions—a shorter version (as in the length of the pole) and a longer version using the standard six-point pole length (9 to 12 feet in length). As with Chi Sim mentioned in chapter 2, Hung Fa Yi's pole was trained first in recognition of meeting actual combat needs.

Some of the modern Wing Chun terms reflected in table 9.1 appear to be the same as their Shaolin counterparts, but they are not. In modern Wing Chun, these terms describe techniques. In Hung Fa Yi and southern Shaolin, they describe complex principles around which extensive exercises are performed and significant knowledge and skill is built. In the true sense of mastering a weapon for hand-to-hand combat, more than techniques and descriptions of movements is needed to survive. The Sam Faat (nature) and Gwan Faat (principles) must both be incorporated for complete knowledge.

Hung Fa Yi's powerful opening move employs full body motion for developing killing energy with proper angulation. This opening motion itself is called Hung Mun Saat Gwan Hei Yin Chan, and the form is named after it, Hung Mun Saat Gwan. It is radically different from the opening move of Popular Wing Chun, as are the Taih, Tan, Hyun, Dim, Chaap, Saat, and Biu motions depicted on pages 186 and 187.

DOU (BUTTERFLY SWORDS)

In Popular Wing Chun of today, learning the butterfly swords is considered to be a highly advanced stage that represents completing the system. In many cases, only a few students are ever taught the sword level of Wing Chun because it requires advanced comprehension of the nature of Popular Wing Chun itself; the sword duplicates many of the single-hand and double-hand techniques of the system. The major difference is that shoulder energy and range are offset to the elbow, elbow energy and range are

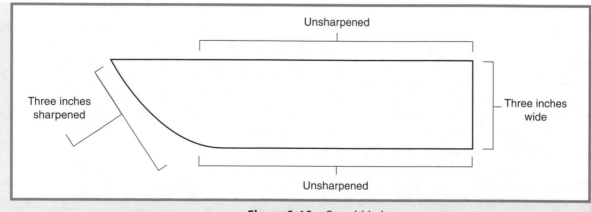

Figure 9.10 Sword blade.

Southern Shaolin 13 Spearing Principles (luhk dím sahp sàam chëung gwan faat) 六點十三槍棍法	Hung Fa Yi Six Oral Commands (hùhng mùhn saat gwan luhk daaih háu kyut) 洪門殺棍六大口訣 "6 Natures" sàm faat 心法	
殺 saat (kill)	心法	sàm faat (Nature)
點 dím (point)	力點法	lihk dím faat (Force Methods)
纏 chìhn (wrap)	圈點法	hyùn dím faat (Circle Point Methods)
擺 báai (place, put)	長短速度距離法	chèuhng dyún chük douh kéuih léih faat (Long Short Speed Distance Methods)
橫 wàahng (side)	生死門法	sáng séi mùhn faat (Life and Death Positioning)
插 chaap (insert)	生死棍法	sang séi gwan faat (Live Vice Dead Pole Methods)
彈 tàahn (strum, pluck)	老嫩棍法	lóuh nyuhn gwan faat (Old and Young Pole Methods) – extension and retraction of the gwan
弔 diu (hang)		
挑 tìu (pick up)		
盆 pùhn (folding)		
拔 baht (pull out)		
抹 mut (wipe)		
帶 daai (carry)		

Table 9.1 Spearing/Pole Principles and Natures

offset to the wrist, and wrist energy and range are expressed on the front edge of the sword. Because of this, the swords of Popular Wing Chun are not taught until after the hand motions have been mastered. See figure 9.10 for an example of a blade.

In contrast, Hung Fa Yi's pole and swords were all trained up front. In chapter 2 it was noted that Chi Sim's pole is also trained first. The message is clear: These systems were intended for battlefield combat use. Weapons were trained first by necessity.

The evolution of the Wing Chun butterfly swords we use today progressed through three primary stages. The first stage was its creation as a defensive, nonkilling weapon created by the Shaolin monks. The original butterfly knife bore only a resemblance to the Wing Chun weapon we see today. The Shaolin version of the butterfly knife was

Figure 9.11 Tàih (raise)

Figure 9.12 Tan (strum)

Figure 9.13 Hyùn (circle)

Figure 9.14 Dím (point – hard or soft)

Grand Master Garrett Gee demonstrates the Gwam.

Figure 9.15 Chaap (insert)

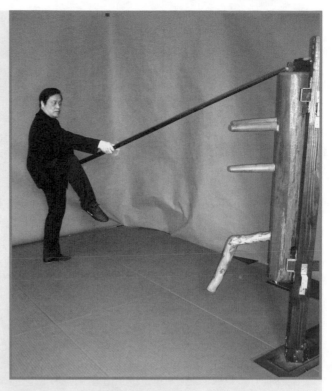

Figure 9.16 Saat (kill)

Figure 9.17 Bìu (thrust)

designed to meet the training and defense needs of Shaolin monks. In harmony with Buddhist philosophy and teachings, the monks designed the weapon for parrying, disarming, and cutting—not for killing. Consequently, the blade was shaped and structured with dull edges on the top and bottom to be used for deflection of an opponent's weapons. As indicated in figure 9.10, only the first three inches (the curved part) of the blade were sharpened. The remainder of the blade, top and bottom, was solid and dull for parrying and nonlethal striking purposes. Today's form still heavily emphasizes parrying, obstructing, or intercepting an opponent's weapon. These remain highly consistent with the original design and intent of the blade itself.

In the Shaolin Temple, the butterfly sword was not mass-produced to a specific length. Rather, the length of each butterfly sword was customized to the practitioner. Specifically, the blade measured from the center of the bony protrusion on the practitioner's wrist to the elbow (this same practice is employed by Hung Fa Yi practitioners today). The monks heavily stressed the need to tailor the butterfly knife to its intended practitioner. An unfitted blade, used as intended, could easily harm the user and limit the mobility of arms and body. In contrast, the width of the blade did not vary. It remained three inches from top to bottom starting at the hilt and extending to the start of the blade curvature near the tip. The three-inch width was selected because it approximates the width of a developed male wrist.

The thickness of the blade varied, depending on the sword maker, but was usually about an eighth of an inch throughout. The handle of the sword sported a guard in the shape of a hook with an open end. The monks used this guard to trap an opponent's weapon and quickly disarm him. Again, this was consistent with Buddhist philosophy, which advocated disarming an enemy when possible rather than killing him.

The Shaolin butterfly sword was considered a small weapon in contrast to its counterparts. This was intentional because the monks (and later the revolutionary fighters) wished to conceal the sword beneath their robes while traveling. They could move about in public without being questioned or creating an improper image in respect to their Buddhist teachings. The ability to conceal this weapon contributed greatly to its favor with southern rebels resisting the Qing Dynasty. As noted earlier, the original Shaolin usage of the blades was deeply rooted in Buddhist beliefs. Killing was not an option. Both the blade and the training methods for using it centered on parrying, disarming, and cutting. It was considered far more humane to surgically cut tendons at the joints, thereby maiming an opponent, rather than killing him.

The change in shape and intended function of the knives was a direct result of the creation of the Wing Chun fighting system with the specific intent of training revolutionaries to engage the imperial troops of the Qing Dynasty. According to Hung Fa Yi Wing Chun Kuen, the double butterfly swords form seen in Shaolin Kung Fu was first created by the Fut Paai Hung Mun (Buddhist Hung Mun). The Fut Paai Hung Mun was a secret society existing within the Southern Shaolin Temple itself. This society's primary goal was to oppose the Qing Dynasty and help restore the Ming family to the throne. They needed a system that was efficient to train and employ and that was complete in that it consistently developed empty hand skills along with both long and short, as well as single to double, weaponry.

These historical events lead us to the second stage of evolution of the traditional Shaolin butterfly sword into today's Baat Jaam Dou. This stage was greatly influenced by the fighting needs of the secret society of Hung Fa Wui (the Red Flower Society) and the Hung Gun Biu family. With the passing of time, revolutionary fighting against the Manchurians and the Qing Dynasty increased in intensity, and the blade began its transition from a defensive parrying weapon to an offensive weapon designed to kill. To make the blade more suitable to warfare, the revolutionary secret society members of the Hung Fa Wui sought to make it more lethal.

According to Hung Fa Yi Wing Chun tradition, Cheung Ng himself modified the Shaolin butterfly sword to create a practical battlefield weapon. Although the changes he made initially were subtle, they did result in a lethal weapon. This new version of the butterfly sword represented a new stage of development for the weapon and its use, but neither Taan Sau Ng nor the Hung Fa Wui ever disclosed the knowledge of the modifications and the training to use them to the general public. The modified swords were known to the Hung Fa Wui as the Hung Fa Yi Wing Chun double butterfly swords.

The Hung Fa Yi Wing Chun swords were very similar to the traditional swords. Most of the top and bottom of the blade remained straight, but the design was altered at the tip to accommodate thrusting and stabbing motions. To this end, the front of the blade was trimmed, adding a curvature and sharpened point that gave the knife the appearance of a large dagger. The notched area was then sharpened, and blood grooves were added to the sides of the blade. This enabled blood to drain more easily when the point of the sword pierced the stomach or other organs.

Although the Hung Fa Yi Wing Chun swords are not generally known to the public, the Hung Fa Yi Wing Chun Kuen still practice with them according to the original form and routines taught by Taan Sau Ng. Their intent is to preserve the knowledge of the swords' use and the methods employed by the revolutionaries to train them.

The third phase of evolution of the Shaolin butterfly swords into the Wing Chun sword and Baat Jaam Dou training form known to Popular Wing Chun practitioners took place in the 20th century. This modern version of the butterfly sword has many variations in shape, but the biggest difference is that all are sharpened the entire length of the blade. Another type of blade, the tiger's head blade, also evolved during this modern period. It shares the same characteristic of sharpness throughout its entire length, but it also incorporates a significant curvature or bow toward the front half of the blade.

In summary, the development of the butterfly swords underwent three primary eras. Out of these eras have come three distinct types of blades heavily influenced by the applications of those periods. The first blade originated from Shaolin. It consisted of a three-inch-wide blade with only the first three inches of the blade sharpened. The next blade originated with the secret societies. It consisted of the same three-inch-wide blade with a modified tip and blood groves to make it more lethal when used for stabbing. The third blade originated in the modern era and is distinguished by the fact that the entire blade is sharpened.

BOOK SUMMATION FROM A CHAN PERSPECTIVE

Principles of cause, condition, and consequence are fundamental to Chan Buddhism. These principles explain the relationship between things happening at different

Figure 9.18 Grand Master Gee demonstrates Seung Gaan Dou.

Figure 9.19 Grand Master Gee demonstrates Gaan Jaam Dou.

189

moments in time, different points of space, and different exchanges of energy. Chan (Zen) considers all phenomena, whether cultural or social, internal or external, physiological or psychological, to be objects of consciousness.

Objects of consciousness are considered dharmas. The six sense organs (the six-petaled flower of Hung Fa Yi) interact with six kinds of sensory objects (i.e., eye sees forms, nose smells fragrances, etc.) to create tangible objects of consciousness. The sixth organ, our consciousness (mind), has thoughts as its object. Objects of the conscious mind include communication, reasoning, symbology, concepts, and so on. This sixth sense is unique to human beings, but its value and use are still bounded by the "experience" gained from the other five.

All dharmas are consequences of cause and condition, including the creation of Weng/Wing Chun. The consequences of disharmony in China some 350 years ago resulted in a life-and-death struggle between two groups of people, the Ming and the Qing. The result of this struggle was the creation of a treasure, Shaolin Weng/Wing Chun. In essence, Shaolin Weng/Wing Chun was a tool intended to bring back or maintain harmony. The combined effort of Grand Master Gee, Grand Master Hoffmann, and the Ving Tsun Museum was intended to preserve and introduce this treasure of Shaolin to the modern world, hoping it will benefit all humanity. This potential for benefit is possible because we are all interconnected. In the 21st century, Shaolin Weng/Wing Chun is a tool that will reintroduce the harmony of time, space, and energy.

EPILOGUE

KINESIOLOGY IN HUNG FA YI WING CHUN: HARMONIZING STRUCTURE AND FUNCTION

Kinesiology is the science and study of movement and the structures that are actively and passively involved in that movement. Hung Fa Yi Wing Chun is the science of human hand-to-hand combat; as such, it stands up to all of the tests of modern day kinesiological science. The martial science of Hung Fa Yi was discovered over three hundred years ago by Shaolin monks and Ming dynasty military leaders. I use the term *science* rather than *art* for a very specific purpose here. Many of today's martial "arts" do not stand up under scientific examination of structures and energies in terms of the optimal efficiency and safety of the person employing them. It is a tribute to the creators of Hung Fa Yi Wing Chun and to the fundamental soundness and truth of their ideas and concepts (across the board) that this system holds up well under examination in the light of contemporary scientific kinesiological knowledge.

As you now know, the purpose of Hung Fa Yi Wing Chun martial science is to achieve maximum effectiveness in hand-to-hand combat ability as quickly and efficiently as possible. In order to achieve maximum effectiveness in striking, the principles of simplicity, directness, and efficiency must be applied and expressed in the structures involved in the movements of Hung Fa Yi Wing Chun. The body structure must be capable of generating and transmitting the strongest possible impact to the target within the limitations of tactically practicable footwork. In order to deliver the maximum force that can be generated by optimal body structure, the strongest and most stable hand structures are required.

Many Hung Fa Yi Wing Chun structural concepts guide the expression of maximal combat ability. All represent a highly precise employment of human body structure. From a kinesiological perspective, they constitute a true optimization of human structure and energetics for the purpose of combat. By way of example, two such concepts are Saam Dim Yat Sin and Saam Dim Bun Kuen. The application of these concepts to the movements of striking allows the entire body structure to support the delivery of a punch or strike for maximal effectiveness.

The Saam Dim Yat Sin concept describes the relationships between the knee, elbow, and tailbone when delivering a strike or punch. Saam Dim Yat Sin means "three points, one line." The three points are the knee, the elbow, and the tailbone. The one line is the strike itself. In Hung Fa Yi Wing Chun, mobile stances and footwork are employed to achieve a tactically advantageous flanking position when striking, thereby avoiding a head-on collision of speed and power. From this position, the strike or punch is delivered with a structure that can be conceptualized as a pyramid, with the strike ("one line") as the tip of the pyramid and the triangle formed by the knee, elbow, and tailbone ("three points") as the base of the pyramid. From the preferred flanking position, the Saam Dim Yat Sin structural concept creates the potential to use body unity and the expression of full body energy for maximal effectiveness in striking.

The key to understanding and expressing this structure is that the knee is outside of the elbow, the elbow is in an intermediate position between the knee and the tailbone, and the strike is delivered along the line connecting the centerline to the target. This structure provides a very strong and stable foundation that allows the maximal generation and transmission of power to the strike. In this structure, if one were to draw vertical lines through the knee, elbow, and tailbone, those lines should never intersect. If the knee line were to intersect the elbow line or the tailbone line, the structure would be weakened and distorted. Similarly, if the elbow line were to intersect either the knee line or the tailbone line, the structure would be distorted and the strike weakened. Finally, delivering the strike anywhere off of the line connecting the centerline and the target weakens the practitioner's ability to deliver maximal force to the target.

Experimentation with the structures and the distortions as described can only lead to the self-discovery that the Saam Dim Yat Sin concept provides the best structure for generating and delivering a strike to an opponent. Indeed, every concept of Hung Fa Yi leads to similar discoveries. They are all deeply rooted in true kinesiological science.

After considering the optimal body structure for generating and transmitting a powerful punch or strike, we must consider the best hand structure for delivering that power to the target. The human hand evolved to create tools and use them, not primarily to be a weapon itself. The structure of the hand is not optimized for function as a weapon, and when the hand is used as a weapon, some risk of injury is unavoidable. Hung Fa Yi Wing Chun fist structure and employment represents an optimal configuration for reducing that risk.

Saam Dim Bun Kuen means "three-and-a-half-point fist" and refers to the striking areas of the three primary Hung Fa Yi hand striking tools. This concept describes the most often used hand structures for delivering force to a target. The three striking tools are the punch, the side palm, and the chop. The corresponding striking structures are the bottom three knuckles and the front portion of the fingers for the punch (the "three" in three-and-a-half-point fist) and the bony protuberance at the bottom of the palm (the "half" in three-and-a-half-point fist).

The Hung Fa Yi three-and-a-half-point fist concept expresses a safe (less chance of self-injury) and effective (strong structure for the efficient delivery of shock energy to a target) means to accomplish the intended function—injuring an opponent.

When punching in Hung Fa Yi Wing Chun, the fist is not bent but held straight, exposing the striking surface, which is the flat surface of the three lower knuckles (proximal phalanges of the middle, ring, and small fingers). The advantages of this position are superior energy transmission by aligning the contact surface of the fist with the long bones of the forearm (radius and ulna) as well as superior stability and protection of the wrist due to the locked position. This locked wrist position prevents the dissipation of energy and the possibility of injury associated with forcefully hyperflexing or hyperextending the wrist. One potential disadvantage of this position is the risk of a fracture to the fourth or fifth metacarpal bones (boxer's fracture). This risk is decreased by striking with the flat surface of the fist rather than with the knuckles. By striking with this structure, the practitioner spreads the potentially injurious counterforce associated with landing a punch over a wider surface area and decreases the likelihood of an injury such as a fracture.

If practitioners condition their hands by striking a heavy bag or other similar surface, they can test other hand structures used for punching against the Hung Fa Yi hand structure and experience the stability of this structure for themselves.

The Hung Fa Yi chop and side palm strike are delivered using the half point in the three-and-a-half-point fist formula. The half point is the small bony knob at the base of the small finger side of the palm. This knob is formed by the pisiform bone, one of the carpal bones of the wrist. As with the fist, this structure facilitates the delivery of force to the target and protects the hand and wrist, although in a different manner. When using the Hung Fa Yi half point for striking, force is delivered directly through the wrist, and the more distal structures in the hand are not involved in contact. This is simpler and more direct than striking with the small finger side of the hand (hypothenar eminence) and precludes the hand acting as a lever arm to deliver injurious force to the supporting ligaments and tendons around the ulnar (small finger side) of the wrist. Martial artists who have broken bricks using both the more traditional knife hand and the Hung Fa Yi half point note a significant difference in wrist stability and less stress to the hand using the Hung Fa Yi structure. As previously noted, there is inherent risk in using the hand as a weapon, and direct force applied to the pisiform bone can result in a fracture. Hung Fa Yi structures provide the best possible minimization of that risk.

Although the science of kinesiology as we know it today did not exist in China 350 years ago, the founders of Hung Fa Yi Wing Chun science were able to discover the most direct and efficient methods of harmonizing the structures of the human body with methods of movement to accomplish hand-to-hand combat efficiency and effectiveness. They could certainly be described as early pioneers of the science of kinesiology. Hung Fa Yi Wing Chun concepts are worthy of admiration as amazing feats of insight, thought, and science.

Pat Keely, MD
Physiologist and kinesiologist

GLOSSARY

INTRODUCTION

The Roman alphabet is the norm for writing Western European and North American languages while the Chinese language uses ideographic symbols. A person unfamiliar with these symbols but who wishes to write down the Chinese sounds according to the way they are heard has to use a phonetic tool commonly termed Romanization. Throughout the lineages of Wing Chun no standard system of Romanization has been used for Cantonese terms. In addition, because translating Chinese terminological subtleties into English depends on an instructor's understanding of both Chinese and English language and culture, students are often given inaccurate or misleading translations of Wing Chun terminology. In an effort to establish higher standards in communication throughout the martial arts community, the Ving Tsun Museum has adopted an organized, researched system for Romanizing all Cantonese terms. This system is known as the Yale system, developed by the Yale-in-China Language Center at the University of Hong Kong.

This pronunciation guide and glossary serves as an aid to students and teachers of the arts of Wing Chun. Following is an introduction to the pronunciation of Cantonese. It is meant as a reference and acts only as an aid to a formal language program from a native speaker or professional teacher.

Many terms used in Chinese martial arts use special meanings or intents for common words. A phrase that might seem simple and straightforward to one lineage might be a secret code phrase symbolizing advanced thinking in another lineage. Also, many terms cannot be directly translated into English without losing much symbolism and intent in the translating.

Take the term 攤 taan (tan) as an example. Taan (tan) means 1) "to spread; to open 2) to divide equally; to apportion." Often it is translated with a short definition of "disperse" but this does not convey much meaning. Taan (tan) can be described through the use of analogy: imaging you are going to put peanut butter on a piece of toast. You toast the bread and put on a big gob of peanut butter. Then you take a knife and spread the peanut butter out to distribute it evenly on the toast. That act of spreading the peanut butter describes the motion of taan (tan) physically, whereas the desire to distribute the peanut butter evenly on the toast describes the intent of taan (tan). Having this understanding of taan (tan) leads to a discussion of the application of taan (tan) physically with intent consistent to both the Chinese term of taan (tan) and the principles and concepts of the Wing Chun System.

In some instances, Pinyin Mandarin has been used instead of the Yale. While most terms in Weng/Wing Chun are Cantonese in origin, some terms are more easily recognized by the general public as Mandarin[1]. Mandarin is the official language of the

---

[1]Terms in Mandarin are noted in italics and are followed by the abbreviation (Md). When both Mandarin and Cantonese are used in the same row, the Cantonese term is followed by the abbreviation (Cn).

Peoples' Republic of China; Pinyin is the official rendering of Mandarin into Roman letters. Throughout this text, whenever Mandarin is used for better-known phrases, the Chinese term is placed into italics.

Wing Chun is a Chinese art in origins—by understanding the original terminology, much insight is provided into the nature of the techniques and the techniques' application.

Cantonese Tones

In pronouncing Cantonese, be aware of the importance of tones in conveying meaning. Basically, there are seven tones, which in the Yale system are represented by the use of diacritics and by the insertion of *h* for the three low tones.

The following chart illustrates the seven tones:

1	2	3	4	5	6	7
High Falling	High Rising	Mid Level	High Level	Low Falling	Low Rising	Low Level
Chàng	Cháng	Chang	Chäng	Chàhng	Cháhng	Chahng
Bàai	Báai	Baai	Bäai	Bàaih	Báaih	Baaih

Below is a chart describing the relative differences between the seven tones:

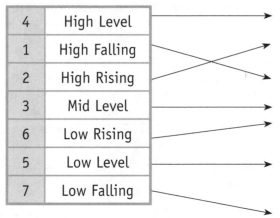

4	High Level
1	High Falling
2	High Rising
3	Mid Level
6	Low Rising
5	Low Level
7	Low Falling

Mandarin Tones

In pronouncing Mandarin, be aware of the importance of tones in conveying meaning. Basically, there are four tones, which in the Pinyin system are represented by the use of diacritics.

The following chart illustrates the four tones:

1	2	3	4
High Level	Mid Rising	Low Falling	High Falling
Mä	Má	Mâ	Mà
Dï	Dí	Dî	Dì

Below is a chart describing the relative differences between the four tones:

1, 4	High
	Middle-High
2	Middle
3	Middle Low
	Low

ä - please note that in most Pinyin writing using diacritics, this tone is noted with a small bar across the vowel. We are limited in character selection and are forced to use two dots to represent the bar. Any vowel with two dots on top should be read as a high, level tone.

â - please note that in most Pinyin writing using diacritics, this tone looks like a small "v" on top of the vowel. We are limited in character selection and are forced to use an upside down "v" with our fonts.

PEOPLE

Romanization	Yale/Pinyin	Meaning	Characters
Chan Biu	chahn bìu	Chan Biu	陳彪
Chan Bo Jung	chahn bóu jùng	Chan Bo Jung	陳保忠
Chan Gan Nan	chahn gahn nàahm	Chan Gan Nan	陳近南
Chan Jing Lin	chahn jing lin	Chan Jing Lin	陳正連
Chan Sai Yuan	chahn sai yán	Chan Sai Yuan	陳世隱
Chan Si Sai Ga	chàhn sih sai gà	Chan family	陳氏世家
Chan Weng Wah	chahn wíhng wàh	Chan Weng Wa	陳永華

Romanization	Yale/Pinyin	Meaning	Characters
Chan Yiu Min	chàhn yúh mìhn	Chan Yiu Min	陳汝棉
Chi Sim Sim Si	ji sihn sihn si	Chan Teacher Chi Sim	至善禪師
Chiu Yun	chìuh yùhn	Chiu Yun	朝元
Damo (Md)	*dá mó*	*Damo* (Bodhidharma)	達摩
Daat Jung	daaht jùng	Daat Jung	達宗
Daai Fa Min Gam	daaih fà mihn gám	"Painted Face" Gam	大花面錦
Fung Siu Ching	fùhng síu chìng	Fung Siu Ching	馮小青
Hung Gun Biu	hùhng gàn bìu	"Hung Gun" Biu	紅巾彪
Hung Hei Gung	hùhng hèi gùn	Hung Hei Gung	鴻熙官
Cheng Sing Gung	jehng sìhng gùng	Cheng Sing Gung	鄭成功
Cheung Bo	jéung bóu	Cheung Bo	張保
Cheung Ng	jéung ñgh	Cheung Ng	張五
Cheung Si	jéung sì	Teacher Cheung	張師
Chu Ming	jyù mìhng	Chu Ming	朱明
Chu Yun Cheung	jyù yùhn jèung	Chu Yun Cheung	朱元璋
Lee Min Mou	léih màhn mauh	Lee Min Mou	李文茂
Leung Yi Dai	lèuhng yih daih	Leung Yi Dai	梁二娣
Maan Wan Lung	maahn wàhn lùhng	Maan Wan Lung	萬雲龍
Mai Gei Wong	máih gèi wòhng	"Rice Machine" Wong	米機王
Ng Dak Hei	ngh däk héi	Ng Dak Hei	吳德起
Ng Jou	ñgh jóu	Five Elders	五祖
Sim Jung	syùn jùng	Sim Jung	宣宗
Taan Sau Ng	tàan sáu ñgh	"Taan Sau" Ng	攤手五
Wong Wa Bou	wòhng wàh bóu	Wong Wa Bou	黃華寶

Romanization	Yale/Pinyin	Meaning	Characters
Yat Chan Daai Si	yät chàhn daaih sì	Grand Teacher Speck of Dust	一塵大師
Yip Kin	yihp gìn	Yip Kin	葉堅
Ip Chun	yihp jéun	Ip Chun	葉準
Ip Man	yihp mahn	Ip Man	葉問
Yuen Chai Wan	yún jai wàhn	Yuen Chai Wan	阮濟雲
Yuen Kay San	yún kèih sàan	Yuen Kay San	阮奇山
Zhongguo (Md)	*zhöng guó*	*China*	中國
Zhongguoren (Md)	*zhöng guó rén*	*Chinese*	中國人
Chu Hsi (Zhu Xi) Chu Hei	*zhü xï* (Md) jyu hèi (Cn)	*Chu Hsi / Zhu Xi* or Chu Hei	朱熹

ORGANIZATIONS

Romanization	Yale/Pinyin	Meaning	Characters
Ching Lin Tong	chìng lìhn tòhng	Green Field Hall	青蓮堂
Fut Paai Hung Mun	faht paai hùhng mùhn	Buddha Sect Magnificent Door	佛派洪門
Hon Seun Tong	hon seuhn tòhng	Submit Hon Hall	漢順堂
Hung Fa Wui	hùhng fà wúih	Red Flower Association	紅花會
Hung Fa Yi Wing Chun Kuen	hùhng fà yih wihng cheùn kyùhn	Red Flower Righteous Praise Spring Fist	紅花義詠春拳
Hung Mun	hùhng mùhn	Magnificent Door	洪門
Hung Suen Hei Baan	hùhng syùhn hei bàan	Red Boat Opera Troupe	紅船戲班
King Fa Wui Gun	kìhng fà wúih gún	Beautiful Jade Flower Association	瓊花會館
Saam Hap Wui	sàam hahp wúih	Three Harmony Association (Triads)	三合會
Tin Dei Wui	tìn deih wúih	Heaven and Earth Society	天地會

STYLES AND FAMILIES OF MARTIAL ARTS

Romanization	Yale/Pinyin	Meaning	Characters
Baak Mei	baahk mèih	White Eyebrow	白眉
Cho Ga	chòuh ga	Cho Family	曹家
Fujian Baihe (Md)	*fú jiàn bái hè*	*Fujian White Crane*	幅建白鶴
Choi Ga	choìh ga kyùhn	Choi Family Fist	蔡家拳
Lau Ga Kuen or Lau Ga	làuh ga kyùhn	Lau Family Fist	劉家拳
Chi Sim Weng Chun Kuen	ji sihn wíhng cheùn kyùhn	Extreme Compassion Eternal Spring Fist	至善永春拳
Jeet Kuen Do	jiht kyùhn douh	Way of the Intercepting Fist	截拳道
Chu Ga	jyù gà	Chu Family	朱家
Lei Ga Kuen or Lei Ga	léih ga kyùhn	Lei Family Fist	李家拳
Lung Kuen	lùhng kyùhn	Dragon Fist	龍拳
Ng Jou Kuen	ñgh jóu kyùhn	Five Ancestor Fist	五祖拳
Pao Fa Lin Wing Chun	pàauh fà lìhn wihng cheùn	Pao Fa Lien Wing Chun	刨花蓮詠春
Shaolin Wing Chun	síu làhm wihng cheùn	Young Forest Praise Spring	少林詠春
Shaolin Weng Chun	síu làhm wíhng cheùn	Young Forest Everlasting Spring	少林永春
Tong Long	tòhng lòhng	Preying Mantis	螳螂

TECHNICAL TERMS

Baak Fu	baahk fu	White Tiger	白虎
Baak Fu Tiu Gaan	baahk fu tiu gaan	White Tiger Jumping Over the Stream	白虎跳澗
Baai Jong Faat	báai jòng faat	Placing Structure Method	擺樁法
Baai Jong Paak Sau	báai jòng paak sáu	Placing Structure Slap Hand	擺樁拍手
Baat Jaam Dou	baat jáam döu	Eight Chopping Knife	八斬刀

Romanization	Yale/Pinyin	Meaning	Characters
Bin Ma	bìn máh	Edge Horse	邊馬
Biu Da Kiu Sau	bìu dä kìuh sáu	Thrust Hit Bridge Hand	標打橋手
Biu Ji	bìu jí	Thrusting Finger	標指
Biu Jong	bìu jong	Thrust Structure	標椿
Biu Sau	bìu sáu	Thrusting Hand	標手
Bong Laap Kiu Sau	bong laahp kìuh sáu	Wing Grabbing Bridge Hand	膀擸橋手
Bun Bou	bun bouh	Half Step	半步
Bun Yeut Ma	bun yuht máh	Half Moon Horse	半月馬
Chu	jyù	Chu (also means red)	朱
Chum Jaang	chàhm jàang	Sink Elbow	沉踭
Chum Kiu	chàhm kìuh	Sink Bridge	沉橋
Chi Jong	chï jong	Stick Structure	黐椿
Chi Sau	chï sáu	Stick Hand	黐手
Chin Gum Sau	chìhn gahm sáu	Front Press Hand	前撳手
Chin Geuk	chìhn geuk	Front Kick	前腳
Ching Lung	chìng lùhng	Green Dragon	青龍
Ching Lung Baak Fu Jong	chìng lùhng baahk fu jong	Green Dragon White Tiger	青龍白虎椿
Chiu Min	chìuh mihn	Open Up to the Face	朝面
Chiu Min Deui Ying	chìuh mihn deui yìhng	Open Up Facing the Shape	朝面對形
Chiu Min Jeui Ying	chìuh mihn jèui yìhng	Open Up Pursuing Shape	朝面追形
Da Xue (Md)	dà xué	Ultimate Learning	大學
Daai Nim	daaih nihm	Universal Self (lit. big idea)	大念
Daai Sing	daaih sìhng	Mahayana (lit. Large Vehicle)	大乘

Romanization	Yale/Pinyin	Meaning	Characters
Daan Chi Sau	dàan chï sáu	Single Stick Hand	單黐手
Tan Jung	daan jùng	Middle Reference Point (lit. center of the chest)	膻中
Daan Paak Sau	dàan paak sáu	Single Slap Hand	單拍手
Daan Tin	daan tìhn	Energy Field	丹田
Dei Pun Kiu Sau	deih pùhn kìuh sáu	Earth Bridge Hand	地盤橋手
Deui Ying	deui yìhng	Facing the Shape	對形
Dim Mak	dím mahk	Death Touch (lit. point pulse)	點脈
Ding Ji Ma	dìng yih máh	"Ding" Character Horse	丁字馬
Dou	döu	Knife	刀
Fa Kuen	fà kyùhn	Flower Fist	花拳
Faat Ging	faat gihng	Focused Power	發勁
Faht Sau Kiu Sau	faht sáu kìuh sáu	Buddha Hand Bridge Hand	佛手橋手
Fau Kiu	fau kìuh	Floating Bridge	浮橋
Fau Kiu Kiu Sau	fau kìuh kìuh sáu	Floating Bridge Bridge Hand	浮橋橋手
Fu Mou Seung Dou	fuh móuh sèung döu	Father Mother Double Knife	父母雙刀
Fong Kiu	fùng kìuh	Attack Bridge	封橋
Gaan Jaam Dou	gaan jáam döu	Chopping Knife	攔斬刀
Gaan Sau	gaan sáu	Making Space Hand	攔手
Gan Sau Kiu Sau	gaan sáu kìuh sáu	Making Space Hand Bridge Hand	攔手橋手
Gum Da	gahm dä	Press Hit	撳打
Gam Gong Wu	gàm gòng wuh	Iron Vest (lit. gold tough protection)	金剛護
Gei Jong	gèi jòng	Mechanical Ability Structure	機樁

Romanization	Yale/Pinyin	Meaning	Characters
Geuk Faat	geuk faat	Kick Method	腳法
Geuk Jong	geuk jòng	Three Half Point Kick Structure	腳樁
Gong Sau	góng sáu	Challenge Match (lit. talking hands)	講手
Kung Fu	gùng fuh	Skill Developed Through Effort	功夫
Gwan	gwan	Pole	棍
Gwan Faat	gwan faat	Principles and Methods of the Pole	棍法
Han (Md) Hon (Cn)	hän hon	Man	漢
Hong (Md) Hung (Cn)	hóng hùhng	Magnificent	洪
Hong (Md) Hung (Cn)	hóng hùhng	Red	紅
Hou Kuet	hou kyut	Oral Idiom	口訣
Hou Ling	hou ling	Oral Command	口令
Hung Mun Saat Gwan	hùhng mùhn saat gwan	Hung Mun Killing Pole	洪門殺棍
Hei Yin Chan	héi yïn chàhn	Raise Smoke and Dust	起煙塵
Hung Mun Saat Gwan	hùhng mùhn saat gwan	Hung Mun Kill Pole	洪門殺棍
Hung Jong	hùng jong	Empty Structure	空樁
Huen Da	hyùn dä	Encircle Hit	圈打
Jaam Jong	jaahm jòng	Stand Structure	站樁
Jaam Ma	jáam máh	Destroy Horse	斬馬
Jaang Dai Lik	jàang daai lihk	Elbow Connect Power	踭帶力
Jut Sau	jaht sáu	Stop Hand	窒手
Jeui Da	jèui dä	Pursuing Hit	追打
Jeui Ying Kiu Sau	jèui yìhng kìuh sáu	Pursue Shape Bridge Hand	追形橋手

Romanization	Yale/Pinyin	Meaning	Characters
Jeui Ying Paak Sau	jèui yìhng paak sáu	Pursue Shape Slap Hand	追形拍手
Jeui Ying Saan Da	jèui yìhng saan dä	Pursue Shape Separate Hit	追形散打
Ji Ng Jung Sin Ma	jih ñgh jùng sin máh	Character Noon Structure Line Horse	字午中線馬
Ji Ng Ma	jih ñgh máh	Character Noon Horse	字午馬
Jit Kiu	jiht kìuh	Intercept Bridge	截橋
Jit Kiu Chi Sau	jiht kìuh chï sáu	Jit Kiu Chi Sau	截橋黐手
Jin Bou	jin bouh	Battle Steps	戰步
Jong Sau	jòng sáu	Structure Hand	樁手
Jung Sin Paak Sau	jùng sin paak sáu	Center Line Slap Hit	中線拍手
Kan Na	kàhn nàh	Seizing Controlling	擒拿
Kiu Jong	kìuh jòng	Bridge Structure	橋樁
Kiu Sau	kìuh sáu	Bridge Hand	橋手
Kiu Sau Saam Gwaan	kìuh sáu sàam gwàan	Bridge Hand Three Boundary	橋手三關
Kuen Chuen Kuen	kyùhn chyùn kyùhn	Fist Thread Through Fist	拳穿拳
Kuen Jong	kyùhn jong	Fist Structure	拳樁
Kuen Tou	kyùhn tou	Form (lit. fist set)	拳套
Laap Da	laahp dä	Grab Hit	擸打
Laap Kiu	laahp kìuh	Grab Bridge	擸橋
Leung Yi Jong	léuhng yih jòng	Two Element Structure	兩儀樁
Leung Yi Ma	léuhng yih máh	Two Element Horse	兩儀馬
Li (Md)	lî	Principle	理
Lin Wan Kuen	lìn wàahn kyùhn	Connect Link Fist	連環拳
Lok Ma	lohk máh	Descend Horse	落馬

Romanization	Yale/Pinyin	Meaning	Characters
Luk Dim Bun Gwan	luhk dím bun gwan	Six Half Point Pole	六點半棍
Luk Dim Sup Saam Cheung	luhk dím sahp sàam chëung	Six Point Thirteen Spear	六點十三槍
Luk Mun Chi Sau	luhk mùhn chï sáu	Six Gate Stick Hand	六門黐手
Mun Jong	mùhn jòng	Gate/Door Structure	門樁
Ng Jong Hei Gung	ñgh jòng hei gùng	Five Posture Energy Skill	五樁氣功
Ng Sin Jong Sau	ñgh sin jòng sáu	Five Line Structure Hand	五線樁手
Paak Da	paak dä	Slap Hit	拍打
Po Jung Sau	po jùng sáu	Break Center Hand	破中手
Qi (Md) Hei (Cn)	qì hei	Life Force	氣
Qi Gong (Md) Hei Gung (Cn)	qì göng hei gùng	Energy Skill	氣功
Quan Fa (Md) Kuen Faat (Cn)	quán fâ kyùhn faat	Fist Methods	拳法
Saam Baai Fut	sàam baai faht	Three Bows to Buddha	三拜佛
Saam Dim Bun Geuk Jong	sàam dím bun geuk jòng	Three Half Point Kick Structure	三點半腳樁
Saam Dim Bun Kuen	sàam dím bun kyùhn	Three Point Half Fist	三點半拳
Saam Dim Yat Sin	sàam dím yät sin	Three Point One Line	三點一線
Saam Jin Bou	sàam jin bouh	Three Battle Step	三戰步
Saam Ming Dim	sàam mìhng dím	Three Bright Point	三明點
Saam Mo Kiu	sàam mò kìuh	Three Connecting Bridge	三摩橋
Saam Sin Chi Sau	sàam sin chï sáu	Three Line Stick Hand	三線黐手
Saan Kiu	saan kìuh	Separate Bridge	散橋
Saan Sau	saan sáu	Separate Hand	散手
Saan Sik	saan sïk	Separate Motions	散式

Romanization	Yale/Pinyin	Meaning	Characters
Saat Geng Sau	saat géng sáu	Kill Neck Hand	殺頸手
Sap Ming Dim Chi Sau	sahp mìhng dím chï sáu	Ten Bright Point Chi Sau	十明點黐手
Sap Yat Kuen	sahp yät kyùhn	Eleven Fist	十一拳
Sap Yi Mou Kiu	sahp yih mó kìuh	Twelve Feet Bridge	十二摸橋
Sau Yan	sáu yan	Hand Print	手印
Sei Mun Chuen Sau	sei mùhn chyùhn sáu	Four Gate Pierce Hand	四門傳手
Sei Pai Da	sei pàaih dä	Four Expel Hit	四排打
Seung Gaan Dou	sèung gaan döu	Double Making Space Knife	雙捫刀
Seung Kung Jong Kuen	sèung gùng jòng kyùhn	Double Skill Structure Fist	雙功椿拳
Sim	sìhm	Chan (Zen)	禪
Siu Nim	síu nihm	Personal Self (lit. small idea)	小念
Siu Nim Tau	síu nihm tàuh	Little Idea Head	小念頭
Siu Sing	síu sìhng	Hinayana (lit. small vehicle)	小乘
Taai Gik	taai gihk (tài jí)	Grand Pole	太極
Taai Ping Tin Gwok	taai pìhng tìn gwok	Great Peace Heaven Country	太平天國
Tin Pun Kiu Sau	tìn pùhn kìuh sáu	Heaven Bridge Hand	天盤橋手
Tin Yan Dei	tìn yàhn deih	Heaven, Man, Earth	天人地
Tit Sa Jeung	tit sà jêung	Iron Palm (lit. iron sand palm)	跌沙掌
Waang Gum Sau	wàahng gahm sáu	Side Press Hand	橫撳手
Wanzi (Md)	wàn zî	Swastika	萬子
Wen (Md)	wén	Literary	文
Weng Kiu	wìhng kìuh	Eternal Bridge	永橋

Romanization	Yale/Pinyin	Meaning	Characters
Wu (Md) Mo (Cn)	*wû* móuh	*Military*	武
Wushu (Md) Mo Seut (Cn)	*wû shù* móuh seuht	*Military Skill*	武術
Wu Sau	wuh sáu	Guarding Hand	護手
Wui Ma	wùih máh	Recover Horse	回馬
Wui Ma Deui Ying	wùih máh deui yìhng	Recovery to Face (lit. recover horse face shape)	回馬對形
Wui Ma Jeui Ying	wùih máh jèui yìhng	Recovery to Pursue (lit. recover horse pursue shape)	回馬追形
Yan Jung	yàhn jùng	High Reference Point (lit. person center)	人中
Yan Pun Kiu Sau	yàhn pùhn kìuh sáu	Bridge Hand	人盤橋手
Yat Kuen	yaht kyùhn	Sun Fist	日拳
Yin Yang	yàm yèuhng	Yin Yang	陰陽
Yat Bou	yät bouh	Full Step	一步
Yat Ji Jeung	yät jih jêung	Character One Palm	一字掌
Yi Ji Kim Yeung Ma	yih jih kìhm yèuhng máh	"Yi" Character Press Goat Horse	二字拑陽馬
Yi Ji Wu Dip Dou	yih jih wùh dihp döu	Character "Yi" Butterfly Knives	二字蝴蝶刀
Yi Sin Jong Sau	yih sin jòng sáu	Two Line Bridge Hand	二線橋手

LOCATIONS

Bei Shaolin Si (Md) Bak Siu Lam Ji (Cn)	*bêi shâo lín sì* bäk síu làhm jih	Northern Young Forest Temple	北少林寺
Bou Man Dim	bóu màhn dihn	Responsible People Temple	保民殿
Gun Yam Tong	gùn yàm tòhng	Gunyam Hall (Gunyam is the Buddha of Mercy)	觀音堂
Hung Fa Ting	hùhng fà thing	Red Flower Pavilion	紅花亭

Romanization	Yale/Pinyin	Meaning	Characters
Nan Shaolin Si (Md) Naam Siu Lam Ji (Cn)	*nán shâo lín sì* nàahm síu làhm jih	Southern Young Forest Temple	南少林寺
Song Shan	*sõng shän*	Song Mountain, location of the Northern Shaolin Temple	嵩山
Weng Chun Dim	wìhng cheùn dihn	Everlasting Spring Temple (another name for Weng Chun Tong)	永春殿
Weng Chun Tong	wìhng cheùn tòhng	Everlasting Spring Hall	永春堂

PROVINCES

Fujian (Md) Fukgin (Cn)	*fú jiàn* fük gin	"Happy Establishment"	幅建
Hebei (Md) Hobak (Cn)	*hé bêi* hòh bäk	"River North"	河北
Henan (Md) Honan (Cn)	*hé nán* hòh nàahm	"River South"	河南
Hubei (Md) Wubak (Cn)	*hú bêi* wùh bäk	"Lake North"	湖北
Hunan (Md) Wunan (Cn)	*hú nán* wùh nàahm	"Lake South"	湖南

CITIES

Beijing	*bêi jïng*	Beijing	北京
Foshan (Md) Fatsan (Cn)	*fó shän* faht sàan	Foshan	佛山
Gulao (Md) Gu Lou (Cn)	*gû láo* gú lòuh	Gulou	古劳

EMPERORS OF THE QING DYNASTY

Shunzhi	*shun zhì*	*Shunzhi* (1644-1661)	順治
Kangxi	*käng xï*	*Kangxi* (1661-1722)	康熙
Yongzheng	*yöng zhèng*	*Yongzheng* (1723-1735)	雍正
Qianlong	*qián long*	*Qianlong* (1736-1795)	乾隆

Romanization	Yale/Pinyin	Meaning	Characters
Jiajing	jiä qíng	Jiajing (1796-1820)	嘉慶
Daoguang	dào guäng	Daoguang (1821-1850)	道光
Xianfeng	xián fëng	Xianfeng (1851-1861)	咸豐
Tongzhi	tong zhì	Tongzhi (1862-1874)	同治
Guangxu	guäng xù	Guangxu (1875-1908)	光緒

PHRASES

Fan Qing Fu Ming	fáan chìng fuhk mìhng	Overthrow the Qing, Return the Ming	反清復明
Dharma	faat	Reality (used for Dharma in Chinese)	法
Hoi Gong	hòi gwòng	Enlightenment (lit. open light)	開光
Hoi Fau	hòi fau	Confusion or Illusion (lit. open floating)	開浮
Gaak Mat Ji Ji	gaak maht ji jì	Within the boundary, Know everything	格物致知
Gei Fa Luk Mun	gèi fa luhk mùhn	Gei Fa Luk Moon	機化六門
Gong Wu	gòng wùh	Martial Arts Community (lit. river lake)	江湖
Hong Wu (Md) Hung Mo (Cn)	hóng wû	Vast Military Power, Imperial name of Chu Yun Cheung	洪武
Hou Chuen San Sau	hou chyùhn sàn sauh	Mouth Passing On/ Teaching Body Receive	口傳身授
Hung Gun	hùhng gàn	Red Bandanna	紅巾
Jaang Dai Lik Bin Fa	jàang daai lihk bin fa	Elbow Connect Power Change Influence	踭帶力變化
Kin Kwan Chi Sau	kìhn kwàn chï sáu	phrase for when one's chi sau skill becomes a natural (lit. heaven earth stick hand)	乾坤黐手
Kiu Sau Bin Fa	kìuh sáu bin fa	Bridge Hand Change Influence	橋手變化

Romanization	Yale/Pinyin	Meaning	Characters
Laam Dung	laahm dung	Blue Lantern	藍燈
Luk Lam Ho Hon	luk làhm hou hon	Green Forest Righteous Man	綠林好漢
Ng Jan Chiu Min Jeui Ying	ñgh jahn chìuh mihn jèui yìhng	Five Battle Formation Face Pursue Shape	五陣朝面追形
Sam Faat	sàm faat	Nature	心法
Sau Ying Bin Fa	sáu yìhng bin fa	Hand Shape Change Influence	手形變化
Taam Lo	taam lou	Seeking the Way	探路
Yim Wing Chun	yìhm wihng cheùn	Discreet Praise Spring, code phrase in the secret societies	嚴詠春
Ying Hung	yìng hùhng	Hero	英雄

PAO FA LIN WING CHUN SAYING

Weng Yin Chi Ji	wìhng yìhn chí ji	Always speak with determination	永言矢志
Mou Mong Hon Juk	mòuh mòhng hon juhk	Vow never to forget the Hon Nation	毋忘漢族
Daai Dei Wui Chun	daaih deih wùih cheùn	Spring will return to the world	大地回春

FIVE MOVEMENTS

Wu Xing (Md) Ng Hang (Cn)	wû xíng ñgh hàhng	Five Movements	五行
Muk	muhk	wood	木
Seui	séui	water	水
Fo	fó	fire	火
Gam	gàm	metal	金
Tou	tóu	earth	土

KUEN KUIT

Kuen Kuit are phrases from within a martial art system that serve to capture the essential nature of experience found in training. These keywords serve to describe theories and strategies.

Romanization	Yale/Pinyin	Meaning	Characters
Yi Sau Daai Geuk	yíh sáu daai geuk	Use Hand Lead Foot	以手帶腳
Yi Geuk Daai Sau	yíh geuk daai sáu	Use Foot Lead Hand	以腳帶手
Loi Lau Heui Sung	lòih làuh heui sung	What Comes, Make Stay; What Goes, Escort	來留去送
Bou Bou Jeui Bik	bouh bouh jèui bïk	Step by Step, Pursue and Pressure (energy)	步步追逼
Kin Kwan Taai Heui	kìhn kwàn taai hèui	Within the changes of Space and Time (lit. Heaven Earth Grand Emptiness)	乾坤太虛
Lau Yam Fa Ming	làuh yam fà mìhng	Harmonize the Yin and Yang to regain superior position (lit. stay shade flower bright)	留蔭花明
Saam Dim Yat Sin, Ding Yun San	sàam dím yät sin dihng yùhn sàhn	Three Points One Line, Establishes Original Nature	三點一線 定元神
Ng Dou Luk Mun, Fa Kin Kwan	ñgh douh luhk mùhn fa kìhn kwàn	Five Ways Six Gates, Influence the Universe	五道六門 化乾坤
Dik Bat Dung Ngo Bat Dung	dihk bät duhng ngóh bät duhng	Enemy Not Move, I Not Move	敵不動 我不動
Dik Dung, Ngo Dung Sin	dihk duhng ngóh duhng sìn	Enemy Move, I Move First	敵動 我動先
Mou Ying Da Yeng	mòuh yìhng dä yíng	No Shape, Hit Shadow	無形打影
Yau Ying Da Ying	yáuh yìhng dä yìhng	Have Shape, Hit Shape	有形打形

TEN SHAOLIN WISDOMS OF CHI SIM WENG CHUN

Romanization	Yale/Pinyin	Meaning	Characters
Sïk	sik	Knowledge	識
Dam	dáam	Courage	膽
Hei or *Qi*	hei / qi	Energy	氣
Ging	gihng	Power	勁
San	sàhn	Spirit	神
Ying	yìhng	Form	形
Yi	yi	Intent or Meaning	意
Lei	léih	Principle	理
Faat	faat	Method or Reality (used for Dharma in Chinese)	法
Seut	seuht	Skill	術

6½ CONCEPTS OF CHI SIM WENG CHUN (SYSTEM CONCEPTS)

Tai	tàih	raise	提
Laan	làahn	to press or take space from an opponent	攔
Dim	dím	point	點
Kit	kit	deflect	揭
Got	got	cut downward, sink	割
Waan	wàahn	circle, absorb	環
Lau	lauh	flowing continuously	漏

6½ POLE CONCEPTS OF CHI SIM WENG CHUN (TANG FAMILY)

Chin	chìhn	wind around	纏
Si	sì	sever	撕
Chau	chàu	pull upward	抽

Romanization	Yale/Pinyin	Meaning	Characters
Taan	tàahn	quick hit	彈
Dik	dihk	drip	滴
Got	got	cut	割
Cheung	chëung	spear	槍

6½ POLE CONCEPTS OF CHI SIM WENG CHUN (LO FAMILY)

Jau	jàu	grasp	揪
Taan	tàahn	rebound	彈
Got	got	sever, cut	割
Saat	saat	stop	殺
Dik	dihk	drip	滴
Lau	lauh	leak	漏
Cheung	chëung	spear	槍

EIGHTEEN SHAOLIN BRIDGE HANDS OF CHI SIM WENG CHUN

Tiu	tìu	pick up	挑
But	buht	sweep aside, push open	撥
Da	dä	strike or hit	打
Pun	pùhn	folding	盆
Jaau	jáau	catch or grasp	抓
Laai	làai	pull	拉
Si	sì	tear / rip, shear	撕
Che	ché	quick pull, jerk	扯
Kan	kàhn	capture	擒
Na	nàh	control	拿

Romanization	Yale/Pinyin	Meaning	Characters
Fung	fùng	prevent free movement	封
Bai	bai	allow no movement	閉
Bik	bïk	press	逼
Hap	häp	follow-up	恰
Tan	tàn	swallow	吞
Tuo	tuo	spit	吐
Bok	bok	attack is your best defense	搏
Saat	saat	eliminate, beat down completely	殺

THIRTEEN SHAOLIN SPEARING PRINCIPLES

Sap Saam Cheung Gwan Faat	sahp sàam chëung gwan faat	13 Spearing Principles	十三槍棍法
Saat	saat	kill	殺
Dim	dím	point	點
Chin	chìhn	wind around	纏
Baai	báai	set up	擺
Waang	wàahng	side	橫
Chaap	chaap	insert	插
Taan	tàahn	strum, pluck	彈
Diu	diu	hang	弔
Tiu	tìu	pick up	挑
Pun	pùhn	folding	盆
Bat	baht	pull out	拔
Mun	mut	wipe	抹
Daai	daai	carry	帶

SIX NATURES OF THE HUNG FA YI POLE

Romanization	Yale/Pinyin	Meaning	Characters
Hung Mun Saat Gwan	hùhng mùhn saat gwan	Hung Mun Killing Pole	洪門殺棍
Luk Daai Hau Kyut	luhk daaih háu kyut	Six Oral Commands	六大口訣
Sam Faat	sàm faat	Heart Methods	心法
Lik Dim Faat	lihk dím faat	Strength Point Methods	力點法
Huen Dim Fat	hyùn dím faat	Circle Point Methods	圈點法
Cheung Dyun Chuk Dou	chèuhng dyún chük douh	Long Short Speed	長短速度距離法
Keui Lei Faat	kéuih léih faat	Distance Methods	
Sang Sei Mun Faat	sáng séi mùhn faat	Life and Death Methods	生死門法
Sang Sei Gwan Faat	sang séi gwan faat	Live Vice Dead Pole Methods	生死棍法
Lou Nyun Gwan Faat	lóuh nyuhn gwan faat	Old and Young Pole Methods	老嫩棍法

6½ POLE CONCEPTS HUNG FA YI

Saat	saat	kill	殺
Tai	tàih	raise	提
Huen	hyùn	circle	圈
Dim	dím	point – hard or soft	點
Taan	tàahn	strum, pluck	彈
Chaap	chaap	insert	插
Biu	bìu	thrust	標

HUNG FA YI TEN ELBOWS

Ngaat	ngaat	Pressing elbow	壓
Biu	bìu	Forward Centerline Thrust Elbow	標
Ji Ng Jaang	jih ñgh jàang	Another Name for Biu Jaang Elbow	字午蹲

Romanization	Yale/Pinyin	Meaning	Characters
Kap	kap	Downward hitting elbow	扱
Ding	ding	Backward centerline thrust elbow	頂
Faan	fàan	Outward turning elbow	翻
Jong	johng	Hitting elbow	撞
Pai	pài	Slicing elbow	批
Suen	syùhn	Inward turning elbow	旋
Tai	tàih	Upward hitting elbow	提
Waang	wàahng	Side elbow	橫

6½ POLE CONCEPTS IP MAN WING CHUN

Tiu	tìu	pick up	挑
Dang	däng	nail	釘
Biu	bìu	thrust	標
Taan	tàan	disperse	攤
Fuhk	fuhk	cover	伏
Laan	làahn	to bar	攔
Huen	hyùn	circle	圈

INDEX

ABOUT THE AUTHORS

Grandmaster **Garrett Gee** comes from a distinguished line of philosophers and martial and military teachers. He is the direct descendant in a family that has consistently studied and taught martial art disciplines for centuries to professional military officers and royal family members of China's greatest dynasties.

Gee began his martial arts training at age five under his father, Grandmaster Peter Kim Ho Chu, and later received full training in Hung Fa Yi Wing Chun Kuen in China. He was the first disciple outside of the founding family to learn this martial science. Now the eighth-generation successor of Hung Fa Yi Wing Chun, he is the first to open the system outside of China or to the public. Gee has been teaching since his move to the United States in 1975.

In January 2001, Gee was inducted into Action Martial Arts Publications Hall of Fame as Martial Artist of the Year in Chinese Martial Arts.

An internationally renowned Wing Chun martial artist, instructor, and researcher, **Benny Meng** has devoted his life to martial arts. He has been featured by national news and major martial arts publications as one of the world's best martial artists.

Meng has had the privilege of training under some of the great grandmasters in the world for judo, taekwondo, and various styles of Wing Chun Kung Fu. He began his Wing Chun training in 1982 and officially started teaching it in 1987. Since then, he has instructed many of this generation's top instructors and tournament grand champions—including Jeremy Roadruck, three-time United States Wushu-Kungfu Federation national champion and the 2002 and 2003

Arnold Battle of Columbus Wing Chun grand champion; Mike Mathews, four-time United States Wushu-Kungfu Federation national champion and 2001 Arnold Battle of Columbus Wing Chun grand champion; and Chango Noaks, two-time United States Wushu-Kungfu Federation national champion and the 1998 Second Pan-American Kung Fu champion.

As curator of the Ving Tsun Museum, Meng is one of the only people to have formally trained directly with the grand masters from the earliest form of Wing Chun to the cutting-edge Hung Fa Yi Wing Chun to today's modern Wing Chun families. His school, Meng's Martial Arts, is one of the first schools in the world to offer the martial science of Hung Fa Yi Wing Chun, and it was chosen for the prestigious Top 200 Schools of North America award out of more than 15,000 contenders in 1994.

A respected military strategist, tactician, leader, and teacher, retired U.S. Air Force Lieutenant Colonel **Richard Loewenhagen** has dedicated more than 30 years to the study and practice of martial arts. While a commissioned officer in the United States Air Force, he taught Wing Chun Kung Fu and Shaolin Kam Na to combat and security personnel. A masters degree graduate of the prestigious Air Force Institute of Technology's advanced Systems and Logisitics School and a graduate of both the United States Marine Corp Command and Staff College, Colonel Loewenhagen possesses military science credentials rarely seen in today's world of martial arts teachers. His research credentials are equally impressive. The world-renowned International Society of Logistics Engineers named him their Graduate Researcher of the Year in 1983. He is the founder of Meng's Martial Arts of Arizona, an official Hung Fa Yi Wing Chun school, which was also chosen for the prestigious Top 200 Schools of North America award from more than 19,000 contenders in 2000.

Loewenhagen serves as the Ving Tsun Museum's director of west coast affairs and as western regional director of the Hung Fa Yi Wing Chun Federation. He is also an inductee into the Martial Arts Hall of Fame with special recognition as Martial Arts Writer of the Year.